KANTIAN HUMILITY

R AE L ANGTON offers a new interpretation and defence of Kant's doctrine of things in themselves. Kant distinguishes things in themselves from phenomena, and in so doing he makes a metaphysical distinction between intrinsic and relational properties of substances. Kant says that phenomena—things as we know them—consist 'entirely of relations'. His claim that we have no knowledge of things in themselves is not idealism, but epistemic humility: we have no knowledge of the intrinsic properties of substances. This humility has its roots in some plausible philosophical beliefs: an empiricist belief in the receptivity of human knowledge and a metaphysical belief in the irreducibility of relational properties. Langton's interpretation vindicates Kant's scientific realism, and shows his primary/secondary quality distinction to be superior even to modern-day competitors. And it answers the famous charge that Kant's tale of things in themselves is one that makes itself untellable.

Kantian Humility

Our Ignorance of Things in Themselves

RAE LANGTON

CLARENDON PRESS · OXFORD

OXFORD

UNIVERSITY PRESS

Great Clarendon Street, Oxford OX2 6DP

Oxford University Press is a department of the University of Oxford
It furthers the University's objective of excellence in research, scholarship,
and education by publishing worldwide in

Oxford New York

Athens Auckland Bangkok Bogotá Buenos Aires Calcutta
Cape Town Chennai Dar es Salaam Delhi Florence Hong Kong Istanbul
Karachi Kuala Lumpur Madrid Melbourne Mexico City Mumbai
Nairobi Paris São Paulo Singapore Taipei Tokyo Toronto Warsaw

with associated companies in Berlin Ibadan

Oxford is a registered trade mark of Oxford University Press
in the UK and in certain other countries

Published in the United States
by Oxford University Press Inc., New York

British Library Cataloguing in Publication Data

Data available

Library of Congress Cataloging in Publication Data
Langton, Rae, 1961–
Kantian humility / Rae Langton.
Includes bibliographical references.
1. Kant, Immanuel, 1724–1804. 2. Kant, Immanuel, 1724–1804—Contributions in doc-
trine of noumenon or ding an sich. 3. Ding an sich. I. Title.
B2799.D5L36 1998 111—dc21 97–51412

ISBN 0–19–823653–0 (hbk.)
ISBN 0–19–924317–4 (pbk.)

1 3 5 7 9 10 8 6 4 2

Typeset by Invisible Ink
Printed in Great Britain
on acid-free paper by
Biddles Ltd.,
Guildford & King's Lynn

Wir sehen das Innere der Dinge gar nicht ein.

We have no insight whatsoever into the
intrinsic nature of things.
(A277/B333)

ACKNOWLEDGEMENTS

Thanks are due to many friends, teachers, and colleagues for patient and constructive comments on earlier thoughts and drafts, without which this book would be much the poorer. The remaining errors are, needless to say, all my own work. The earliest inklings of this story about Kant came to me in Sydney in 1985, encouraged by Keith Campbell (who first inspired my interest in Kant) and David Stove (who warned me that Kant was a Black Hole—encouragement enough for the countersuggestible). Later on, at Princeton and thereafter, I was lucky to have had the advice of Margaret Wilson, who supervised the dissertation which was ancestor to this book. Her patience and thoroughness saved me from many errors and over-glib generalizations. I was fortunate to receive comments from others, including Mark Johnston, Eckart Förster, Michael Friedman, and Béatrice Longuenesse. Conversations with Alison Laywine were also very helpful. Since my return to Australia in 1990, the Philosophy Department at Monash University, and the Philosophy Program at the Research School of Social Sciences, Australian National University, have each provided me with the great luxury of teaching-free time, a semester's leave at Monash in 1994, and a Fellowship at the Research School which began in 1997. I have bene-fited enormously from interaction with my colleagues at both institutions, especially John Bigelow, Jamie Dreier, Frank Jackson, and Michael Smith. Without Lloyd Humberstone and David Lewis I would have been mud-dled—or more muddled—about the metaphysics of intrinsic properties. Simon Blackburn has been particularly helpful on the subject of powers and unknowable somethings. I have enjoyed conversations with Michael Ayers about Kantian epistemic humility and its Lockean analogues. I am grateful for the detailed and constructive advice I received from the readers of Oxford University Press, Robert Stern and Peter Strawson. The book has been much improved by the wise editorial hand of Angela Blackburn. Richard Holton has helped philosophically and practically in ways that I cannot even begin to count. Eleanor Holton, whose impending arrival spurred this book to completion, has helped in a very practical way. This book is dedicated to the memory of my father, David Langton, who once said I should write a book; though I somehow doubt he had this one in mind.

CONTENTS

NOTE ON SOURCES AND ABBREVIATIONS

References to Kant's *Critique of Pure Reason* follow the customary practice of citing the pagination of the 1781 (A) edition and the 1787 (B) edition. Translations of the *Critique* are chiefly my own, following the German edition by Raymund Schmidt, though influenced by Norman Kemp Smith's translation. Citations of other writings by Kant give their location in the Academy edition of Kant's works, and (usually) an English translation. Unless otherwise indicated, quotations from the *Prolegomena*, the *Metaphysical Foundations of Natural Science*, the *Letters*, and *On a Discovery* follow the translations by Peter Lucas, J. Ellington, Arnulf Zweig, and Henry Allison, respectively. Translations from all other works by Kant are my own, though influenced by the English translations given in the Bibliography. Kant's *Reflexionen zur Metaphysik* are cited by the numbers assigned to them in the Academy edition; dates given are those suggested by Erich Adickes (in the Preface to volume xvii of the Academy edition), or by Arthur Melnick (in *Space, Time and Thought in Kant*, 547–9), signified by the letters 'A' and 'M' respectively. In addition the following abbreviations are used for works by Kant (full publication details can be found in the Bibliography):

Ak.	*Gesammelte Schriften*, Academy edition
Allison	*The Kant-Eberhard Controversy*, trans. Henry Allison
Beck	*Kant's Latin Writings*, trans. L. W. Beck et al.
Ellington	*Metaphysical Foundations of Natural Science*, trans. J. Ellington
Inaugural Dissertation	*De mundi sensibilis atque intelligibilis forma et principiis* (1770)
Kerferd and Walford	*Selected Pre-Critical Writings*, trans. G. B. Kerferd and D. E. Walford
Living Forces	*Gedanken von der wahren Schätzung der lebendige Kräfte* (1747)
Lucas	*Prolegomena*, trans. Peter G. Lucas
Metaphysical Foundations	*Metaphysische Anfangsgründe der Naturwissenschaft* (1786)
New Exposition	*Principiorum primorum cognitionis metaphysicae nova dilucidatio* (1755)

On a Discovery	*Über eine Entdeckung nach der alle neue Kritik der reinen Vernunft durch eine ältere entbehrlich gemacht werden soll* (1790)
Physical Monadology	*Metaphysicae cum geometria iunctae usus in philosophia naturali, cuius specimen I. continet monadologiam physicam* (1756)
R	*Reflexionen zur Metaphysik*
Regions in Space	*Von dem ersten Grunde des Unterschiedes der Gegenden in Raume* (1768)
What Real Progress?	*Welches sind die wirklichen Fortschritte, die die Metaphysik seit Leibnizens und Wolf's Zeiten in Deutschland gemacht hat?* (1791/1804)
Zweig	*Kant's Philosophical Correspondence 1759–99*, trans. Arnulf Zweig.

Works by Leibniz are cited by original language source and English translation. Unless otherwise indicated, quotations of Leibniz follow the translations cited. The following abbreviations are used for works by Leibniz:

Ariew and Garber	*Philosophical Essays*, trans. R. Ariew and D. Garber
Bodemann	*Die Leibniz-Handschriften der königlichen öffentlichen Bibliothek zu Hannover*, ed. E. Bodemann
Couturat	*Opuscules et fragments inédits de Leibniz*, ed. L. Couturat
Gerhardt	*Die philosophischen Schriften*, ed. C. I. Gerhardt
Gerhardt M	*Mathematische Schriften*, ed. C. I. Gerhardt
Grua	*Textes inédits d'après les manuscrits de la bibliothèque provinciale de Hanovre*, ed. G. Grua
Loemker	*Philosophical Papers and Letters*, trans. L. Loemker
Remnant and Bennett	*New Essays on Human Understanding* (1765), trans. P. Remnant and J. Bennett.

INTRODUCTION

> Many historians of philosophy, with all their intended praise, let the philosophers speak mere nonsense. They do not guess the purpose of the philosophers . . . They cannot see beyond what the philosophers actually said, to what they really meant to say.
>
> *On a Discovery* (1790)

Kant is rather scathing of a certain kind of history of philosophy. Alert to the possibility that interpretive charity and interpretive fidelity may sometimes pull in different directions, he favourably contrasts the stance of intelligent and charitable engagement with the stance of an uncritical devotee. If Kant is right to value the former, then the history of philosophy since his time has been fortunate, since there has been no lack of intelligent and charitable engagement. This is perhaps especially true with respect to interpretations of Kant himself. What did Kant himself actually say, or mean to say? He said that there is a distinction between appearances and things in themselves, that things in themselves exist, and that we have no knowledge of things in themselves. This has seemed to come dangerously close to nonsense, and there has accordingly been no lack of charitable interpreters only too willing to suppose that he did not mean quite what he said, and that a different purpose must be guessed. Kant's purpose must be to say something else, something mild, and sane, and wise. Kant gives some licence, as we can see, for this kind of rational reconstruction: he gives licence for seeing beyond what the philosopher actually said, to what he really meant to say.

It seems unlikely, though, that a philosopher did not mean to say what he said, when he said it over and over again. And it is worth bearing in mind that Kant himself did not appear to think his philosophy was mild, and sane, and wise. Startling, yes; frustrating, yes; wise, perhaps; mild, no.[1] Faced with this stubborn fact, there is a choice. One can let the philosopher speak nonsense. One can turn an indulgent blind eye to the metaphysical lapses. Or, best of all, one can aim for an alternative which achieves both fidelity and charity, which accepts that this is what the philosopher actually said, and that it is what the philosopher meant to say, and that it is not nonsense after all.

---

[1] Kant says it is 'startling' (A285/B341), and admits that it leaves unsatisfied an 'inextinguishable yearning' (A796/B824). An example of a sane and mild interpretation will be discussed in Chapter 1.

Kant says that there is a distinction between things in themselves and phenomena. What he says is admittedly metaphysics, but none the worse, I think, for that. He says that things as we know them consist 'wholly of relations' (A285/B341). He says that we have no insight into 'the inner' of things (A277/B233). He has a distinction between substances, bearers of intrinsic properties, on the one hand; and relational properties of substances on the other. He says that we have no knowledge of the intrinsic properties of substances. This, as it stands, is not idealism, but a kind of epistemic humility. There are inevitable constraints on what we can know, inevitable limits on what we can become acquainted with. And while those limits could be correctly described, in Strawson's phrase, as 'the bounds of sense', such a description fails to capture Kant's thought that there is a particular sort of thing that is beyond the bounds of sense, something abstractly characterizable in metaphysical rather than epistemological terms: not simply as 'that which is beyond the bounds of sense', but as 'that which has an intrinsic nature'.

I introduce this way of understanding Kant by suggesting that it can help to dissolve a very old contradiction: things in themselves exist, and are the causes of phenomena, and we have no knowledge of things as they are in themselves. This problem has been described as presenting the 'acid test' for any interpretation of things in themselves.[2] The problem and my suggested solution is the topic of Chapter 1. In Chapter 2 I state and explain in more detail three of the fundamental Kantian theses which will be the focus of my attention. The first is the distinction between phenomena and things in themselves. The second is Kant's denial of knowledge of things as they are in themselves, his thesis of epistemic humility. And the third is the empiricist strand in Kant's philosophy, his belief that we are receptive creatures, who must be affected by the things of which we come to have knowledge. Kant believes that humility follows from this fact of receptivity: he believes, as Strawson has remarked,[3] that our ignorance of things as they are in themselves follows from the fact that we must be affected by things if we are to achieve knowledge of them. If this is correct, then our ignorance of things as they are in themselves is not supposed to be a special consequence of the arguments about space, or time, or the categories: it is supposed to be a general consequence of the fact that human knowledge is receptive.

This has two implications. The first is dialectical. Many philosophers would agree with Kant about the receptivity of human knowledge; many

[2] Henry Allison, *Kant's Transcendental Idealism* (New Haven, Conn.: Yale University Press, 1983), 247.

[3] P. F. Strawson, *The Bounds of Sense* (London: Methuen, 1966), 250.

who would raise an eyebrow at other doctrines of the *Critique* will find common ground here. But if there is anything to Kant's belief that humility follows from receptivity, then this poses a rather immediate threat to ordinary epistemological ambition. The premise which is supposed to lead us to humility is true, or widely accepted to be true. If Kant is right, then many philosophers are closer than they think to the Kantian conclusion that we have no knowledge of things as they are in themselves.

The second implication is exegetical. Suppose we are interested in the question of why Kant believes we have no knowledge of things as they are in themselves. If humility is supposed to follow from receptivity, then it should be possible to explore this question without exploring in detail the arguments about space, time, and the categories, for which Kant is (perhaps justly) most famous. The arguments from the Aesthetic and Analytic are accordingly given little detailed attention in the following discussion, since, notwithstanding their importance, they are separable from the conclusion about our ignorance.

However, there is an obvious problem, and it is raised at the end of Chapter 2. Although Kant believes that humility follows from receptivity, it does not appear to do so. Strawson calls this a fundamental unargued premise of the *Critique*. From the fact that we must be affected if we are to have knowledge it does not directly follow that we must be ignorant of things in themselves—or not at any rate without some *further* premise. The search for that missing premise is the task of Chapters 4 to 6. Before it can be pursued, there is a potential stumbling block to be removed. According to Kant's distinction, as I interpret him, things in themselves are substances. What then of Kant's claim in the *Critique* that substance, phenomenal substance, is in the world that we experience? In Chapter 3 I explain how this commitment to phenomenal substance should be understood, in light of Kant's basic distinction.

The problem raised at the end of Chapter 2 is taken up in Chapter 4: the problem of how epistemic humility is supposed to be a consequence of receptivity. Some of the clearest expressions of Kantian humility are to be found in the context of Kant's critique of Leibnizian philosophy. This suggests a clue—a possible path to a solution, a possible link between Kant's attitude to Leibniz and his belief in our ignorance of things as they are in themselves. So in this fourth chapter I offer an interpretation of Leibniz that attempts to show what, in Kant's opinion, Leibniz was doing—and what he was doing wrong.

There are four notable features to Leibniz's philosophy, or at least to Kant's version of it. There is a metaphysical distinction between things in themselves and phenomena, which coincides with a distinction between substances and their relational properties. There is a commitment to the reducibility of relations. There is a denial of causation, and hence a denial of sensory receptivity. And finally, there is an extraordinary ambition that is quite the antithesis of epistemic humility. Leibniz believes that there are no bounds of sense, and that we are each acquainted, through the senses, with everything there is, although our sensory acquaintance is confused. To what extent do Kant and Leibniz share common ground? They agree about certain metaphysical theses: in particular about the distinction between phenomena and things in themselves. They disagree about epistemology: about receptivity, and humility. Kant says, contrary to Leibniz, that human knowledge is receptive, and that we have no knowledge of things as they are in themselves. A question mark stands, though, over the metaphysics of the reducibility of relations. Is this a point of similarity between the two philosophers, or a point of difference? Some critics affirm the former. Some even suggest that a Leibnizian view about relations led Kant to his mature philosophy. If they were right, then Kant's attitude to Leibniz would indeed provide a clue as to why he believes we have no knowledge of things as they are in themselves.

To discover whether they are right, and what Kant's attitude to Leibniz has to do with the thesis of humility, I turn in Chapter 5 to the *New Exposition* (1755). Two of the above Leibnizian themes are addressed explicitly in this early work. There is an explicit distinction between phenomena and things in themselves which has much in common with that of Leibniz. Kant's arguments hinge on a contrast between how a substance is when it is by itself, and how it is when it is in a relation to other things: a contrast between the intrinsic and relational properties of a substance. Kant's matter theory—his theory of force—is intricately connected with this basic distinction between phenomena and things in themselves, and this early work helps to show how.

Moreover, there is an explicit focus here on the issue of the reducibility of relations. Kant's argument is of considerable interest and sophistication, and deserves close attention. However, contrary to the suggestions of the aforementioned critics, it does *not* endorse a Leibnizian view about relations. Its conclusion is that relations, or relational properties, are *irreducible*. Kant believes that relational properties, causal powers in particular, are not reducible to intrinsic properties—and he seems to believe that intrinsic properties are therefore causally inert. He says that it is *never through its own intrinsic properties* that a substance has the capacity to affect other things.

On the two metaphysical themes there is thus partial agreement and partial disagreement with Leibniz: agreement about the basic distinction between phenomena and things in themselves, disagreement about the reducibility of relations. The arguments of this work also have implications for the two epistemological themes, one drawn by Kant, the other not—or at least, not yet. There is, already, the theme of receptivity. The *New Exposition*, notwithstanding its status as an essay in dogmatic metaphysics, contains a seed of empiricism: it offers an anti-Leibnizian argument which implies that human knowledge is essentially receptive, and Kant explicitly draws this conclusion.

Most important of all, there is an apparent implication—which Kant does not yet draw—for epistemic humility. The conclusion about relations, together with the conclusion about receptivity, has the potential to yield the conclusion about humility. If this is so, then Kant's attitude to Leibniz does indeed provide a clue as to why he believes we have no knowledge of things as they are in themselves: but, contrary to the critics, the clue is to be found not in his agreement with Leibniz about the metaphysics of relations, but rather in his disagreement.

How these pieces fit together is the topic of Chapter 6. Receptivity implies that we can have knowledge only of what can affect us. Irreducibility implies, in Kant's view, that intrinsic properties cannot affect us. If Kant maintains this view throughout his philosophical career—as I shall argue he does—then one can trace a path to humility. If substances affect us, but it is not through their intrinsic properties that we are affected, then their intrinsic properties remain unknown.

One might put the argument in terms of a familiar Leibnizian metaphor. If perception were to mirror bodies, and bodies were to mirror the intrinsic properties of monadic substances, then perception would mirror the intrinsic properties of substances. Our minds would, through perception, mirror the monadic realm of things in themselves. The intrinsic properties of substances would be known through perception (albeit confusedly). The epistemological ambition of Leibniz's philosophy—his denial of humility—arguably depends on this commitment to the reducibility of relations. But if, as Kant says, the relations that constitute bodies are *not* reducible, then bodies do not after all mirror the intrinsic properties of substances. The mirror is broken. Perception cannot mirror the intrinsic properties of substances. Their intrinsic properties must remain unknown.

Chapters 7 to 9 explore the implications of this understanding of Kant for an otherwise surprising feature of his philosophy, namely his scientific realism. One aspect of this realism is an apparent commitment to a distinction between primary and secondary qualities that applies within the phenomenal world. This is surprising in a supposed idealist, and appears to conflict with Kant's apparently Berkeleyan claim in the *Prolegomena* that he makes all the qualities secondary. In Chapter 7 I resolve the conflict: Kant does not mean that he makes the qualities ideas, but that he makes them powers. The result is that Kant has a version of the primary/secondary quality distinction that is novel, interesting, and has considerable advantages over many of its competitors, whether of his own time or of ours. Kant's version of this distinction, and its merits, is the topic of Chapter 8. Kant's argument in the Critical period against a more traditional view of primary qualities draws on the early irreducibility argument of the *New Exposition*. It has the potential to challenge some of our own contemporary philosophical orthodoxies, or so it seems to me. Chapter 9 turns to a further aspect of Kant's scientific realism, namely his commitment to the unobservables of science. This commitment is permitted by his understanding of receptivity: we can have knowledge of anything that can affect us. Kant's scientific realism, and his humility, thus have a common origin.

Does the interpretation I offer in these pages amount to a rational reconstruction of Kant—is it an attempt to see beyond what the philosopher actually said, to what he really meant to say? It is my sincere hope and belief that the answer to this question is *no*. The interpretation aims to be firmly grounded in what the philosopher actually said. However, it does ascribe to a notorious idealist a position that is not idealism, not anti-realism of any kind, but rather epistemic humility. It does make a metaphysician of a philosopher who is supposed to have abandoned metaphysics. And it does ascribe to a philosopher of long ago a view that has contemporary resonance: many philosophers today are indeed closer than they think to the Kantian conclusion that we have no knowledge of things as they are in themselves. There is a gulf between Kant the notorious idealist, and the realist Kant who emerges in the pages that follow, but that gulf can sometimes be explained. Many apparent expressions of idealism turn out to be expressions of epistemic humility—many, but admittedly not all. Many apparent expressions of idealism rest on dubious interpretive assumptions about what phenomena must be—many, but admittedly not all. Some qualifications and caveats are called for, and these are raised in the final chapter. They complicate the story, but they do not, I believe, undermine it. It remains as the story of what I find to be the central stream of Kant's thinking—or of what I hope others may find to be, at the very least, one driving current within it.

I

An Old Problem

1. *Introduction*

Kant affirms the existence of things in themselves and speaks of them affecting our minds, and being the cause of appearances. Since the earliest days, this has been seen as the fundamental sticking point in Kant's philosophy.[1] If Kant's philosophy is right, then we have no knowledge of things in themselves: we cannot know that they exist, nor can we know that they are causes of appearances, and affect us.[2] Kant's philosophy has been thought to imply two relations of affection, empirical and transcendental. We are affected by bodies; and we are affected by things in themselves. Both relations of affection seem illegitimate on the assumption of idealism, since the first requires causal agency of a mere representation, and the second is supposed to be unknown. Our concern here will be chiefly with the problem raised by things in themselves.

The problem, thus described, attributes to Kant two metaphysical theses.

K1 Things in themselves exist.

K2 Things in themselves are the causes of phenomenal appearances.

And it attributes to Kant an epistemological thesis.

K3 We can have no knowledge of things in themselves.

Trouble comes with the conjunction of the three. For the epistemological thesis appears to imply these corollaries:

---

[1] Jacobi being one of the first to draw attention to it; F. H. Jacobi, *Werke* (Leipzig: Gerhard Fleischer, 1815), ii. 304. See Allison's discussion of this problem, *Kant's Transcendental Idealism*, 247–54. Paul Guyer shares my suspicion of what he calls Allison's 'anodyne conceptual analysis', though he does not give the same reasons for suspicion. He too thinks that Allison's attempted solution to the problem fails. See Guyer, *Kant and the Claims of Knowledge* (Cambridge: Cambridge University Press, 1987), ch. 15, especially p. 338. My explanation of Allison's proposal draws partly on Guyer's helpful discussion, though he would disagree with my proposed solution.

[2] The 'double affection' interpretation of Kant is developed by Erich Adickes, who (oddly) sees double affection not as a problem but as a solution. See *Kants Lehre von der doppelten Affektion unseres Ich als Schlüssel zu seiner Erkenntnistheorie* (Tübingen: J. C. Mohr, 1929).

C1 We cannot know that things in themselves exist.
C2 We cannot know that things in themselves are the causes of phe-
     nomenal appearances.

We cannot know K1 and K2. Kant's story makes itself untellable.

2. *Allison's Deflationary Proposal*

In Chapter 11 of *Kant's Transcendental Idealism*, Henry Allison confronts
these problems. His response to the alleged problem of empirical causation
is swift. It is a mistake, he says, to suppose that Kant cannot legitimately
speak of affection by empirical objects: 'Kant *not only can but does* speak
about the mind as affected by empirical objects.'[3] He gives examples. But
Allison cannot argue by equivocation—even if he not only can but does.
Allison's 'can' is equivocatory. That Kant *does* something implies that he *can*
do something in one sense, but not in the other. As Kant reminds us, should
reminders be needed, doing and legitimately doing are not the same.[4] There
is more, though, to Allison's defence. He says, and I think rightly, that a
problem of empirical affection would arise only for a Berkeleyan Kant, for
whom appearances are just ideas, and he says that the Berkeleyan Kant is a
fiction. And he saves his most elegant solution for the most fundamental
problem, the one that concerns us here: namely, the existence of, and affection by, unknowable things in themselves.

The mistake, says Allison, is to construe Kant's basic theses as metaphysical theses. Construed metaphysically, the contrast between phenomenal appearance and thing in itself lands us with 'two distinct entities' or 'two
kinds of entity'.[5] That is where the trouble starts, and that is where we can
stop it in its tracks. Kant is not interested in making existence claims, says
Allison. He is interested in philosophical methodology. It is not that there
exist two kinds of thing, phenomena and things in themselves. Rather, there
are two ways of considering things. We can consider things, at the empirical level, in relation to our sensibility. And we can consider things, at the
transcendental level, in abstraction from that relation. When doing science
we sometimes consider a thing in abstraction from certain properties it has,

---

[3] Allison, *Kant's Transcendental Idealism*, 249, emphasis added. My objection is not to the
overall strategy of his defence of empirical affection, but to this particular punning argument.

[4] Kant distinguishes the question of right (*quid juris*) from the question of fact (*quid facti*)
at the beginning of the Transcendental Deduction (A84/B116).

[5] Allison, *Kant's Transcendental Idealism*, 240, 248.

such as weight: but this does not show that there are weightless things. When evaluating an applicant for a job, we sometimes consider the applicant in abstraction from certain properties she has, such as height; but this does not show that there are people who have no height. When doing philosophy, we sometimes consider things in abstraction from their relation to our sensibility, in abstraction from their spatial, temporal, categorial properties; but this does not show that there are non-spatial, atemporal, non-causal things. Kant's distinction between phenomena and things in themselves is a distinction between two ways we have of considering things, and from that distinction no metaphysical theses follow. In the absence of metaphysical theses, no further problems arise.

In place of the metaphysical K1 and K2, we have the following anodyne theses:

> A1 We can consider things 'in themselves', i.e. in abstraction from the conditions of our sensibility.
> A2 Things considered in abstraction from the conditions of our sensibility can be considered only as something that affects the mind.

Allison's view makes it analytic that things in themselves are not describable spatiotemporally. Statements about things in themselves are, by definition, statements that abstract from any talk of space, time, and the categories. This kind of abstraction is just what constitutes the transcendental level of considering things. Since knowledge arises only with the concrete application of the forms and categories, Kant's thesis K3 about our ignorance of things in themselves becomes nothing more than this:

> A3 Things considered in abstraction from their relation to our sensibility are things considered in abstraction from their relation to our sensibility.

On Allison's view, there are no unknowable entities in the picture. If we are asked to say more about the 'something' in A2 that is supposed to affect the mind, we must refuse. To say anything more at the transcendental level would be to make oneself guilty of a kind of methodological impurity. We can say nothing more until we stop abstracting, until we descend to the empirical level. Then, of course, our answer to the question 'What affects the mind?' must be an empirical answer. Light, air, elements, and all the familiar denizens of the globe are the things that affect our minds. There is no problem of affection. The 'something' in A2 is not something over and above the familiar phenomenal objects: it is identical with the class of phenomenal objects 'referred to collectively'. It is the class of those objects, considered in an abstract way.

3. *Reasons for Suspicion*

Allison's is an ingenious and attractive solution to an old and ugly problem. But I would like to suggest that there are reasons for suspicion. I have an ulterior motive. I have up my sleeve a solution that is, though less ingenious, more attractive.

First, there is a problem about analyticity. Allison's approach makes it analytic that we have no knowledge of things in themselves. To consider things in themselves is simply to consider things in abstraction from the conditions of our knowledge: K3 has become the tautological A3. From one point of view this is an advantage, but from another it is a grave defect, for it fails to do justice to an aspect of Kant that ought not to be ignored. What I have in mind is not exactly a Kantian philosophical thesis, in the sense that K1–K3 are philosophical theses. Rather, it is a Kantian attitude to these philosophical theses, and in particular to the third. When Kant tells us that we have no knowledge of things in themselves, he thinks he is telling us something new and important. The truth of K3 is a major philosophical discovery. Moreover, it is not just a discovery with a definite, non-trivial content. It is a depressing discovery. Kant thinks we are missing out on something in not knowing things as they are in themselves. Kant speaks of our yearning for something more, he speaks of doomed aspirations, he speaks of 'our inextinguishable desire to find firm footing somewhere beyond the bounds of experience' (A796/B824). It is not easy to see how this inextinguishable desire could be for the falsity of A3.

It is not inconceivable, of course, that we might have a futile yearning for the falsity of an analytic truth. The proposition that 'All men are mortal' may be analytically true, and greatly mourned for all that. So too the proposition that 'There is no triune God', believed and mourned by the new apostate.[6] We can always cry for the moon, want the impossible—even the logically impossible. But I say that it *is* inconceivable that we could have a yearning for the falsity of A3—it is inconceivable that we could have an 'inextinguishable desire' to consider things abstractly without considering things abstractly. I think this is reason enough to reject Allison's anodyne interpretation.

There is a further problem with the analyticity. If K3 were really just A3, then the question of how anyone or anything *could* have knowledge of things in themselves would be nonsense. If Allison were right, then Kant would not attempt to say what it could be to have knowledge of things as they are

---

[6] I imagine an apostate unmoved by attempts to save the Trinity by appeal to notions of relative identity. Cf. Peter Geach, ch. 7 of *Logic Matters* (Oxford: Blackwell, 1972).

in themselves. He would not attempt to give any content to what is being denied by K3. But he does. He says, for example, that to have knowledge of a thing in itself would be to be able to ascribe to it 'distinctive and inner predicates' (A565/B593).[7] The fact that Kant says anything at all about this question is hard to reconcile with Allison's interpretation. On Allison's view, to speak of a thing in itself is *ipso facto* to speak of a thing in *abstraction* from any distinctive predicates whatsoever.

Second, there is a problem about causality. Allison says that we render the causal claim about things in themselves innocuous by the simple assertion of A2, which does not commit us to non-spatial, atemporal, unknowable things. That is true. A2 does not require a causal relationship between our minds and some non-spatial, atemporal, unknowable existents. Allison avoids the traditional problem of affection. But there is a new problem in its place. A2 remains a causal claim: something affects the mind. And the question must be raised whether one is entitled to make any causal claims at all while 'considering things' at the transcendental level. If A2 is a causal claim, and causality is a category of things considered only in relation to our sensibility, then Allison seems to be failing by his own lights. In asserting A2, we fail to abstract completely from the relations things have to our sensibility. We fail to keep to the transcendental level. In ascending to the transcendental level, we are supposed to abstract from all the 'conditions of sensibility', namely space, time, and the categories. But in ascribing causality to things, we fail to abstract from the categories.

There is a further problem with the causal claim in A3. Allison's idea, if it worked, would make sense of the claim that things in themselves affect us. But it renders false the Kantian claim that things in themselves are the causes of phenomenal empirical objects. If a first thing is identical with a second thing, then it cannot be its cause.[8] And if the 'something' in A2 is *identical* with the class of phenomenal objects, referred to in an abstract collective way, then that 'something' cannot be their cause.

I have given grounds for suspicion, but they are not conclusive. They suggest that Allison is trying to see beyond what the philosopher actually said, to what he really meant to say: they suggest that Allison's project, like others before him, is rational reconstruction after all. But Allison does indeed have

---

[7] To have knowledge of a thing in itself would be to know it as 'ein durch seine unterscheidenden und inneren Prädikate bestimmbares Ding' (A565/B593), a thing determinable through its distinctive and inner, or intrinsic, predicates.

[8] This happens to be endorsed by Kant in a very early philosophical work. 'It is inconsistent that anything should have the reason for its existence in itself', he says in Proposition VI of *A New Exposition of the First Principles of Metaphysical Knowledge* (1755), Ak. i. 394, Beck 69. He there draws the implication that God is not his own cause.

a solution, where others have failed. And he thinks that non-deflationary attempts are bound to fail. He thinks Kant's problems will go away only if we stop injecting him with the poison of metaphysics. Otherwise we are bound to be left with a philosophy that crudely divides the world into different entities, that supposes an incoherent double affection, that attempts to tell the untellable. If we abandon metaphysical interpretations, and accept Allison's deflationary proposal, we will be saved much philosophical embarrassment.

I have suggested that the price of acceptance is too high. If it is, we shall need to find an alternative. I have an alternative. It is not deflationary. It does not avoid metaphysics. But it does offer a solution to the old problem.

4. *A Metaphysical Proposal, and an Acid Test Passed*

Are there two worlds, or one world considered two ways? Are appearance and thing in itself the very same? Kant seems ambivalent. Consider the following passage.

> We call certain objects, as appearances, sensible entities (phenomena), thereby distinguishing the way that we intuit them from the nature they have in themselves, we place these (considered according to this latter nature) . . . in opposition to the former, and . . . call them intelligible entities (noumena). (B306)

If we pursue the thread of Kant's anaphors we find one answer. When we call objects, as appearances, sensible entities (phenomena), we distinguish the way that we intuit *them* from the nature that belongs to *them* in themselves. The objects that have a nature that belongs to them in themselves are the same as the objects that we intuit. The labels 'noumena' and 'phenomena' refer to the same things. So it seems at first sight. However, one can find in the same passage a different answer. Phenomenal and noumenal 'entities' are described and put 'in opposition' to each other, as if they are two non-overlapping sets of things. One world or two? This ambivalence needs an explanation.

The explanation I would like to suggest draws on what Kant says elsewhere, and its defence is the topic of chapters to come. There is one world: there are simply, as Kant says with appropriate vagueness, objects, or things. But there are two, non-overlapping sets of properties. Kant speaks in this passage of the nature that things have in themselves, as he speaks elsewhere of the 'distinctive and inner predicates' of things (A565/B593). The nature things have in themselves is different from what we encounter when we intuit them: the inner or *intrinsic* predicates are different from the predicates encountered by us. There is one world, one set of things, but two kinds of properties: intrinsic properties, and properties that are 'in opposition' to the intrinsic, namely relational properties. The labels 'phenomena' and 'noumena' seem to label different entities, but really they label different classes of properties of the same set of entities. This helps to explain the ambivalence.

A distinction between two sets of properties is a metaphysical distinction, but this one has epistemological significance. To have knowledge of a thing in itself, Kant says, would be to be able to ascribe to it distinctive intrinsic predicates (A565/B593), which we cannot do. K1–K3 should be understood something like this:

> M1 There exist things in themselves, i.e. things that have intrinsic properties.
> M2 The things that have intrinsic properties also have relational properties: causal powers that constitute phenomenal appearances.
> M3 We have no knowledge of the intrinsic properties of things.

Instead of an inconsistent triad, we have a consistent one. The old and ugly problem disappears. The third claim about knowledge does not undermine the first two. It has no unwelcome corollaries. Kant's story does not make itself untellable.

Kant's existence claim in K1 looked incompatible with the knowledge claim of K3: if we literally have no knowledge of things in themselves, then we do not even know that they exist. If K3 is true, then K1 is false. But interpreted as M3 and M1 there is no inconsistency. We can know *that* there are things that have intrinsic properties without knowing *what* those properties are. Knowledge of things *as* they are in themselves involves the ability to ascribe 'distinctive intrinsic predicates' to a thing. That involves more than simply knowing that there are things that have intrinsic properties.

Kant's causal claim in K2 looked incompatible with the knowledge claim of K3. The claim that things in themselves affect us, and that things in themselves are the cause of phenomena, conflicts with the claim that we have no knowledge of things as they are in themselves. If K3 is true, then K2 is false. Interpreted as M3 and M2, however, there is no inconsistency, at least on a certain assumption. On the assumption that causal powers are not intrinsic properties, we can know that a thing has certain causal powers without knowing what its intrinsic properties are. We can know that things are in certain causal relations with other things without being able to ascribe to them any 'distinctive and intrinsic predicates'. If this is so, there is no problem of affection here.

Finally, we do not need to ignore Kant's sense of loss. Kant's attitude to K3 is not the attitude of a man doing conceptual analysis. We have no knowledge of things in themselves despite having an 'inextinguishable desire' for such knowledge. This attitude makes more sense on the assumption that K_3 is really M_3. There is indeed an entire aspect of the world that remains hidden from us. We are indeed missing out on something. It may be a trivial, analytic thesis to say, with Allison, that we can have no knowledge of things in abstraction from the conditions of knowledge. It is by no means trivial, analytic, that we have 'no insight whatsoever into the intrinsic nature of things' (A277/B333). That is a substantial philosophical discovery, and, in Kant's eyes, a cause for mourning.

2

Three Kantian Theses

1. *Introduction*

The problem of the previous chapter, and the two solutions considered, hinge on a distinction that is at the heart of Kant's philosophy, although some have wanted to excise it. Kant says that the 'object as appearance' is to be distinguished from 'the object as it is in itself' (B69). It is easy to think that Kant means to draw a distinction between what is dependent on the mind, and what is independent of the mind. Kant's distinction cannot help but conjure up a vision of the veil of appearance, with ideas, or impressions, or representations, on one side of the veil, and things that are independent of us hidden for ever behind it. That vision is at its most provoking in passages like these.

External things, namely matter, are . . . nothing but mere appearances, that is, representations in us, of whose reality we are directly conscious . . . Objects . . . in themselves remain unknown to us . . . If I remove the thinking subject, the whole corporeal world must vanish. (A371–2, A379, A383)

Here we have Kant's apparent idealism expressed at its most extreme—and the claim that objects in themselves are unknown to us seems to be part and parcel of that apparent idealism. Kant's philosophy can be made to look like the worst of all veil of appearance philosophies: Berkeley plus unknowable things in themselves. Kant can seem to make the physical world a world of mere ideas, that will vanish on the removal of the thinker. But we know that Kant vehemently rejected the charge that he was a Berkeley in disguise, and he rejected it not simply because the Berkeleyan interpretations ignored the existence of things in themselves, and not simply because they ignored the claims to objectivity established in the Analytic. There is something in principle quite wrong about understanding Kant's distinction in any way that resembles a traditional veil of appearance. That is something I hope to make more evident in time, but for the moment I want to begin by drawing out a different picture, a picture that I introduced in Chapter 1, but did not attempt to explain or justify. Let me place a typical expression of Kant's distinction in the company of some passages which I believe illuminate it.

(1) This object as appearance is to be distinguished from itself as object in itself. (B69)

(2) The understanding, when it calls an object in a relation mere phenomenon, at the same time forms, apart from that relation, a representation of an object in itself. (B306)

(3) Concepts of relation presuppose things which are absolutely [i.e. independently] given, and without these are impossible. (A284/B340)

(4) Substance is that which is . . . an absolute subject, the last subject, which does not as predicate presuppose another further subject. (*R* 5295)

(5) The pure concept [of] substance would mean simply a something that can be thought only as a subject, never as a predicate of something else. (A147/B186)

(6) Substances in general must have some intrinsic nature, which is therefore free from all external relations. (A274/B330)

(7) The substantial is the thing in itself and unknown. (*R* 5292)

(8) We have no insight whatsoever into the intrinsic nature of things. (A277/B333)[1]

A fuller context for these passages will need to be considered in due course. Each passage, I believe, represents an aspect of Kant's own philosophical view, even when (as in some cases) the context is one in which Kant is discussing the views of others. For now let me merely note that my belief that each of these represents an aspect of Kant's own view is not particularly idiosyncratic, and is at least in partial agreement with a number of other commentators.[2]

[1] Note D. P. Dryer's translation of B69: 'The object has then to be distinguished *as presenting itself* from what it is as object *in itself.*' (Dryer, *Kant's Solution for Verification in Metaphysics* (London: George Allen & Unwin, 1966), 513 n 3.) *R* 5295 and *R* 5292 (Ak. xviii. 145) are dated M 1777–80, i.e. probably the period of the writing of the *Critique*, whose first edition appeared in 1781.

[2] Compare the following commentators, who seem to agree that Kant is endorsing some of the views he attributes to Leibniz in the Amphiboly of the Concepts of Reflection: Dryer, who says, 'By a thing in itself is meant any thing whatever considered apart from relations in which it stands', *Kant's Solution*, 514; Norman Kemp Smith, who says of such passages in the Amphiboly of the Concepts of Reflection, 'Kant . . . is profoundly convinced of the essential truth of the Leibnizian position', *Commentary to Kant's Critique of Pure Reason* (London: Macmillan, 1923), 418–19; Jill Vance Buroker, who says of A284/B340, 'It is a conceptual truth about real relations that they presuppose non-relational properties of existing things . . . Leibniz had that much right', *Space and Incongruence* (Dordrecht: Reidel, 1981), 84–5; Paul Guyer, who says of a passage similar to those quoted (A249–52) that 'the very notion of an appearance—a relation in which something stands to me—implies the independent existence of something which appears', *Kant and the Claims*, 455 n. 22; Heinz Heimsoeth, who says that Kant denies us 'genuine knowledge of substantiality', in 'Metaphysical Motives in the Development of Critical Idealism', Moltke Gram, ed., *Kant: Disputed Questions* (Chicago: Quadrangle Books, 1967); and James van Cleve, who takes seriously, though ultimately rejects, the interpretive possibility of 'things in themselves as things apart from relation', in 'Incongruent Counterparts and Things in Themselves', G. Funke and T. M. Seebohm, eds., *Proceedings of the Sixth International Kant Congress*, vol. ii. Pt. 2 (Washington, D.C.: Center for Advanced Research in Phenomenology and University Press of Amer-

The first of the above passages, with its awkward idea that we must distinguish an object 'from itself', asserts Kant's fundamental distinction. We must distinguish two aspects of an object: the object as it appears to us, and the object as it is in itself. We must distinguish the object as it is in relation to us from the same object as it is in itself.

The second passage shows how we should understand this. We must, in general, distinguish the way an object is in relation to something else, from the way that object is 'in itself', that is to say, 'apart from that relation'. Kant uses the word 'phenomenon' in this second passage to signify simply 'an object in a relation'. Kemp Smith's translation makes an insertion here: 'an object in a [certain] relation', implying perhaps that the relation Kant has in mind is exclusively the 'certain' relation that holds between a thing and a human mind. There is no need for this interpolation. Kant has something quite general in mind. There is, however, a prima facie difficulty with this idea of an object at once existing 'in a relation' and 'apart from that relation'. One natural way of understanding the idea that an object exists 'apart from a relation' to something else is precisely as a *denial* of the idea that it bears a relation to something else. This makes Kant's statement incoherent: we must think of an object as at once bearing a relation to something else, and not bearing a relation to something else. We need to find a different way of interpreting the phrase 'apart from that relation'.

The third passage gives us what we need, and at the same time supports the very general interpretation we gave to the second passage. Concepts of relation, Kant says, 'presuppose things which are absolutely [i.e. independently] given': that is to say, concepts of relation presuppose the existence of relata whose existence is independent of the relation. That means we must distinguish between a thing as it is in relation to something else, and a thing as it is 'absolutely', or (with Kemp Smith's gloss on *schlechthin*) 'independently' of that relation. Instead of the incoherent idea of an object that is at once in a relation to something else, and not in a relation to something else, we have the coherent idea of an object whose existence is independent of its relations to other things. An 'object in itself' could exist even in the absence of those other things. It need not coexist with any other distinct thing: its existence, let us say, does not imply *accompaniment*. Its existence is compatible with its being the only thing: its existence is compatible, let us say, with *loneliness*.[3]

---

ica, 1989), 33–45; in 'Inner States and Outer Relations: Kant and the Case for Monadism', Peter H. Hare, ed., *Doing Philosophy Historically* (Buffalo, N.Y.: Prometheus Books, 1988); and in 'Putnam, Kant, and Secondary Qualities', *Philosophical Papers* 24 (1995), 83–109.

[3] The terms 'accompaniment' and 'loneliness' are from David Lewis, 'Extrinsic Properties', *Philosophical Studies* 44 (1983), 197–200. Lewis uses these to define, not the notion of substance, but Jaegwon Kim's notion of an intrinsic property, discussed below.

The idea of a thing that exists 'absolutely' or independently is the idea of a substance. And this brings us to the fourth and fifth passages: a thing that is an 'absolute subject' is a substance, something that can be thought only as a subject, never as a 'predicate' of something else. Here, as elsewhere, Kant means property by 'predicate'. So the idea of a substance is the idea of something that is an ultimate property bearer, that cannot itself be borne by anything else. The fifth passage says in addition that this is the 'pure concept' of a substance, the concept of a substance in general. The implicit contrast here is with the schematized concept of a substance, about which we shall have more to say in the next chapter.

The sixth passage says something more about the pure concept, the notion of a substance in general. 'Substances in general must have some intrinsic nature, which is therefore free from all external relations.'[4] Substances, things that exist independently of relations to other things, 'absolute' subjects which cannot be thought of as predicates of something else, are things that have some 'intrinsic nature' (*etwas Inneres*). They must have properties that are 'free' of the substance's external relations (*äußere Verhältnisse*): free of relations the substance bears to things other than itself.[5] And they must have properties that are not simply relational, or extrinsic, properties. Substances must have intrinsic properties. What does Kant have in mind here, with this notion of 'something intrinsic' to a substance, something which is 'free of all external relations'? Let us say, as a first approximation, that intrinsic properties are those which do not imply coexistence with any other thing—they are properties which do not imply accompaniment, and (equivalently) are compatible with loneliness. Properties which do imply accompaniment, and (equivalently) are incompatible with loneliness, are the extrinsic, or relational, properties. This understanding of intrinsicness (suggested by Jaegwon Kim, and explored by David Lewis)[6]

---

[4] I translate *äußere Verhältnisse* as 'external relations'. It should convey the idea of a relation to something else, and should be regarded as neutral as to any doctrine of the internality or externality of relations, construed as a thesis about the reducibility of relations (whether to intrinsic properties of terms, or to terms themselves). The issue of reducibility/irreducibility will be central to the later arguments of Chapters 5 and 6, but because of associations with the British Idealists, I avoid the 'internality/externality' labels in that discussion. One could translate *außer* as *outer* (as Kemp Smith does), but it is important to avoid a purely spatial implication.

[5] A possible contrast here might be a relation, e.g. identity, that a thing bears to itself.

[6] Jaegwon Kim, 'Psychophysical Supervenience', *Philosophical Studies* 41 (1982), 51–70; David Lewis, 'Extrinsic Properties'. Lewis, on Kim's behalf, defines accompaniment as the property of coexisting with some *wholly* distinct *contingent* object. I find Kim's account of the intrinsic/extrinsic distinction—as interpreted by Lewis—a close enough approximation to Kant's for present purposes. But as we shall see shortly, if we are to attribute something like it to Kant, the word 'wholly' probably ought to be omitted, to account for Kant's apparent view that spatial properties are extrinsic because part-dependent (and likewise, as we shall

seems like a reasonable first attempt to capture the notion of intrinsicness Kant has in mind.

On this way of thinking, there is a close connection between the notion of a substance and the notion of a bearer of intrinsic properties. A substance is a thing which can exist absolutely, independently of its relations to other things. A substance is the kind of thing that can exist on its own: it can exist and be lonely. But nothing can exist without having properties. If a substance can exist on its own, it must have properties that are compatible with its existing on its own. If a substance can be lonely, it must have properties compatible with loneliness. So a substance must have intrinsic properties.

At this stage let us pause and, putting together what we have so far, see what conclusion we reach for Kant's distinction between 'appearance' and 'object in itself'. An object in itself is a thing that exists independently of its relations to other things. An object in itself is a substance, which has intrinsic properties. A phenomenon is an object in a relation to something else. The same object can be described both as phenomenon and as object in itself, precisely because the same object that has relations to other things also has an 'intrinsic nature'. If we keep the label 'phenomenon' for the general case of an object in a relation to something else, as suggested in the second of the above passages, then 'appearance' to a human mind can be thought of as a special case. An object that is in a relation to human sensibility is an object that is in a relation: and if we must *in general* distinguish an object as it is 'in a relation', from an object as it is 'in itself' (B307), then we must also in this case 'distinguish this object as appearance' from the object 'as object in itself'.

This understanding of phenomena can be linked with another description offered by Kant in a context where his aim is to distinguish phenomena, not from things in themselves, but from subjective appearances: a context where his purpose is epistemological rather than metaphysical. Phenomena, he says, are appearances that are objective: 'appearances, in so far as they are thought to be objects, in accordance with the unity of the categories, are called phenomena' (A249). Appearances are not phenomena if

---

see in Chapter 4, for Leibniz). Lewis showed the Kim definition to be inadequate: 'lonely' is an extrinsic property, but intrinsic on Kim's definition. However, for a recent and more optimistic defence of a Kim-style definition, see Rae Langton and David Lewis, 'Defining 'Intrinsic'', *Philosophy and Phenomenological Research*, 58 (1998). Langton and Lewis define a *basic intrinsic property* as a property *independent* of loneliness and accompaniment, where independence means that all four cases are possible: something can have the property and be lonely, something can lack the property and be lonely, something can have the property and be accompanied, something can lack the property and be accompanied. We propose that intrinsic properties supervene on basic intrinsic properties. For an excellent (and different) discussion of Kant's notion of intrinsicness, see van Cleve, 'Putnam, Kant, and Secondary Qualities'.

they are not objective, not thought to be objects. The two descriptions are compatible: an objective appearance (a phenomenon according to A249) may also be an object in a relation (a phenomenon according to B306). Phenomena may be objects in a relation, where the relation is something with which we are acquainted: phenomena may thus be both objective, and appearances.

Considered this way, phenomenon may be viewed as the genus of which appearance to human sensibility is the species. Considered this way, Kant's distinction between phenomena and things in themselves is very far from being a phenomenalistic distinction between mental representations and things independent of the mind. It can be summarized thus.

> *Distinction*: Things in themselves are substances that have intrinsic properties; phenomena are relational properties of substances.

Here we have a metaphysical thesis, and it is the first of the three theses of my title. For ease of reference I shall use it with a capital initial, as a proper name, from now on.

Some clarification is called for. If Kant says 'an object in a relation' is to be entitled a phenomenon, and such an object is a substance, then there is good reason for identifying phenomena with substances, rather than with properties. So one could say that Kant's Distinction should instead be understood like this. Things in themselves are substances *qua* bearers of intrinsic properties; phenomena are those substances *qua* bearers of relational properties. This, I think, would be basically right. But it would also be potentially misleading, since it would bring with it a temptation to think that substances are somehow in the phenomenal world. There are some delicate issues to negotiate here. This notion of substance is so closely tied to the notion of a bearer of intrinsic properties that Kant can also say, in the seventh passage above, that 'the substantial *is* the thing in itself' (*R* 5292, emphasis added). And he can say that phenomena consist 'wholly of relations' (A265/B321). If substance is the substantial, and the substantial is the thing in itself, and the thing in itself is the bearer of intrinsic properties, then any temptation to locate substance—in *this* sense—in the phenomenal world is to be avoided. For this reason, I propose to identify phenomena with the relational properties of the substances, and with whatever things are constituted by those relational properties.

While the first thesis of this chapter is solely metaphysical, the others, while partly metaphysical, also concern epistemology. Consider again the seventh of the passages quoted at the outset. Kant says 'the substantial is the thing in itself and *unknown*'(emphasis added). And consider the eighth passage. Kant says that 'we have *no insight whatsoever* into the intrinsic nature of things' (emphasis added). Kant thinks we have no knowledge of things as they are in themselves. But here that does not express idealism, but something else—the second of the three Kantian theses.

> *Humility*: We have no knowledge of the intrinsic properties of substances.

These two theses evidently lay behind the argument of Chapter 1. M1 and M2 both drew on the Distinction: the former asserts the existence of things in themselves as things that have intrinsic properties; the latter says that those things also have relational properties that constitute phenomenal appearances. And M3 of that argument amounts to the thesis of Humility. Together, these two theses are what made it possible to avoid that old and ugly problem: to avoid ascribing to Kant tales of the untellable, and to pass what Allison described as the 'acid test' for an interpretation of Kant's philosophy.

This way of understanding Kant helps us to see why he thinks it would be so absurd to deny the existence of things in themselves—and why the wise and sane course adopted by many of his philosophical successors, the course of jettisoning things in themselves, would seem to him so ludicrous. One often finds in Kant an argument that the very notion of an appearance—an objective appearance, a phenomenon—implies the existence of a thing in itself.

Although we cannot know these objects [i.e. objects of experience] as things in themselves, we are required to be able to think of them as things in themselves. Otherwise we should have the absurd conclusion that there could be appearance without there being something that appears. (Bxxvi)

Now we should bear in mind that the concept of appearance . . . itself establishes the objective reality of noumena, and justifies the division of objects into phenomena and noumena, and indeed in such a way that the distinction does not refer simply to the logical form of our knowledge . . . but to the way in which they are themselves generically distinct from each other. For if the senses represent to us something merely as it appears, this something must also be a thing in itself. (A249)

It follows naturally from the concept of an appearance in general that something which is not itself appearance must correspond to it. For an appearance can be nothing on its own . . . Unless we are to move in an endless circle, the word 'appearance' must already indicate a relation to something . . . which, however, must be something in itself. (A251–2)

In regarding objects of the senses merely as appearances, we thereby acknowledge that a thing in itself underlies them, although we have no knowledge of how it is in itself . . . Thus, through the very admission of appearances, the intellect acknowledges the existence of things in themselves as well; and we can say that to this extent the thought of such beings underlying the appearances is not only permissible, but unavoidable.[7]

These passages convey a line of thinking which bears close similarities to what we have just encountered. Notice that they make little sense on a phenomenalistic interpretation, according to which appearances are sense data, or conscious states of mind: what could be easier to suppose than that there could be an appearance without there being something that exists in itself, apart from our states of mind? But if an appearance is a phenomenon, an object in a relation (B307), and if concepts of relation presuppose something that exists in itself, independently of the relation (A284/B340), then appearance presupposes something that exists in itself, independently of the relation that is involved in appearance. We have here a particular application of the more general principle. As a general rule, relations, and relational properties, imply the existence of independent bearers: substances capable of existence in the absence of relations to other things, having properties capable of existence in the absence of relations to other things. The inference from appearance to the existence of a thing in itself is an application of this general rule. The inference is not incompatible with the epistemological thesis of Humility. The final passage, from the *Prolegomena*, explicitly distinguishes claims about the existence of things in themselves from claims about how the things are in themselves. Although we cannot know *how* a thing is in itself (*wie es an sich beschaffen sei*), we must none the less acknowledge the *existence* of things in themselves (*das Dasein von Dingen an sich selbst*). There exist things in themselves, there exist things that have an intrinsic nature. But we do not know them as they are in themselves: we do not know how they are intrinsically constituted, we do not know what their intrinsic nature is.

We can see here what care must be taken when considering Kantian claims about our ignorance or knowledge of 'things in themselves'. Sometimes the phrase (and its German equivalents) may be taken to function as a name for the things: a shorthand for 'things that have an intrinsic nature'. Sometimes it may be taken to work differently, so that 'in themselves' applies not simply to the things, but to the content of our knowledge of the things: we know them, or do not know them, *as* they are in themselves. 'We have no knowledge of things in themselves' is then ambiguous between 'we have no knowledge of the things that have an intrinsic nature', and 'we have no knowledge of what their intrinsic nature is'. On these disambiguations, the first reading is false: we do have some knowledge of the things that have an intrinsic nature. We know that such things exist. Moreover we are acquainted with

---

[7] *Prolegomena*, Ak. iv. 314–15, Lucas 75–6.

some of the properties of the things that have an intrinsic nature—we are acquainted with their relational properties, which make up phenomenal appearances. And on these disambiguations, the second reading is true: we have no knowledge of what their intrinsic nature is. The issues here are delicate, both philosophically and terminologically: but I shall try to capture the second kind of usage with the phrase 'things *as* they are in themselves'. It is then no contradiction to say: we have knowledge of things in themselves (i.e. of things that have an intrinsic nature), yet we have no knowledge of things *as* they are in themselves (i.e. of how they are, intrinsically).

Kant seems to believe that our ignorance of things as they are in themselves follows directly from the fact that we have knowledge only in so far as things are given to the *senses*: 'Properties that belong to things as they are in themselves can never be given to us through the senses' (A36/B52). The epistemological thesis of Humility appears to be linked to a certain view about what the senses can give us. What is at stake, then, in this notion of the *senses?*

To say that knowledge of things depends on the senses is to say that it depends on our being *affected* by things.[8]

(Human) intuition . . . is always sensible, that is . . . affected by objects. (A35/B51)

The receptivity of our mind, its power of receiving representations in so far as it is affected in any way, is called 'sensibility'. . . . Our nature is such that our intuition can never be other than sensible, that is, it contains only the way in which we are affected by objects. (A51/B75)

Here we come to the empiricist strand in Kant's thinking, and the third Kantian thesis of this chapter.

> *Receptivity*: Human knowledge depends on sensibility, and sensibility is receptive: we can have knowledge of an object only in so far as it affects us.

Kant believes that our ignorance of the intrinsic properties of things follows from the fact that knowledge depends on our being affected by things: he thinks that Humility follows from Receptivity.

In the remainder of this chapter I shall try to explain and defend these three theses, as interpretations of Kant, and show how they raise a particular problem. Section 2 is devoted to a philosophical exploration of the Distinction, comparing it with a similar metaphysical distinction cautiously

---

[8] The understanding of receptivity developed here conflicts with Wilfrid Sellars's suggestion that receptivity, for Kant, is 'a peculiar blend of the passivity of sense and the the spontaneity of the understanding', a suggestion which I do not find very Kantian. See Sellars, *Essays on Philosophy and its History* (Dordrecht: Reidel, 1974), 49.

attributed to Kant by Jonathan Bennett, according to which the thing in itself/phenomenon distinction is, roughly, a substance/property distinction. Section 3 marshals additional textual support for all three Kantian theses, discussing each of the three in turn, and showing how they raise a problem. The problem can be simply stated: Kant appears to believe that Humility follows directly from Receptivity, but it does not so follow. This is the belief which Strawson calls a fundamental and unargued premise of the *Critique*.[9] I conclude that the problem to which Strawson draws our attention is one that sorely needs an answer. What is needed, I suggest, is a premise which, conjoined with Kant's Distinction, and the thesis of Receptivity, will imply Humility. What is needed is something that will allow us to see why, granted a division between the intrinsic and the relational properties of substances, the mere fact that we are receptive creatures implies our ignorance of the intrinsic properties of substances, and thereby implies our ignorance of things as they are in themselves. The search for that missing premise is among the chief tasks of this enquiry, and it is the subject of Chapters 4 to 6.

That the notion of a thing in itself functions as the notion of a substance in Kant is not an unfamiliar idea, and has been remarked upon, and complained about, by many commentators, among whom Jonathan Bennett has been particularly enlightening. Something very like the contrast between the Distinction I attribute to Kant, and the phenomenalistic 'veil of appearance' distinction more commonly attributed to Kant, is explicitly drawn in both of his commentaries.[10] Although Bennett in the end takes his rational reconstruction down a phenomenalistic path, his discussion provides a useful way of locating the Distinction I want to attribute to Kant, and it also offers a potentially plausible alternative. So the next section has an extended discussion and evaluation of Bennett's suggestion, as a means of gaining a better philosophical understanding of what Kant's Distinction amounts to, with a particular focus on one side of the Distinction: the thing in itself.

2. Bennett on Two Distinctions and their Conflation

Bennett finds a long tradition of confusion about notions of substance and substratum throughout the history of philosophy, a confusion 'endemic' to the thought of practically all the philosophers he considers, and he finds

---

[9] Strawson, *Bounds of Sense*, 250.

[10] Jonathan Bennett, *Kant's Analytic* (Cambridge: Cambridge University Press, 1966), 184–7; Bennett, *Kant's Dialectic* (Cambridge: Cambridge University Press, 1974), 105–8. The discussion on which I focus is in the latter. The widespread philosophical conflation of the two distinctions is also a theme of his book *Locke, Berkeley, Hume* (Oxford: Oxford

Kant no exception to this confusion. There is a tendency, he says, to conflate the following two distinctions:

(a) the distinction between things, and the sensory states which are
their appearances;
(b) the distinction between substrata, and the properties they support.

According to Bennett, the conflation of these two has much to answer for in
philosophy's history (Berkeley's idealism being just one of its pernicious
effects), and he traces the confusion to two sources. First, a certain slipper-
iness with such terms as 'idea' in the British tradition enabled the same label
to refer both to sensory states and to properties, with the result that substances could be viewed as the supporters of 'ideas' in both of those senses.
Second, the apparent similarity of two plausible claims, that we know things
only through their appearances, and that we know things only through their
properties, paved the way for the identification of appearances with properties. To one in the grip of this confusion, the notion of substance steps in
to fill the dual functions of both (a) thing as it is apart from the sensory states
which are its appearance, and (b) substratum, or bearer, of properties.

Kant belongs firmly within this confused tradition, according to Bennett.
He uses 'substratum' sometimes to mean bearer of properties, and sometimes to mean the thing in itself behind the appearance.[11] The conflation of
properties with appearances is illustrated, he thinks, in these remarks on
rational psychology, whose other implications need not concern us here
(though we shall return to them in Chapter 10).

If I understand by soul a thinking being in itself, the question whether or not it is
the same in kind as matter—matter not being a thing in itself, but merely a species
of representations in us—is by its very terms illegitimate. For it is obvious that a
thing in itself is of a different nature from the determinations which constitute only
its state. (A360)[12]

The thing in itself is here contrasted with, on the one hand, representations
in us, and, on the other hand, the 'determinations' or properties that 'constitute' the 'state' of the thing itself. Kant's argument appears to move
directly from representations in us, to the properties or state of a thing, as
if these were the same. He thus appears to conflate Bennett's first distinction (a) above, with the second, (b).

University Press, 1971), and his article 'Substance, Reality and Primary Qualities', *American
Philosophical Quarterly* 2 (1965), 1–17.
    [11] Bennett finds examples at B225, B231, A359, B645, B225.
    [12] This is Kemp Smith's translation; the passage is translated somewhat differently when
it is discussed again in Chapter 10.

Bennett is right to say that the conflation of those two distinctions would be a confusion. And he may be right to suggest that the conflation is, if not 'endemic' to philosophy, at least more prevalent than one would like. Postponing for the moment the question of whether Kant is guilty, it seems that some of his commentators may be. Heinz Heimsoeth, more sensitive than many commentators to the metaphysical dimensions of Kant's thought, nevertheless moves indiscriminately between 'appearances' to us, 'representations' in us, and 'properties' of things in themselves, as if these words and phrases were synonymous.[13] This kind of talk is the target of Bennett's complaint. If Kant is guilty of confusion here, he is not the only one. And if Kant is guilty of confusion here, then one might hope that it is the business of his commentators to try to diagnose it and understand it, not merely to perpetuate it.

This brings us to the question of whether Kant is in fact guilty as charged. First, suppose that he is. What then? If Bennett is right, then Kant is interested in two issues which he fails clearly to distinguish. One concerns the gap between sensory states and things independent of them (Bennett's (a) distinction). The other concerns the instantiation of properties in a substance (Bennett's (b) distinction). Kant is interested in the veil of appearance, and the metaphysics of property instantiation, and fails to distinguish these two issues clearly. The thing in itself, as a substance, is made to fill the two distinct roles of mind-independent reality, and bearer of properties. How should one respond to this (alleged) confusion? Bennett, like many of Kant's critics, advocates ignoring the thing in itself altogether, and therefore ignoring it in either of those two identified roles. We should focus on what is then left of the first distinction: namely, sensory states. According to Bennett, Kant should be understood as advocating a kind of phenomenalism: objects are logical constructions out of actual and possible sensory states. The (b) distinction, concerning objects and properties, will then have application for these phenomenal objects, but that has nothing to do with the banished thing in itself.

That is not the only possible response. Bennett has discovered, let us suppose, two streams in Kant's thinking. He pursues one, and leaves the other behind. But what of the stream which Bennett identifies and then goes on to ignore? Kant's idea that appearances are *properties of a substance* gets short shrift with Bennett. It will not get such short shrift here.

All this is on the assumption that Bennett's complaint is correct, and that there are in fact two incompatible streams in Kant's thought. But it is far from evident that the complaint is correct. It seems to me that Kant's Dis-

---

[13] Heimsoeth, 'Metaphysical Motives', 164, 168, 169.

tinction, as I understand it, makes it possible to avoid the mere conflation that Bennett sees. If the thing in itself is a substance, then it will be able to fulfil both roles identified by Bennett. It will be able to fulfil the role of bearer of properties, and the role of mind-independent reality, for if a substance is independent of other things in general, then it is, *a fortiori*, independent of human minds. Moreover, on this interpretation it is easier to move from property talk to appearance talk than Bennett's approach would allow. Bennett assumes that appearances are sensations, or constructions thereof, and on that assumption a move from 'appearances' to properties of substances is a conflation. But we can avoid this problem if appearances are, in the first place, properties of a substance: relational properties of a substance, and in particular, those relational properties with which we can be acquainted. One can interpret Kant's contrast in A360 between the 'nature' of a thing 'in itself', and the 'determinations' that make up its 'state' or situation (*Zustand*), as precisely a contrast between the intrinsic and the relational properties of the thing. There is nothing in what has been said so far to imply that appearances are, as Bennett thinks, sensations, and there is much to oppose it. This does not, I concede, explain why Kant sometimes wants to move from talk of appearances to talk of 'representations in us'. It does not explain why Kant wants to make colourful counterfactual statements about the vanishing of the corporeal world. There are possible explanations for these statements, but I am afraid they are to be postponed until the final chapter.

I said that Bennett's pair of distinctions resemble the two competing interpretations of Kant with which I began, the traditional 'veil of appearance' view, and the Distinction I attribute to him. That is not quite right. Bennett's first distinction (a) between sensations and mind-independent things does coincide with the traditional veil of appearance distinction. However, his second distinction (b) does not quite match the Distinction that I attribute to Kant. To say that Kant distinguishes a substance from its properties (Bennett's (b) distinction), is not exactly to say that Kant distinguishes a substance as bearer of intrinsic properties from the relational properties of the substance (the Distinction). Bennett's (b) distinction has much in common with the one I propose: both are basically metaphysical distinctions; both provide an alternative to the veil of appearance; both give a role to the thing in itself as substance, and as bearer of properties; both say that phenomena are properties of a substance. But according to the Distinction I attribute to Kant, phenomena are some, not all, of the properties—they are only the relational properties. And things as they are in themselves are not simply substances, but substances as bearers of intrinsic properties. So the Distinction adds to Bennett's (b) distinction a division between different kinds of properties.

Bennett's simpler distinction raises the possibility of a different line of argument for the thing in itself which Bennett himself does not pursue. There are some grounds for attributing it to Kant, and it has one very great virtue, as an interpretation of Kant's distinction: as we shall see in a moment, it leads immediately and uncontentiously to the conclusion that we cannot possibly know a thing in itself. This is a virtue sadly lacking in the Distinction I want to attribute to Kant. Given the apparent similarities between Bennett's substance/property distinction and the Distinction, and this apparent virtue of his, Bennett's substance/property distinction deserves more careful attention. It is worth playing devil's advocate on its behalf, though careful reflection will bring us back to the Distinction in the end.

3. *A Case For, and Against, the 'Bare Substratum'*

Kant may be trying to distinguish substance as property-bearer from the properties a substance bears: that was Bennett's (b) suggestion. On this hypothesis, what Kant means by 'thing in itself' is simply substance as property-bearer. If this were correct, then it would place Kant in a long tradition of metaphysicians who hold that such a distinction must be made.

Whenever a property is instantiated, it is possessed by a particular or substance that is ontologically distinct from the property it possesses. When we say that the pencil is red, we think of the possessor of the property as being distinct from the redness we attribute to it. But what goes for this property goes for all properties: so we must think of the bearer as distinct from the redness, colouredness, length, shape, smoothness, or any other property we care to name. What then is this substance to which we attribute these various properties? Every candidate answer will 'merely' attribute some further property to the substance. It will not tell us what the substance *is*. It will 'merely' tell us what properties the substance possesses. This is the 'naked lady' theory of substance, satirized thus by Peter Geach, who says the theory invites metaphysicians to 'mentally strip off' the characteristics or properties of a thing to reveal, ultimately, the 'bare particular' in all her glory. But in place of glory there is frustration and bathos: the particular vanishes, leaving nothing at all (except, perhaps, some grist to a feminist mill).[14]

---

[14] See e.g. Genevieve Lloyd, *The Man of Reason* (London: Methuen, 1984), and Jane Flax, 'Philosophy and the Patriarchal Unconscious', in S. Harding and M. Hintikka, eds., *Discovering Reality: Feminist Perspectives in Epistemology, Metaphysics, Methodology, and Philosophy of Science* (Dordrecht: Reidel, 1983), for two among many recent feminist explorations of the political and psychoanalytic implications of metaphor in philosophy.

Geach's conclusion is that philosophers have, yet again, been beguiled by language: 'some people are so hypnotized by mere words that even without jargon they will think to avoid contradiction by change of the stress: "A substance can have no *qualities* because *it* is *what has* the qualities"!'[15] This may be a conception of substance to be found in Locke as well, explained and possibly satirized by him too in the following famous passage:

[I]f any one will examine himself concerning his *Notion of pure Substance in general,* he will find he has no other Idea of it at all, but only a supposition of he knows not what support of such Qualities which are capable of producing simple Ideas in us; which Qualities are commonly called Accidents. If anyone should be asked, what is the subject wherein Colour or Weight inheres, he would have nothing to say, but the solid extended parts; and if it were demanded, what is it, that the Solidity and Extension inhere in, he would not be in a much better case, than the *Indian . . .* who, saying that the World was supported by a great Elephant, was asked what the Elephant rested on; to which his answer was, a great Tortoise; But being again pressed to know what gave support to the broad-back'd Tortoise replied, something, he knew not what. And thus here . . . we talk like Children; who, being questioned, what such a thing is, which they know not, readily give this satisfactory answer, That it is *something*; which in truth signifies no more, when so used, either by Children or Men, but that they know not what . . . The *Idea* then we have, to which we give the general name Substance, being nothing, but the supposed, but unknown support of those Qualities, we find existing, which we imagine cannot subsist, *sine re substante,* without something to support them, we call that Support *Substantia*; which, according to the true import of the Word, is in plain *English, standing under,* or *upholding*.[16]

Mockery is a possible response to this metaphysical picture, the response of Geach and (less certainly) Locke. But another response might be to accept the picture, accept the claim that there are indeed substrata, and deny that it is in principle possible to know them. Since knowledge involves the ascription of properties to a distinct substance, of course the substance in so far as it is distinct from properties will be unknown: there is nothing to know. Questions about what a bare substratum is *like* do not make any sense, as Bennett says. In short, if the thing in itself were a bare substratum, then it would be plausible for Kant to both assert its existence and deny knowledge of it.

A first thing to be said in favour of this interpretation is that Heimsoeth, with specialist knowledge of Kant's metaphysics, sometimes seems to

---

[15] P. T. Geach, *Truth, Love and Immortality* (Hutchinson: London, 1979), 47. A more sympathetic discussion of the bare substratum theory of substance is to be found in Michael J. Loux, *Substance and Attribute* (Dordrecht: Reidel, 1978), 108–12.

[16] *Essay* II. xxiii. § 2.

attribute it to him. Heimsoeth says that according to Kant 'the finite subject grasps other substances only through . . . "properties"'.[17] He has in mind such passages as the following: 'Since we know a thing only through its predicates, we cannot know the subject in itself alone' (*R* 5290).[18] Since this is suggestive of a bare substratum interpretation of the thing in itself, Heimsoeth attributes to Kant the view that we have knowledge only of predicates or properties of things, and therefore do not have knowledge of any substance distinct from those predicates or properties.

Unfortunately Heimsoeth at the same time attributes to Kant the view that we are thereby *missing out* on something. He attributes to Kant the view that there could be such a thing as knowledge of a substance that was not knowledge of its predicates: hence the *wistfulness* of tone—'only' through properties—and the hinted possibility of 'genuine knowledge' that is not only through properties. This air of disappointment, which is indeed present in Kant (as I observed in Chapter 1), does not sit well with any 'bare substratum' interpretation of the thing in itself. There is nothing to miss out on.[19]

Leaving Heimsoeth aside, there may be more to be said in favour of the 'bare substratum' interpretation: there may be textual support for it within the *Critique* itself. Perhaps it is what Kant means when he says that 'Matter . . . is mere external appearance, the *substratum* of which cannot be known through any *predicate* . . .' (A359, emphasis added). If Kant really means that the thing in itself cannot be known through *any* predicate, then this would be perfectly intelligible on a bare substratum interpretation.

Moreover, it may be that we can find in Kant precisely the train of thought that Geach describes, particularly if we keep in mind Bennett's hypothesis that Kant may sometimes conflate 'representation' with 'property'. Consider the following typical passage about the transcendental object. If we experimentally substitute 'property' for 'representation' (*Vorstellung*), taking seriously Bennett's hypothesis, we have a line of thinking which appears to have close affinities with the bare substratum view.

---

[17] 'Metaphysical Motives', 164, my emphasis.

[18] Ak. xviii. 146, M 1777–80.

[19] There are some reasons for thinking that this is not Heimsoeth's considered, or at least not his only, interpretation. For Heimsoeth appears to run together a number of different interpretations of the thing in itself, and while it is possible (though uncharitable) to believe that Kant holds them all at once, Heimsoeth does not seem alert to their differences. In addition to the 'bare substratum' idea of the thing in itself are two other very different ideas, one of the thing in itself as having *intrinsic* or 'inner properties' of which we are necessarily ignorant, and another idea of the thing in itself as having *essential* properties of which we are necessarily ignorant. All three may have interpretive merits, but they are hardly the same.

All [properties] are, it is true, referred by the understanding to some object; and since appearances are nothing but [properties], the understanding refers them to a something, as the object . . . But this something, thus conceived, is only the transcendental object; and by that is meant a something = x, of which we know . . . nothing whatsoever, but which . . . can serve only for the unity of the manifold . . . By means of this unity the understanding combines the manifold into the concept of an object. This transcendental object cannot be separated from the . . . data, for nothing is then left through which it might be thought. Consequently it is not in itself an object of knowledge. (A250)

On this interpretation, a transcendental object, *ein Etwas* = *x*, is the particular to which properties are ascribed, the item to which the manifold and various properties are attributed, the 'something' conceived of as bearer of properties, but not really separable from the properties we attribute to it. Independently of the properties we attribute to it, we can think of it only as a 'something': not an object of knowledge. It is tempting here to borrow Geach's parody: the transcendental object *has* no properties because *it* is *what has* the properties. But that would be unfair to Kant, I think. He would be guilty of no contradiction if he thought of the transcendental object as bare substratum, as far as I can see. The transcendental object would be knowable in so far as we attribute properties to it, but conceived of as a particular 'something' distinct from the properties, not knowable. Can we identify Kant's transcendental object with the thing in itself? Kant's doctrine of the transcendental object has been frowned upon. Kemp Smith, for example, dismisses it as a 'pre-Critical or semi-Critical survival [which] must not be taken as forming part of Kant's final and considered position'.[20] Whether or not that is so, what seems clear, and is indeed emphasized by Kemp Smith, is that Kant does use 'transcendental object' and 'thing in itself' as synonyms.[21] So passages like A250 might well be thought to support the interpretation we are considering: the transcendental object, and therefore the thing in itself, is a bare substratum.

Finally, it is worth noting in its favour that the 'bare substratum' interpretation may, at a stretch, be compatible with the first three of the four passages with which I began this chapter.

This object as *appearance* is to be distinguished from itself as object *in itself*. (B69)

The understanding, when it entitles an object in a relation mere phenomenon, at the same time forms, apart from that relation, a representation of an *object in itself*. (B307)

---

[20] Kemp Smith, *Commentary*, 218.
[21] See, for example, A191/B236, A277/B333 ff., A288/B344, A358, A361, A366, A372, A379, A390, A393, A394. These are all cited by Kemp Smith.

Concepts of relation presuppose things which are absolutely [i.e. independently] given, and without these are impossible. (A284/B340)

The idea of an object in itself could conceivably be interpreted as the idea of a property bearer that is distinct from (exists apart from, independently of) any properties whatsoever. It could therefore conceivably be interpreted as the idea of a 'bare substratum'.

However, the bare substratum interpretation creaks and strains at this point, and it collapses completely when we include the fourth passage.

Substances in general must have some intrinsic nature, which is therefore free from all external relations. (A274/B330)

If the thing in itself is a substance, then it is not a substance conceived of as a bare substratum, but a substance conceived of as having 'some intrinsic nature', *etwas Inneres*. And if we stop cheating on behalf of the devil and fill in the ellipses in the passages at A359 and A250, we find that 'matter is mere external appearance, the substratum of which cannot be known through any predicate *that we can assign to it*' (A359, emphasis added). Kant does not mean that the substratum cannot be known through any predicate at all. He means that it cannot be known through any predicate or property that we are in a position to ascribe to it. And when we turn to A250, we find that Kant means by 'transcendental object', 'a something = x, of which we know, and *with the present constitution of our understanding can know*, nothing whatsoever . . .' (A250, emphasis added). It is quite evident that Kant thinks that there is something to know, but that we cannot know it—not at any rate with the 'present constitution of our understanding'. This is incompatible with the bare substratum interpretation. And the passage from the *Reflexionen* can be reinterpreted in light of this as an expression of Humility: 'since we know a thing only through its [relational] predicates, we cannot know the subject as it is in itself alone' (*R* 5290).

In short, the point made against Allison in the last chapter holds equally here. It is patently obvious that Kant thinks we are missing out on something: there *is* something to know that we cannot know. That is why he is a chastened and disappointed metaphysician, as Heimsoeth rightly implied, but wrongly explained. For it makes no sense to suppose that anything could in principle—no matter what the 'constitution' of its understanding (A250)—have knowledge of a bare substratum. My conclusion is that, while the 'bare substratum' interpretation of the thing in itself has some prima facie plausibility, it fails. The thing in itself is not unknowable in virtue of its 'bareness' of properties: it is unknowable in virtue of its having intrinsic properties that we cannot know.

4. *Three Theses: Some Further Texts*

So far I have described Kant's Distinction rather abstractly, with little attention to the question of what phenomena and things in themselves are like,
which now emerges as the question of what the relational and intrinsic properties of substances are. The task of remedying this will be a long one, and
will take us beyond the scope of this chapter. We can begin, though, by mar-
shalling some additional texts, some of which are more complete versions
of those considered earlier. Our interest is in their implications for all three
theses, to be taken one at a time.

(9) The *Intrinsic* and *Extrinsic*.—In an object of the pure understanding the
intrinsic is only that which has no relation whatsoever (so far as its existence is
concerned) to anything different from itself. It is quite otherwise with a *substantia phaenomenon* in space; its intrinsic properties are nothing but relations,
and it itself is entirely made up of mere relations. We are acquainted with substance in space only through forces which are active in this and that space, either
drawing other objects (attraction) or preventing their penetration (repulsion
and impenetrability). We are not acquainted with any other properties constituting the concept of the substance which appears in space and which we call
matter. As object of pure understanding, on the other hand, every substance
must have intrinsic properties and powers which concern its inner reality.
(A265/B321)

(10) Substances in general must have some intrinsic nature, which is therefore free
from all external relations . . . But what is intrinsic to the state of a substance
cannot consist in place, shape, contact, or motion (these determinations being
all external relations). (A274/B330)

(11) Matter is *substantia phaenomenon*. I search for that which belongs to it intrinsically in all parts of the space which it occupies, and in all the actions it performs, and these of course can only be appearances to external sense. So I have
nothing that is absolutely intrinsic, but only what is comparatively intrinsic,
and that is itself again constituted by external relations. It is silly to suppose
that matter has an absolute intrinsic nature of the sort conceived by pure understanding, for matter is not an object of pure understanding. On the other hand,
the transcendental object which may be the ground of this appearance that we
call matter is a mere something. We would not understand what it was, even if
someone could tell us . . . If the complaints that 'we have no insight whatsoever into the intrinsic nature of things' are supposed to mean that we cannot
grasp by pure understanding what the things which appear to us may be in
themselves, they are completely unreasonable and stupid. They want us to be
able to be acquainted with things without senses! (A277/B333)

(12) All that we know in matter is merely relations (what we call its intrinsic prop-

erties are intrinsic only in a comparative sense), but among these relations some
are . . . enduring, and through these we are given a determinate object . . . It is
certainly startling to hear that a thing is to be taken as consisting wholly of relations. Such a thing is, however, mere appearance. (A285/B341)

(13) Everything in our knowledge which belongs to intuition . . . contains nothing
but mere relations, of locations in an intuition (extension), of change of location (motion), and of laws according to which this change is determined (moving forces). What presents itself in this or that location, or, beyond this change
of location, what activities occur within the things themselves, is not given
through these relations. Now through mere relations one cannot be acquainted
with a thing as it is in itself. We may therefore conclude that since external sense
gives us nothing but representations of mere relations, this sense can contain
in its representation only the relation of an object upon the subject, and not
the intrinsic properties that belong to the object as it is in itself. (B67)[22]

These passages are taken from Kant's discussion of metaphysics in The
Amphiboly of the Concepts of Reflection, except for the last, which is from
the Transcendental Aesthetic.

5. *The Distinction*

Consider the subtitle in (9), 'The *Intrinsic* and *Extrinsic*' (*Das Innere und
Äußere*). Kant draws a distinction between two classes of properties (*Eigen-
schaften, Bestimmungen, Akzidenzen*). He draws a contrast between properties a thing has when it has 'no relation whatsoever . . . to anything different
from itself', and properties a thing has when it does have some relation to
something 'different from itself'. He thus draws a distinction between properties that are intrinsic and those that are not. Kant does not distinguish very
clearly between relations and relational properties, referring to forces, for
example, as both. But a basic distinction is clearly being made between the
intrinsic and extrinsic, or relational—somehow construed. We shall have
more to say about this in a moment. The distinction itself is not offered by

---

[22] The fourth sentence in passage (11) is more literally: 'the absolute intrinsic nature,
according to pure reason, of matter, is a silly idea, a mere fantasy (*Grille*)'. With respect to
the first ellipses of passage (12), Kant actually says 'selbständige und beharrliche', which
Kemp Smith translates 'self-subsistent and permanent'. Given that the purpose of the passage is to show among other things that phenomenal substance is precisely *not* self-
subsistent in the manner of a true substance, I would translate this as 'independent and permanent', where the independence in question is not taken to be absolute independence, but
independence from the flux of change, in line with the First Analogy and the B Refutation
of Idealism. Independence of this kind is required for the arguments of the Analytic, but the
absolute independence of a thing 'that exists apart from all relation' is not. This point is
developed in the argument of the next chapter.

Kant as something novel. As a matter of fact, it is present in the metaphysics textbook that Kant himself used, in teaching, for most of his life. Baumgarten distinguishes intrinsic properties from extrinsic, describing the former as inner, absolute determinations, the latter as external, relative determinations, or (equivalently) relations.[23] While the distinction between two classes of properties is not offered as something novel, something else is.

What is novel—what is indeed *startling*, according to Kant—is his own proposal that there is something that consists wholly of relations. Matter, phenomenal substance, 'consists wholly of relations' (12), is 'constituted by external relations' (11), is 'entirely made up of mere relations' (9), is 'nothing but mere relations' (13). He refers briefly in (9) to the 'intrinsic properties' of matter, but that is swiftly undermined: what we call its intrinsic properties are intrinsic only in a comparative sense, and it is silly to suppose that matter is the sort of thing that could have an absolutely intrinsic nature (11 and 12). In all of these passages there is a clear expression of one side of the Distinction: phenomena are constituted by relations, or relational properties.[24]

What of the other side of the Distinction? Consider (13), an important and complex passage to which we shall have reason to return. What presents itself as matter in space is not given through the relations that constitute matter: the intrinsic properties that belong to the object as it in itself are absent from matter in space. Any activities occurring within the things themselves are not given through the relations. Kant seems clearly to be talking about two aspects of the one thing: the thing that presents itself to us as matter—as something constituted by relations—is the same as the thing that has 'activities' occurring within it, 'intrinsic properties belonging to the object as it is in itself'. In (11) this thought recurs. There is a transcendental object, a ground of this appearance that we call matter, a ground which has an intrinsic nature; but the object is for us a mere something, since the

---

[23] Baumgarten says that relations are external 'determinations', which may be why, in Kant's usage, relations seem to be viewed as properties. '§ 37. *Relationes* [Verhältnisse] . . . sunt . . . *determinationes externae* [äussre] (relativae, ad extra, extrinsecae), reliquae omnes, *internae* [innre Bestimmungen].' A. G. Baumgarten, *Metaphysica* (1757), reprinted in the Academy edition of Kant's works, Ak. xvii. 35. Square brackets contain the original German annotations. Baumgarten also says that if determinations are considered as belonging to a thing in the absence of a nexus they are 'absolute', whereas if they are considered to belong to a thing only when it is in a nexus, they are 'respective'. Ermanno Bencivenga draws attention to Baumgarten's text in *Kant's Copernican Revolution* (New York: Oxford University Press, 1981), 32.

[24] For a different interpretation of these passages see Harold Langsam, who argues that properties of phenomenal things are intrinsic, but relational in their concepts, in 'Kant, Hume, and Our Ordinary Concept of Causation', *Philosophy and Phenomenological Research* 54 (1994), 625–47.

intrinsic nature is unknown. Passage (9), in light of these, bears a similar interpretation. The substance which appears in space and which we call matter must also have another aspect: it must have intrinsic properties and powers that concern its inner reality.

These passages have implications for different aspects of our understanding of phenomena: for phenomenena as external appearance; for phenomena as matter; and for phenomenal substance. The first two of these topics can be attended to here; the third is a large one, and needs the more detailed attention I give it in the next chapter.

Kant often refers to phenomena as external appearance (*äußere Erscheinung*), and one might wonder whether Kant's discussion in the passages above sheds any light on this notion. The phrase is usually interpreted in a *spatial* sense—'outer appearance'. And the phrase is usually interpreted in such a way that 'external' means 'external *to us*'. The notion of an *external appearance* is thus taken to convey the idea of appearances *outside us, in space*. However, Kant's discussion in the above passages gives us reason to reconsider the notion of external appearance, and to ask whether it may sometimes mean something rather different.

Kant here describes a certain class of properties as *extrinsic* (*außer,* or nominalized as *das Äußere*). If appearances are external because they are phenomena, and phenomena are external because they are extrinsic, or relational, properties, then the usage of *außer* in the notion of 'external appearance' may well be connected with the usage of *außer* here. There are two potential ambiguities. The first is noted by Kant himself elsewhere, who says that the idea can sometimes carry an implication of *outerness* and sometimes an implication of *otherness* (A373). Suppose we deem 'external' to be an equally ambiguous English translation: then to say that x is external to y can be to say that x is outside y, located in a different part of space to y; or it can be to say that x involves something other than y, something distinct from y. These two notions are not the same, though it is part of the argument of Kant's Aesthetic that the two are closely connected in human experience.[25] Kant says: 'By means of outer sense . . . we represent to ourselves objects as distinct from us (*außer uns*), and all without exception in space' (A22/B37). Kemp Smith's translation of the *außer uns* is spatial, 'outside us', but this makes a tautology of something Kant does not appear to be offering as a tautology.[26] What Kant means by outer sense, or external

---

[25] This connection has been fruitfully explored by many, including Strawson, *Bounds of Sense*; Strawson, *Individuals* (London: Methuen, 1959); Gareth Evans, 'Things Without the Mind', in Zak van Straaten, ed., *Philosophical Subjects* (Oxford: Oxford University Press, 1980), 76–116; Bennett, *Kant's Analytic*; Guyer, *Kant and the Claims*.

[26] Cf. Guyer, *Kant and the Claims*, 311.

sense, is our capacity to be affected by things external to us, distinct from us, other than us. By means of outer, or external, sense, we represent these distinct objects that affect us *as* distinct from us, by representing them in space.

The *Äußere* of the subtitle is potentially ambiguous in a similar manner, between having to do with *space*, and having to do with *something else*. 'External' can have a spatial sense, or it can have the more general sense of extrinsic (when Kant speaks of 'relational or external properties'—*Verhältnis- oder äußeren Bestimmungen* (B339/A283)). It is important to avoid the mistake of taking it for granted that extrinsic properties are *ipso facto* spatial properties. And when Kant speaks of external appearance throughout the *Critique*, it should not be taken for granted that by 'external' he means simply 'in space'.

There is a second ambiguity to note. Assuming that 'external' is sometimes to be taken as meaning 'extrinsic', a further question is: external to *what*? In A22/B37 , Kant clearly means external to *us*—but in the numbered passages listed above 'external' means external, or extrinsic, to *a substance*. To be sure, the properties in question of shape, contact, attraction, repulsion, are also external to us: but what is relevant, given the contrast Kant wants to draw, is that they are external, or extrinsic, to a substance, a thing in itself, whose intrinsic properties are unknown. When Kant refers throughout the *Critique* to external or outer appearance (*äußere Erscheinung*), it is not always evident which of the two possibilities he means. But if appearances are constituted by properties of a substance, and in particular, by extrinsic or relational properties of a substance, then while 'external appearance' may well be external to us, what Kant may sometimes mean is that appearance is external to the substance, the thing in itself. This understanding of Kant thus allows us a rather different interpretation of the notion of an external appearance. To say that we know the external appearances of things, but not the things as they are in themselves, is to say that we know the extrinsic, but not the intrinsic, properties of substances.

There are also implications here for our understanding of the realm of phenomena as the realm of *matter*. Phenomenal properties are physical properties, and Kant says in these passages that physical properties are all relational. Kant mentions two kinds of physical property, in (9) and (13): spatial properties of 'place, shape . . . motion', and dynamical properties, forces of attraction and repulsion, or impenetrability. These, he says, are 'all relations', 'nothing but relations', 'mere relations'. Elsewhere he says that what is given to us in space are 'merely relations, formal, or also real' (A284/B340), again distinguishing between spatial (formal) and dynamical (real) relations. In what sense are spatial and dynamical properties 'nothing but relations'?

Kant seems to believe that spatial properties, even apparently intrinsic

properties such as shape, are extrinsic, or relational, because they depend
on the parts of the shaped body: 'Corporeal things are never anything but
relations only, at least of their parts external to one another' (A283/B339).
This suggests that Kant's understanding of intrinsicness is to be interpreted
in a particular way. It was suggested that an intrinsic property is a property
something can have even when unaccompanied by another distinct thing:
but what counts as another distinct thing? A proper part of a thing is not
identical with the whole it is part of: so it is, in one sense, a distinct thing,
even if not a wholly distinct thing. If the spatial properties of an extended
object depend on the parts of the object, and if a part is a distinct thing for
the purposes of Kant's notion of intrinsicness, then spatial properties are
extrinsic properties. So perhaps that is how Kant's notion of intrinsicness
is to be understood.

Dynamical properties are relational for very different reasons. In explaining why they are 'mere relations', Kant says that forces 'are active in this or
that space, either drawing other objects (attraction) or preventing their penetration (repulsion and impenetrability)' (A265/B321). Now this notion of
force (*Kraft*) which is so central to Kant's matter theory is not easy to clas-
sify; or rather, there seems to be more than one feature of the physical world
that is picked out by his notion of force. Is force a relation—for example,
the relation a thing bears to another when a thing *attracts* another? Or is it
a causal power to enter into such relations—for example, the *power* a thing
has to attract another? Kant seems to think of forces as both. He thinks of
them as relations (of attraction and repulsion), and as causal powers (of
attraction and repulsion)—and either way, as relational properties. Certainly
the notion of force, however construed, is a causal notion. Kant describes it
as a predicable of the relational categories of causality and (in the case of
reciprocal attraction and repulsion) community (A82/B108). Some philosophers in our own time have argued that force is to be understood as a species
of the causal relation itself.[27]

The notion of force can also be understood as the notion of a power—
which is itself to be thought of as a certain kind of relational property.
Forces, construed this way, are relational, because they are powers to act in
certain ways towards other things: something has a force of attraction when
it has a power to attract something else; something has a force of impenetrability when it has a power to repel something else. Something can have a
power to attract without actually attracting, so the power is not to be identified with the relation itself. All the same, there is something relational,
something other-directed, about the *concept* of a force, construed as a power.

---

[27] See, for example, John Bigelow, Brian Ellis, and Robert Pargetter, 'Forces', *Philosophy
of Science* **55** (1988), 614–30.

There is, we can say, something *conceptually* relational about a force, thus construed: something has an attractive power if and only if it would attract other things in certain circumstances. That is a fact about the concept of a force, or power. Does that prove that force, construed this way, is an extrinsic property? No. The relationality of concepts is not the same as the extrinsicness of properties. Whether a power is to be classified as an extrinsic property will depend on what we take intrinsicness to be: and on the definition so far considered, it will depend on whether something could have a power in the absence of other distinct things. Answers to that complex question may well differ, even among philosophers today—so I propose for now to postpone considering it until a more appropriate occasion arises (in Chapter 5). What seems clear enough, and adequate for our present purposes, is that forces—understood as causal powers—are regarded by Kant himself as properties that are not only conceptually relational, but also extrinsic.[28]

We here encounter Kant's dynamical theory of matter, which he endorsed in some form throughout the length of his philosophical career, and which forms a backdrop to some of the more puzzling parts of the *Critique*. This theory, and some of its merits, will be discussed in more detail later (Chapters 5 and 8). According to Kant, matter is constituted by fundamental forces of attraction and repulsion. Matter requires the interaction of both forces: for if attraction existed alone, matter would coalesce to a point, and if repulsion existed alone it would be dispersed to infinity. Matter is thus constituted by a 'conflict' of forces:

Since all given matter must fill its space with a determinate degree of repulsive force, in order to constitute a determinate material thing, only an original attraction in conflict with an original repulsion can make possible a determinate degree of the filling of space, which is matter.[29]

Kant sees matter as made up, not of atoms, but centres of force. Since forces are relational properties, according to Kant, and since the realm of matter is the phenomenal realm, the phenomenal realm is thus constituted by relational properties, just as the Distinction says. And this brings us back to the previous point: the realm of *matter* is what Kant describes as '*external*

[28] Lloyd Humberstone advises that the 'intrinsic/extrinsic' distinction be distinguished from the 'non-relational/relational' distinction, the former being a label for properties of properties, the latter for properties of concepts. However, I use 'relational' and 'extrinsic' as synonyms, for convenience, and Humberstone's label of 'relational' becomes my label of 'conceptually relational'. The distinction becomes especially important for cases where intrinsic properties are designated by relational concepts: e.g. the property of being shaped like the Eiffel Tower. (Some philosophers may think powers may belong in this category, but Kant, so I argue, does not.) See Humberstone, 'Intrinsic/Extrinsic', *Synthese* **108** (1996), 205–67.
[29] *Metaphysical Foundations*, Ak. iv. 518, Ellington 69.

appearance, the substratum of which cannot be known through any predicate that we can assign to it' (A359, emphasis added). Matter is external appearance, constituted by forces, constituted by the extrinsic properties of the substance or substratum of matter—the thing in itself. Kant's matter theory was significant in the historical development of physics, being a descendant of that of Leibniz, cousin to that of Boscovich, and ancestor of Faraday's field theory. A further complexity in the notion of force that he is working with is that it is, historically, a precursor to the notion of energy. What is important for us here, however, is the connection with Kant's broader philosophy. If matter is force, and force is a 'relation', Kant's matter theory and his Distinction are closely intertwined.[30]

These passages support the Distinction I attribute to Kant, but they also raise a difficulty. According to the Distinction there are things in themselves, that is to say, substances having intrinsic properties: but what could this possibly mean? These passages have given us some indication of what the relational properties might be that constitute phenomena, but they have also made it very difficult to see what Kant can possibly have in mind when he speaks of *das Innere*, since none of the traditional paradigms count, for him, as intrinsic properties. Shape is traditionally thought to be an intrinsic property: but not for Kant. Solidity is traditionally thought to be an intrinsic property: but in matter, according to Kant, there is no solidity, merely impenetrability, one of the two fundamental forces he describes as 'mere relations'. For the moment I want simply to acknowledge this difficulty, but maintain none the less that it does not undermine the Distinction. For it would be surprising if apparently familiar properties of shape and solidity were to be counted amongst the intrinsic properties referred to in the Distinction, if—as Humility advises—we have no knowledge of them whatsoever.

---

[30] This connection between Kant's matter theory and his philosophy is made by Ian Hacking, who suggests that Kant's development of field theory went hand in hand with his rejection of knowable noumena (Hacking, *Representing and Intervening* (Cambridge: Cambridge University Press, 1983), 100). The suggestion is partly right, though Hacking's speculation about Kant's own supposedly positivist attitudes to theoretical entities is not (101). For an excellent recent study of Kant's theory of physics, emphasizing Kant's relation to Newton, and emphasizing space rather than force, see Michael Friedman, *Kant and the Exact Sciences* (Cambridge, Mass.: Harvard University Press, 1992). For the contribution of Kant's dynamism to the history of science and to field theory, see Max Jammer, *Concepts of Force* (Cambridge, Mass.: Harvard University Press, 1957); Mary Hesse, *Forces and Fields* (London: Thomas Nelson, 1961); W. Berkson, *Fields of Force* (London: Routledge & Kegan Paul, 1974); and especially L. P. Williams, *Michael Faraday: A Biography* (London: Chapman & Hall, 1965). See also, for comparison, R. J. Boscovich, *A Theory of Natural Philosophy* (1763), trans. J. M. Child (Cambridge, Mass.: MIT Press, 1966).

6. *Humility*

Besides supporting the Distinction, the above passages evidently have something to say about knowledge, and the limits on what we can know. Kant says, 'We are *acquainted* with substance in space only through forces' (9), 'All that we *know* in matter is merely relations' (11), 'Everything in our *knowledge* which belongs to intuition . . . contains nothing but mere relations' (13) (emphasis added). He denies that we have knowledge of things in themselves by saying that we have no knowledge of the intrinsic properties of substances (9, 11, 13). These passages express Humility. Note that in (9) and (11) Kant describes these unknown bearers of intrinsic properties as 'objects of pure understanding'.

In an object of the pure understanding the intrinsic is only that which has no relation whatsoever (so far as its existence is concerned) to anything different from itself. It is quite otherwise with a *substantia phaenomenon* in space; its intrinsic properties are nothing but relations, and it itself is entirely made up of mere relations. (A265/B321)

This usage points to a more epistemic characterization of Kant's basically metaphysical distinction. It concerns how it is in principle possible for a knower to know a thing. It contrasts the sensible and the intelligible.

It is already implicit in our concepts that, if we call certain objects, as appearances, sensible entities (phenomena), thereby distinguishing the way that we intuit them from their intrinsic nature, we place the latter (considered in their own nature) . . . in opposition to the former, and . . . call them intelligible entities (noumena). (B306)

Doubtless indeed there are intelligible entities corresponding to the sensible entities. (B309)

Kant is not non-committal here. He asserts the existence of things in themselves, speaks of them having a 'nature' that belongs to them in themselves, and calls them 'intelligible entities'. For some critics this kind of talk is on a par with talk of the 'transcendental object': an illegitimate relic of dogmatic metaphysics, a fossil that harks back to a past era when Kant did indeed hold that things in themselves were intelligible to human minds. But by calling them intelligible Kant does not mean to imply that their properties are knowable to us. He may be implying that reason requires us to infer their existence, and thus to 'think' them: but that is not to know them, for knowledge would require knowing what they are like in themselves. One main purpose of his label is to make a contrast: it is to emphasize that they are not sensible, that their intrinsic nature is epistemically inaccessible to receptive creatures. That is not dogmatism but Humility.

The passages illustrate the link in Kant's thinking between Humility and the relational character of the physical world. Let us first reconsider (13):

Everything in our knowledge which belongs to intuition . . . contains nothing but mere relations, of locations in an intuition (extension), of change of location (motion) and of laws according to which this change is determined (moving forces). What presents itself in this or that location, or, beyond this change of location, what activities occur within the things themselves, is not given through these relations. Now through mere relations one cannot be acquainted with a thing as it is in itself. We may therefore conclude that since external sense gives us nothing but representations of mere relations, this sense can contain in its representation only the relation of an object upon the subject, and not the intrinsic properties that belong to the object as it is in itself. (B67)

Kant here has something general to say about our knowledge of relational and intrinsic properties. Through knowledge of mere relations we cannot be acquainted with a thing as it is in itself. We cannot, merely through knowledge of the relational properties of an object, be acquainted with 'the intrinsic properties that belong to the object as it is in itself'. He concludes that our acquaintance in intuition with 'mere relations' of an object leaves us ignorant of the intrinsic properties that belong to the object in itself.

And consider again passage (11).

Matter is *substantia phaenomenon*. I search for that which belongs to it intrinsically in all parts of the space which it occupies, and in all the actions it performs, and these of course can only be appearances to outer sense. So I have nothing that is absolutely intrinsic, but only what is comparatively intrinsic, and that is itself again constituted by external relations. It is silly to suppose that matter has an absolute intrinsic nature of the sort conceived by pure understanding, for matter is not an object of pure understanding. On the other hand, the transcendental object which may be the ground of this appearance that we call matter is a mere something. We would not understand what it was, even if someone could tell us . . . If the complaints that 'we have no insight whatsoever into the intrinsic nature of things' are supposed to mean that we cannot grasp by pure understanding what the things which appear to us may be in themselves, they are completely unreasonable and stupid. They want us to be able to be acquainted with things without senses! (A277/B333)

The 'unreasonable and stupid' demand that we should have knowledge of the 'intrinsic nature' of things is a demand for which Kant has sympathy, despite his sarcasm. He feels the pull of that demand himself, which is why he can elsewhere speak so powerfully of the philosopher's yearning, his 'inextinguishable desire to find firm footing somewhere beyond the bounds of experience' (A796/B824). That desire, he says, is doomed. And it is unreasonable to lament our fate unduly. What is unreasonable is not the assertion that 'we have no insight whatsoever into the intrinsic nature of things', for Kant too asserts that we cannot know 'what the things which appear to us may be in themselves'. But it is unreasonable to spend our time complaining. Why? Because our ignorance follows from the fact that our knowledge depends on our *senses*. The 'unreasonable and stupid' demand that we have knowledge of the intrinsic properties of things is a demand that we should be able to be 'acquainted with things without senses' (A277/B333). It is, in other words, an unreasonable and stupid wish that our knowledge were not *receptive*.

7. *Receptivity*

Let us begin here with some further expressions of the thesis of Receptivity.

Properties that belong to things as they are in themselves can never be given to us through the senses. (A36/B52)

It is not that through sensibility we are acquainted in a merely confused way with the nature of things as they are in themselves; we are not acquainted with that nature in any way at all. (A44/B62)

Here we have the empiricist Kant who begins his *Critique* with a resounding declaration of the indispensability of the senses to the acquisition of knowledge:

There is no doubt that all our knowledge begins with experience. For how should our capacity for knowledge be awakened into action, if objects did not affect our senses, and partly of themselves produce representations, and partly arouse the activity of our understanding to compare these representations, combine and separate them, and thus work up the raw material of sensory impressions into that knowledge of objects which is called experience? (B1)

This is the thesis of Receptivity implicit in the numbered passages, not only in (11), with its indignation directed towards the stupid wish of those who hoped for something other than receptivity, but also in others. It is present in (13) in the mention of external *sense*; in the mention of 'intuition' (which can only be sensible), and in the thought that external sense represents the relation of an object 'upon' (*auf*) the subject—the causal action of an object upon a receptive sensibility. The latter thought can be understood in terms of the general point made in (9) that 'we are acquainted with substance in space only through forces': forces being causal powers things have to affect each other (9), and to affect our own senses (9 and 13).

Kant clearly thinks that there is something about his empiricist starting-point, something about the *senses*, that prevents us from having knowledge

of the intrinsic natures of things. But why should he think so? The answer
is not easy to come by.

Strawson is keenly aware of the importance of this question, or his version of it, and he says that Kant never offers an answer. According to Kant,
says Strawson,

knowledge through perception of things . . . as they are in themselves is impossible. For the only perceptions which could yield us any knowledge at all of such
things must be the outcome of our being affected by those things; and for this reason
such knowledge can be knowledge only of those things as they appear . . . and not
of those things as they . . . are in themselves. The above is a fundamental and unargued complex premise of the *Critique*.[31]

Strawson is absolutely right, I think, to emphasize that it is the mere
requirement that *we are affected* by things that is supposed to preclude knowledge of how those things are in themselves.

In this remark Strawson draws attention to a fundamental unanswered
question in Kant's philosophy—and also to a distinctive aspect of Kant's
empiricist assumption. Kant thinks that knowledge depends on the senses,
but in thinking of sensibility he does not begin with the familiar data of
sense, as Berkeley does: the cherry, red, and round, and sweet. He begins
with the most abstract characterization possible. The basic fact about sensibility, in Kant's view, is that it is *passive*, a capacity to be affected by things.
His notion of sensibility is essentially a causal notion. He does not, of course,
think that being affected by something is a sufficient condition for having
knowledge of it: in addition to Receptivity there is a complex doctrine of the
spontaneity of the understanding, and its application of categories. But
Receptivity is at least a *necessary* condition for knowledge. Here are some
representative passages.

The receptivity of our mind, its power of receiving representations in so far as it is
affected in any way, is to be called sensibility . . . Our nature is so constituted that
our intuition can never be other than sensible, that is, it contains only the way in
which we are affected by objects. (A51/B75)

(Human) intuition . . . is always sensible, that is . . . affected by objects. (A35/B51)

The receptivity of the subject [is] its capacity to be affected by objects. (A26/B42)

Human knowledge depends on sensibility, and sensibility is receptive. We
can have knowledge of an object only in so far as it affects us.

Now it might be wondered why anyone would think it worth making such
a fuss about the passivity of sensibility. Once one has accepted the empiricist presumption that knowledge depends on the senses, the rest of the

---

[31] P. F. Strawson, *Bounds of Sense*, 250.

thesis looks easy. What could it mean for something to be 'given to us through the senses' (A36/B52) if not that we are receptive to and affected by objects? The thesis of Receptivity, its abstractness notwithstanding, looks obvious, trivial.

It is not, though. One can easily imagine a competing empiricist picture, a cautious phenomenalism perhaps, that turns its back on metaphysical-sounding talk of human faculties (whether active or passive), admits the existence of sense data, professes agnosticism about causality generally, and therefore questions the meaningfulness of statements asserting causal relations between sense data and the world. Such a phenomenalism[32] would admit that something is given to the senses, but admits no passive sensibility. It would admit that something is given to the senses without thereby admitting that something *affects* the senses. It does not go without saying that an empiricist presumption must express itself in a *causal* thesis like that of Receptivity. Kant's endorsement of Receptivity, taken on its own, would yield a particular kind of empiricism: something that more closely resembles a causal theory of knowledge than a phenomenalism.

Kant does not think it goes without saying that knowledge requires a passive sensibility either, and he writes of a different contrast, one that has already been implicitly encountered in the contrast between the sensible and the intelligible. When Kant asserts of human beings that we have a passive sensibility, he compares that with another way of achieving knowledge, impossible for us, but not for God, who has an 'original' or 'active' intuition, and is a being to whose view 'all things lie open . . . with total clarity'.[33] Intelligible entities are indeed intelligible—to him.

Our way of intuiting is dependent upon the existence of the object. So it is possible *only if the subject's faculty of representation is affected by that object* . . . However universal this may be, it does not cease to be sensibility. It is derivative (*intuitus derivativus*), not original (*intuitus originarius*), and therefore not an intellectual intuition . . . Such intellectual intuition . . . can never be ascribed to a dependent being. (B72, first italics added)

Here, in the concept of the original intuition, we strike depths which I have no ambition to plumb, merely pausing to note the significance which Kant evidently attaches to his apparently obvious premise of Receptivity. A further sign is to be found in the startling implications he takes Receptivity to have for knowledge of the mind itself.

---

[32] Perhaps Hume, perhaps the Russell of the logical atomism phase ('Philosophy of Logical Atomism' (1918), in R. C. Marsh, ed., *Logic and Knowledge* (London: Allen & Unwin, 1956), 175–281). Most relevantly for Kant (as we shall see in the ensuing chapters) it is *Leibniz* who denies Receptivity.

[33] *New Exposition* (1755), Ak. i. 391, Beck 64, an early expression admittedly.

If the capacity of becoming self-conscious is the capacity of seeking out (appre-
hending) what lies in the mind, the mind must affect itself . . . it then intuits itself . . .
as it is affected by itself, therefore as it appears to itself, not as it is. (B69)

Here again we strike deep and murky waters, and here again my aim is simply to emphasize the *seriousness* with which Kant treats his apparently obvious premise of Receptivity, and to emphasize the very general implications
he sees it as having for Humility in every sphere of knowledge. The most
fundamental fact about our intuition is that it is receptive: our way of intuiting is dependent upon the existence of the object, and so it is 'possible only
if the subject's faculty of representation is affected by that object'. Kant says
that 'our intuition can never be other than sensible, that is, it contains only
the way in which we are affected by objects' (A51/B75). If this is indeed the
most fundamental fact about our intuition, then when Kant says that an
existing thing is presented in intuition, he means, first and foremost, that it
affects our sensibility.

   We only know objects in so far as they affect us: therefore we do not know
them as they are in themselves. We have knowledge of things only through
the senses: therefore we do not know their intrinsic properties. Kant seems
to think these are valid inferences, but if Strawson is right, he gives us no
good reason at all for thinking they are.

   In the absence of any justification from Kant, it might be possible to safely
disentangle the good Kantian empiricism from its dubious *alter ego*, which
is just what Strawson does. His Kant is a kind of Janus, sane and mad, whose
benign empiricist face vies with the face of an ugly idealism, which invokes
a supersensible realm only to banish us from it for ever. Strawson thinks one
face can be safely ignored. Kant thinks there are not two faces but one. He
thinks that *because* we have knowledge only through the senses, there *must*
be aspects of reality that are necessarily beyond our grasp. He thinks that
Receptivity implies Humility. If Kant is right, we cannot separate these two
in the way that Strawson hoped.

   At the other end of the interpretive spectrum we find, again, Heimsoeth,
who embraces the metaphysical Kant with open arms. He shows some testi-
ness towards the empiricist thieves who have stolen Kant in the misguided
belief that he is one of their own. 'One can no longer believe', he says, 'that
Kant's "critical" attitude can be taken as a model for one's own avoidance
of all metaphysical problems.'[34] Heimsoeth, with formidable scholarship,
traces every wrinkle on the face that so repelled Strawson, and in the process
gives full acknowledgement to Kant's inference from Receptivity to Humility. But he acknowledges it and simply endorses it. He offers this as his own

---

[34] 'Metaphysical Motives', 158.

commentary on Kant's inference: 'finite knowledge . . . must make contact with its object only by Receptivity. It follows from this that no finite knowledge is knowledge of the thing as it is in itself.'[35] This is simply to assert what Strawson called the fundamental unargued premise. Kant certainly believes that 'it follows from this': that is to say, Kant believes our ignorance of things in themselves follows from the fact of Receptivity. But we want to know *why*. Heimsoeth gives no answer, but repeats Kant's inference without philosophical qualm. One might wish he had taken his own severe advice: none of Kant's attitudes, whether critical or otherwise, can be taken as excuses for one's own avoidance of metaphysical problems. To take Kant's more enigmatic statements and repeat them in assertoric mode does little to advance understanding. Humility does not, contrary to Heimsoeth, simply 'follow' from Receptivity. Strawson is right to say that Kant's inference, as it stands, presents a problem. Humility does not follow from Receptivity: or not, at any rate, without some other premise. But what?

This brings us to new business. What is needed, I suggest, is a premise that will allow us to move from the premises we already have to the conclusion about Humility. On the assumption that there is a distinction between the intrinsic and relational properties of things, and on the assumption that human beings are receptive creatures, we need something to fill the gap: something that will show us why, from this starting-point, we have no knowledge of the intrinsic properties of things.

Before embarking on this journey, however, there is a potential challenge to meet. For the texts we have just been considering make use of a notion of *substantia phaenomenon*, which has some as yet unremarked implications. If the contrast between things in themselves and phenomena is supposed, in part, to be a contrast between substance and not-substance, what is to be made of this notion of phenomenal substance?

---

[35] Ibid. 162.

3

Substance and Phenomenal Substance

1. *Introduction*

Does the Distinction I attribute to Kant conflict with Kant's commitment to *phenomenal* substance? In this chapter I shall address that question by exploring the status of substance as phenomenon. This is a large topic, and my aim is not to analyse or evaluate the arguments of the First Analogy, nor to begin to do justice to the vast and complex literature on this subject, but rather to show how Kant's Distinction is compatible with a commitment to phenomenal substance as something enduring in the appearances. In the process of addressing this problem, more support is offered for two theses of the previous chapter: the Distinction itself, and the thesis of Humility.

Some cautionary remarks are in order. The notion of a 'phenomenon' tends to call to mind nowadays the notion of something of which we are aware. Because of its historical association with philosophical doctrines that take the name 'phenomenalism' it calls to mind sense data, and logical constructions thereof. Because of its association in the philosophy of science with the *phenomena* or observable regularities that may or may not need to be saved, it calls to mind what can be seen or at least detected. However it has not always been so, and it seems to me that in Kant's own rationalist philosophical background the primary sense of phenomenon is metaphysical: to say that something is a phenomenon is to say that it is not fundamental, that it is in some way dependent or derivative. The Distinction offers a metaphysical conception of phenomena. Kant says, in a quite general manner, that the understanding tends to 'entitle an object in a relation mere phenomenon' (B307); and confirmation of a broadly metaphysical conception of phenomena will be found in this chapter.

2. *The Pure Concept of Substance vs. the Schematized*

To attribute to Kant the view that things in themselves are substances is to ignore the conception of substance for which Kant is most famous, and for which he argues in the First Analogy. The Distinction draws on a general conception of substance which is also to be found in Kant's writings, which is not the same as the substance of the First Analogy. This general conception, or pure concept, of substance is described in such passages as these:

The pure concept [of] substance would mean a something that can be thought only as a subject, never as a predicate of something else. (A147/B186)

Substance is that which is . . . an absolute subject, the last subject, which does not as predicate presuppose another further subject. (*R* 5295)[1]

Substances in general must have some intrinsic nature, which is therefore free from all external relations. (A274/B330)

Kant says, at the end of the chapter on Schematism, that we can find no use for this pure concept of substance in experience. The concept of substance can be applied to the empirical world only when it is interpreted through the schematism:

The schema of substance is permanence of the real in time, that is, the representation of the real as a substratum of empirical determination of time in general, and so as enduring when all else changes. (A143/B183)

We apply the concept of substance in experience when we represent 'the real' that is given to us in experience as a substratum, or bearer, of properties that change over time, and as something that endures throughout all this change.

Substance, once the sensible property of permanence is taken away, would mean simply a something that can be thought only as a subject, never as a predicate of something else. Now I cannot put this representation to any use, because it doesn't show me at all which properties belong to the thing whose role is to be a first subject of this kind. (A147/B186)

Kant says that we cannot put the pure concept of substance to use in a way that will allow us to have knowledge of a substance of this kind. The reason is that we are not shown 'which properties belong to the thing whose role is to be a first subject'. What properties are we not shown? Evidently, the properties required in something 'whose role is to be a first subject'. And what properties are required in a first subject, a substance that conforms to the pure concept? The answer is clear: intrinsic properties. A substance that conforms to the pure concept is an independent thing, that can exist by itself, and must thus have properties compatible with its existing by itself. We are not able to put the pure concept of substance to use in a manner that will yield knowledge, because we are not shown the intrinsic properties of such a substance. This understanding of the above passage is in keeping with Kant's statement about what would be involved in having knowledge of a thing as it is in itself. Such knowledge, he says, would involve being able to 'think of it as a thing that can be determined through its distinctive and

---

[1] Ak. xviii. 145, M 1777–80.

intrinsic predicates' (A565/B593). To 'determine' a thing is to ascribe predicates or properties to it,[2] and such knowledge would involve determining the substance by ascribing to it distinctive intrinsic predicates. Kant says that we can determine objects of the senses, but only with respect to the predicates that are possible in the field of appearance—which he says are all relational. In the absence of acquaintance with intrinsic properties, we are unable to determine things as they are in themselves.

This is what helps to provide a means of deflecting that famous charge of inconsistency: that Kant has no right to say anything at all about the substances that are things in themselves. When Kant says that we can have no knowledge of things in themselves, he means that we cannot make use of the pure concept of a substance in a manner that will enable us to determine a thing 'through distinctive and intrinsic predicates'. It is compatible with this that one can use the pure concept in a manner which will allow one to assert the existence of substances, and to assert that they must have intrinsic properties: for this use falls short of a use that attempts to determine a thing by ascribing to it particular distinctive and intrinsic predicates.

The schematized concept of substance, in contrast to the pure concept, is one that we can unproblematically put to use in the field of experience. What is central to the schematized concept of substance is the notion of an *enduring substratum of change*. In the First Analogy Kant says:

In all change of appearances substance persists, and its quantity in nature is neither increased nor diminished. All appearances contain the enduring (substance) as the object itself, and the transitory as its mere determination, that is, a way in which the object exists . . . The enduring is substance in the [field of] appearance, that is, the real in appearance, and as the substratum of all change, remains always the same. Since it cannot change in its being, its quantity in nature can neither be increased nor diminished . . . In all appearances the enduring is the object itself, that is, the substance as phenomenon. (A182/B224, B225, A183/B227)

Phenomenal substance is something in the field of appearance: the substratum of change, the bearer of changing properties, the 'real' in the field of appearance, matter, something whose quantity is conserved. The schematism of the pure concept of substance yields not simply the abstract notion of a something that can be thought as a subject, but the notion of an *enduring something* that can be thought as a subject.

What is this enduring something? On the assumption that the First Analogy is compatible with Kant's dynamical theory, then matter, the phenom-

---

[2] This is at least one sense of 'determine' to be found in Kant. To determine a thing *completely* would be this, according to the 'principle of complete determination': for each given thing, if all the possible predicates of things in general are listed together with their opposites, to ascribe to the thing one from each pair of contradictory opposites (A572/B600).

enal substance of the First Analogy, is *force*. The conservation principle of the First Analogy thus comes close to a principle of the conservation of energy, as Guyer suggests.[3] Kant says, recall:

All that we know in matter is merely relations (what we call its intrinsic properties are intrinsic only in a comparative sense), but *among these relations some are . . . enduring.* (A285/B341, emphasis added)

Kant describes the relations as forces of attraction and impenetrability. And in the Anticipations of Perception (to be discussed in Chapter 8), Kant says that 'the real' is force. What endures in the field of appearance is force.

Kant, according to Guyer, 'employs endurance as the primary criterion of substance—indeed, perhaps even *endurance of action*'.[4] Guyer sees close interconnections between the analogies, in particular between the concepts of phenomenal substance and causality, and he cites a neglected discussion of substance in the Second Analogy:[5]

The concept of causality leads to the concept of action, this leads to the concept of force, and thereby to the concept of substance . . . I cannot leave unconsidered the criterion of substance in experience, in so far as substance seems to make itself manifest not through the permanence of appearance, but better and more obviously through action. *Where there is action, and therefore activity and force, there is also substance* . . . How can one infer directly from action to the endurance of action? For endurance is the fundamental characteristic mark of substance (as phenomenon) . . . Action proves substantiality, and is its adequate empirical criterion. (A204/B249–A205/B250, emphasis added)[6]

Concepts of causality, action, force, substance are here seen to be inextricably connected. Kant says 'where there is action, and therefore . . . force, there is also substance'. We can take Kant to be making an *identity* statement here: enduring action, or force, *is* substance (as phenomenon). This suggestion makes good sense of the assumption that the matter of the First Analogy is also the matter of Kant's dynamical theory, and we shall see that there is still more to be said in its favour.

---

[3] Guyer, *Kant and the Claims*, 233.

[4] Ibid. 233.

[5] I say neglected because Kemp Smith is dismissive ('not of any very real importance . . . we may omit all treatment of it', *Commentary*, 380); so too is Allison (it is 'elliptical', *Kant's Transcendental Idealism*, 214), despite the fact that this passage appears to undermine Allison's own interpretation of substance as a merely spatial enduring thing; H. J. Paton expresses deep uncertainty about it (*Kant's Metaphysic of Experience* (London: Allen & Unwin, 1936), 216 n. 6). A very good discussion, on the other hand, is to be found in Gordon Brittan, *Kant's Theory of Science* (Princeton, N.J.: Princeton University Press, 1978).

[6] The translation is guided by Guyer's suggestion.

So far we have two broad conceptions of substance: the pure concept of substance, and the schematized concept of phenomenal substance discussed in the First Analogy. Allison draws attention to these two notions of substance in a passage which aims to defend Kant from the criticisms his First Analogy arguments have attracted. Allison says that, far from merely conflating a number of distinct conceptions of substance, Kant in fact draws on a relatively univocal conception of substance that is 'more or less common to the Western philosophical tradition'. Substance, on this conception, is regarded as

a subject of predication or *bearer of attributes that cannot itself be borne by anything else* [and] as an *enduring substratum of change*. These two characterizations are of course not equivalent . . . Nevertheless, they can be said to constitute two sides of a conception of substance that is more or less common to the Western philosophical tradition, to which Kant is obviously an heir. Indeed, the subject aspect of the conception is reflected in his *nominal definition* of substance, and the enduring substratum aspect is reflected in his characterization of the *schema*.[7]

By 'nominal definition' of substance Allison means what Kant calls the 'pure concept' (A147/B186). Allison thinks that these two conceptions of substance are brought together in the First Analogy. According to the Distinction however, substance is not in the field of appearance, but is the thing in itself. This means that there must be a sense in which Kant thinks phenomenal substance is not a substance: that the enduring substratum is not a first subject, and does not conform to the pure concept (or 'nominal definition'). This has implications for the debate about the First Analogy, although it is not my task here to spell out those implications. For if the argument of this chapter is correct, then far from being, as Allison says, an 'heir' to this Western philosophical tradition, Kant is a drastic departure from it. Both characterizations of substance are to be found in Kant's philosophy, as Allison rightly says: but the enduring substratum of change is *not* a bearer of attributes that cannot itself be borne by anything else. Matter is not a first subject.

---

[7] Allison, *Kant's Transcendental Idealism*, 214, emphasis added. The chief accusation levelled at the First Analogy is the alleged illegitimacy of the move from a bearer of properties to something sempiternal. (See e.g. Bennett, *Kant's Analytic*, 197–201; Strawson, *Bounds of Sense*, 125–32). Gordon Brittan also thinks there are two conceptions of substance at work in the First Analogy, the Aristotelian (which is supposed to combine the ideas of first subject and substratum of change) and the Cartesian (the idea of a self-subsistent thing). As far as I can see, what Brittan describes as the Cartesian is part of the pure concept of a first subject. I agree with Allison that these distinctions are less important than the distinction between the pure and the schematized concepts. See Brittan, *Kant's Theory of Science*, 143–4.

3. *The Concept of Phenomenal Substance in General*

Implicit in Kant's label of 'phenomenal substance' is the implication of something that is *not a substance*. There is a general conception of phenomenal substance that has a significance in Kant's own metaphysical background, quite apart from the particular content he wants to give it in the First Analogy. In general, and quite apart from any distinctive theses of the *Critique of Pure Reason*, it is possible to give a tolerably clear explanation of what it means to call something a phenomenal substance. I call it a concept of phenomenal substance in general because it is quite abstract, and because in describing it one does not need to mention time, as one does for the schematized concept of the First Analogy. It can be drawn from the passages that follow.[8]

Kant says that

a phenomenon that is a substratum for other phenomena is not thereby a substance, or is only a substance *comparatively* speaking. (*R* 5312)[9]

Kant here describes a certain notion of phenomenal substance to be found in the textbook he used to teach metaphysics, written by Baumgarten:

§ 193. If accidents are viewed as subsisting in themselves, they are *phaenomena substantiata*.[10]

When accidents are viewed this way, they are so to speak 'substantiated' or reified—hence the Latin label of *phaenomena substantiata*, phenomena that are made substance. This is what I shall here call the notion of phenomenal substance in general. Kant has these marginal comments on Baumgarten's definition: 'A real subject is substance. An accident can be a logical subject'

---

[8] I first learned of this general conception of phenomenal substance from Ermanno Bencivenga's reference to Baumgarten's definition, quoted below. See Bencivenga, *Kant's Copernican Revolution*, 33. He emphasizes the influence of Baumgarten's *Metaphysica* on Kant's thought, but thinks Kant disagrees with Baumgarten, retaining none the less much of his terminology: 'many of the obscurities of the *Critique* can be explained (away) as the result of forcing Kant's new wine into Baumgarten's old bottle' (224–5 n. 1). Although I disagree with Bencivenga's interpretation of Kant, I have benefited from his interesting and wide-ranging discussion. He draws attention to the basic conceptual distinction in Kant/Baumgarten metaphysics between internal and external determinations of substances, but offers a different suggestion about its implications for Kant's mature philosophy. On the assumption that *cognitions* are determinations of a substance, the question arises: are they internal or external determinations? According to Bencivenga, the fact that neither answer is satisfactory shows that 'the old conceptual framework' has no adequate account of knowledge, and this is part of what provoked Kant's 'Copernican revolution' (ch. 2, sects. 1 and 2).

[9] Ak. xviii. 150, M 1777–80.

[10] '§ 193. Accidentia si videntur per se subsistentia, sunt *phaenomena substantiata*', Baumgarten, *Metaphysica*, Ak. xvii. 67. See also § 233, Ak. xvii. 78.

(*R* 3573, 3574).[11] The concept of a phenomenal substance in general is that of something that can be thought of as a substance, which is ultimately not a substance. We can treat things that are not substances as if they were. That is what we do when we view something that is not itself a substance as 'a substratum for other phenomena'. That is what we do when we view 'accidents' as 'subsisting in themselves'. That is what we do when we regard an 'accident' as a 'logical subject' of some other predicate. Kant describes this broad use of the concept of substance in the *Critique*: 'I can say of anything and everything that it is a substance, in so far as I distinguish it from mere predicates and properties' (A349). I can treat anything at all as a substance— as a logical subject—if I treat it as though it were distinct from mere predicates and properties.

This general conception of phenomenal substance is to be sharply distinguished from the pure concept of substance. The pure concept of a substance is of a 'something which can be thought only as a subject, never as a predicate of something else' (A147/B186); 'substance is that which is . . . an absolute subject, the last subject, which does not as predicate presuppose another further subject' (*R* 5295). The general concept of a phenomenal substance, by contrast, is of a something which can indeed be thought as a subject, but as a subject that must in turn be thought of as a predicate of something else. This notion of a something treated as substance, that does not really deserve the name, is associated with the labels of *comparative* substance, or *phaenomena substantiata*.

Kant says that the poets reify qualities in this manner. He says that 'all properties that the poets personify are *phaenomena substantiata*'.[12] Shakespeare says that love is a spirit all compact of fire, that love is blind, that love is too young to know what conscience is. Love is spoken of as if it were a thing, indeed as if it were a person. Someone might also say of a battle, that it was fierce, and treat the battle as a subject of a predicate. One might say of a battle, that it *lasted* for three days, and that two brothers were killed in the *same* battle. One might think of the battle as if it were a comparatively self-subsistent individual thing. But battles are adjectival on the existence and actions of soldiers, and if we reify them they are merely phenomenal substances. One can say of a rainbow that it is bright and beautiful, and treat the rainbow as a subject of certain predicates. The rainbow is, so to speak, a 'phenomenon that is a substratum for other phenomena': for although one treats the rainbow as the subject of certain predicates (hence as 'substratum for other phenomena'), it is in turn adjectival on something else, the drops of rain, and so itself a phenomenon. Raindrops in their turn serve as the

---

[11] Ak. xvii. 67, A 1769–71?
[12] Ak. xvii. 291, A 1768?

'substratum' for the 'phenomenon' of the rainbow, which may be what Kant means in the Aesthetic when he says: 'The rainbow in a sunny shower may be called a mere appearance, and the rain the thing in itself' (A45/B63). Raindrops themselves are bodies, and are in turn adjectival upon something else, namely matter, constituted by the fundamental forces. Something other than a body serves as the substratum for the phenomenon of body. That is why Kant says:

Body . . . is a *phaenomenon substantiatum.*
Bodies are the phenomena of external presences [i.e. forces].
Bodies are comparative substances, *substrata phaenomenorum* [i.e. substrata of phenomena]. (R4421, R4422, R5294)[13]

Bodies can be viewed as substances, because they can be viewed as the bearers of properties: a house is large, a ship moves downstream. They can be viewed as self-subsistent in so far as they persist for a certain, if finite, length of time. Bodies, such as raindrops, can be the substrata for other phenomena, such as the rainbow. However, bodies are not substances, since they are adjectival on something else: bodies are the phenomenon of matter, or forces. In so far as they are things that are thought of as if they were substances, without really being substances in their own right, bodies are *phaenomena substantiata.*

In all of these examples we have something that is not a true substance, that can nevertheless in certain circumstances serve the purpose of substance. There may be different reasons for supposing that the thing in question is not truly a substance: perhaps it is because it is a property or relation (love); perhaps it is because it is reducible to, or supervenient on, other particulars and their properties or relations (a rainbow, a battle). There may be different ways in which the thing that is not a substance is treated as if it were one: perhaps the thing is treated as the logical subject of a predicate; perhaps it is viewed as a bearer of properties, or a relatively enduring bearer of changing properties. There may be different degrees of seriousness with which the thing that is not a substance is viewed as if it were one. (It is no surprise that we never see love walking with a white stick. It can be a surprise that we never reach the foot of a rainbow.) The broad notion we are considering is insensitive to these differences: in all these cases, whatever the differences, we have something that is not a true substance, that is in some sense treated as if it were one. In these examples we have things—love,

[13] Ak. xvii. 540, M 1772; Ak. xviii. 145, M 1777–80. Compare Bennett's discussion of substance as category of subject predicate statements: 'anything counts as a substance which can be referred to by a subject term', for example 'His amiability cloys' (*Kant's Analytic*, 183). The amiability of Bennett's example is a *phaenomenon substantiatum*, in Kant's sense.

rainbows, raindrops, battles—that conform to what I have called the concept of phenomenal substance in general. They are *phaenomena substantiata*, though none mentioned so far are phenomenal substance in the sense of the First Analogy, since none endure.

We now have three conceptions of substance before us: (1) the pure concept of substance as an absolute subject, (2) the schematized concept of substance as the enduring subject of change, associated with the First Analogy, and (3) the concept of a phenomenal substance in general, a merely comparative subject. The third of these notions is defined by contrast to the first. Our question concerns the status of the second: the status of phenomenal substance as an enduring subject of change.

We are now in a position to see how it might be possible for enduring phenomenal substance not to be a true substance. In the section that follows I shall try to show that substance in sense (2) is an instance of substance in sense (3): the enduring in appearance is, according to Kant, a merely comparative subject, a *phaenomenon substantiatum*. Substance in the First Analogy sense is something that is not substance, that can none the less be regarded as substance. The substance which is 'the real in the appearance', which persists through all time, whose quantity is conserved, and which Kant says we call 'matter', is also phenomenal substance in the general sense described in the quotations above. That is to say, it is 'a phenomenon that is a substratum for other phenomena' and 'not thereby a substance, or only a substance comparatively speaking' (*R* 5312). It is not a substance, because it is a property of a substance. It is an 'accident' that is viewed as subsisting in itself. It is an accident that is viewed as a subject (*R* 3573-4). It is indeed 'a something that can be thought . . . as a subject'; but not 'a something that can be thought *only* as a subject, never as a predicate of something else' (A147/B186, emphasis added).

4. *Matter as a Merely Comparative Subject*

First, it can be admitted that matter is indeed something that can be thought 'as a subject'. This can be freely acknowledged, for this is part of what it means for something to be a phenomenal substance in the general sense. Matter can be treated as a subject of certain predicates: parts of it are heavy and dense, and arranged in structures that we call raindrops and houses and ships, all of which are adjectival on matter in the way that battles are adjectival on soldiers. Matter is 'an abiding appearance in space (impenetrable extension) [and] can . . . be the primary substratum of all outer perception' (A284/B339). The *endurance* of matter distinguishes it from other *phaenomena substantiata*, the rainbows and raindrops, for it enables matter not only to be thought as a subject, but to serve the task of a substratum that under-lies *all* the changing properties with which we can become acquainted. Kant says in the First Analogy:

All appearances contain the enduring (substance) . . . and the transitory as its mere determination . . . The enduring is substance in the [field of] appearance, that is, the real in appearance, and as the substrate of all change, remains always the same. (A182/B225)

When particular bodies change, when logs are heated, glow, and disappear in flames and smoke, matter itself persists through the changes. Transitory things are determinations of substance: transitory things are temporary arrangements of matter, which itself endures through all change. Matter is the subject to which a changing series of predicates are attributed. The endurance of matter guarantees that matter will *always* be available to serve the role of substratum of any changing property. It gives matter a special status, among *phaenomena substantiata*. Kant comments on this special status in the second Paralogism, where his purpose (which does not concern us here) is to deny that we have any notion of substance that can be used to yield knowledge of properties of the soul as a simple substance. He says

So far from being able to infer these properties [i.e. of a soul] merely from the pure category of substance, we must, on the contrary, take our start from the endurance of an object given in experience, if we want to apply the concept of substance in a manner that is empirically serviceable. (A349)

Kant says here that matter is the only thing to which we can apply the con-cept of substance in a manner which is 'empirically serviceable', and it is empirically serviceable precisely because it endures.

Although matter can serve the function of a subject, note the apparent reservations in Kant's description of matter, even in such passages as these. He speaks here and in the First Analogy as if we must find something that will serve the function of a substance, as a bearer of properties, and the only thing available to us to serve this function is matter. In matter we find some-thing 'in the [field of] appearance which we name substance', we 'give an appearance the title "substance" just for the reason that we presuppose its existence throughout all time' (A185/B228). Matter is something which we *name* substance, something to which we give the *title* 'substance', something to which we can apply the concept of substance in an *empirically serviceable* manner. All these ways of speaking suggest that matter, the phenomenal substance of the First Analogy, is something that can do the job of substance well enough; but they express caution.

The reasons for caution become evident when we see that Kant in fact denies that matter is substance. He explicitly denies in the *Critique* that matter, the enduring subject of changing predicates in the field of appearance, is a 'something which can be thought only as subject, never as a predicate of something else'. He explicitly denies that matter is 'that which is . . . an absolute subject, the last subject, which does not as predicate presuppose some further subject'. Matter, he says, is substance in the appearance, and 'substance in the appearance . . . is *not an absolute subject*' (A525/B553). This admission means that the schematized concept of substance, notwithstanding its empirical serviceability, falls short of the requirements given by the pure concept of substance. The pure concept is a concept of something that is an absolute subject, which is not a predicate of something else; the schematized concept, of the First Analogy, is not.

The denial that matter is substance is to be found in a variety of Kant's writings, and is a common thread throughout different stages of his thinking.

Matter is no substance, but only a phenomenon of substance. That which endures in appearance, what lies at the basis of the manifold in bodies, we call substance. We find in bodies substances which we call substances only by analogy.[14]

This discussion assumes the dynamical theory of matter, according to which matter is constituted by forces of attraction and repulsion, that are not themselves substances but rather relational properties or powers of substances. Matter is 'that which persists in appearance, what lies at the basis of the manifold in bodies'. Matter is thus the phenomenal substance of the First Analogy, that which persists, and is the 'substratum' of the various changes that bodies undergo. Matter is that which 'we call substance'. Matter serves the task of being a subject of (changing) predicates, and to that extent it is appropriate to call it substance. The reservations implicit in this way of talking are here made explicit. Matter is not truly substance, but 'only a phenomenon of substance'. Matter can be thought of as substance, but only 'by analogy'. Here Kant says that matter is something that we *call* substance, that is in fact only a phenomenon of substance: a description that conforms precisely to his description of a *phaenomenon substantiatum*.

Compare the immediately preceding discussion with some of the passages from the Amphiboly:

All that we know in matter is merely relations (what we call its intrinsic properties are intrinsic *only in a comparative sense*), but among these relations some are . . . enduring, and through these we are given a determinate object. (A285/B341, emphasis added)

---

[14] Guyer gives a tentative date of 1778. The passage is from *Metaphysik L₁*, Ak. xxviii. 209, cited and discussed in Guyer, *Kant and the Claims*, 234–5. Guyer offers a different interpretation.

An abiding appearance in space (impenetrable extension) can contain only relations and nothing at all that is absolutely intrinsic, and yet be the primary substratum of all outer perception. (A284/B339)

Compare also the following passages, which I quoted only in part above.

Body is not composed of substances, but is a *phaenomenon substantiatum*.
Bodies are the phenomena of the external presences [i.e. forces] *of . . . substances*.
(*R* 4421, *R* 4422, final emphasis added)[15]

Kant does not always seem to distinguish very clearly between bodies, particular ephemeral arrangements of matter, and matter itself, the enduring. But both alike count as mere *phaenomena substantiata*. This is true of bodies, since they have matter, or force, as their substratum. However, what is true of bodies is also true of matter itself. Bodies are a phenomenon of matter, matter (force, 'external presence') is in turn a property of something else, in which case matter itself is therefore substance only 'comparatively speaking'.

This understanding of phenomenal substance finds clear support in many passages in the *Reflexionen*, of which the following are a sample.

All external appearances are *phaenomena substantiata*, for we treat them as substances. (*R* 4494)

Bodies, that is to say, external appearances, are *phaenomena substantiata*, that is to say, enduring substrata of other phenomena. (*R* 4495)

Bodies are *phaenomena substantiata* . . . because they are external appearances, in which the first subject is absent. (*R* 4699)

In the field of phenomena one can certainly come upon comparative substance, and *phaenomena substantiata*. But one cannot come upon the substances themselves. (*R* 4830)

The substantial is completely unknown. (*R* 4054)[16]

Although Kant sometimes refers to matter as 'bodies' in these passages, the reference to *endurance*, and to the realm of appearance in its *entirety*, suggest that it is strictly matter, substance of the First Analogy, that he has in mind. Here we have the same themes: something in appearance which is not a substance, but treated as a substance, something that is a substratum of other phenomena, but not itself a first subject, only a comparative subject.

---

[15] Ak. xvii. 540, M 1772. That Kant means 'force' by 'external presence' becomes clear in the discussion of Chapter 5 (the terms are used synonymously in the *Physical Monadology*).

[16] Ak. xvii. 572, M 1773; Ak. xvii. 573, M 1773; Ak. xvii. 679, M 1775; Ak. xvii. 740, M 1775; Ak. xvii. 399, A 1769–70.

These passages help us to understand what Kant means when he says in the *Critique*:

If, in thought, we were to take away all compositeness from matter, nothing at all would be left. This does not seem compatible with the concept of a substance, for a substance is really supposed to be the subject of all composition, and ought to remain, as elements, even when the connection in space through which it constitutes a body is taken away. This would be true if we were thinking of a thing in itself, through pure concepts. But it does not hold for what, in the appearance, we call substance. For this is not an absolute subject, but only a *sensible abiding picture* [of an absolute subject]. (A525/B553, emphasis added)

Kant says here that phenomenal substance 'is not an absolute subject, but only a . . . picture'. How are we to understand this way of speaking? It has the form: not an *F*, but only a picture. If I were to say, 'this is not a real flower, but only a picture', I would say something with a similar form: and the implication would be, merely a picture of a flower. When Kant says that phenomenal substance 'is not an absolute subject, but only a . . . picture', the implication is similar: merely a picture of an absolute subject. Kemp Smith translates the phrase *berharrliches Bild der Sinnlichkeit* as 'an abiding image of sensibility', but this is ambiguous between two thoughts: the first about how phenomenal substance is presented to us (via sensibility?); and the second about what phenomenal substance is an image or picture of (of sensibility?). The most plausible reading of the passage is not the latter, but the former, hence my disambiguation. Phenomenal substance is something abiding that is presented to our sensibility (and therefore of sensibility, sensible); and it is a picture, or image, of an absolute subject, hence my bracketed interpolation. This is in keeping with the usages we have noted: matter is something we 'call substance', but it is substance only 'by analogy', 'comparatively speaking'.

The pure concept of substance is the concept of an absolute subject, something independent of its relations and connections to other things, hence something that would remain even if all the things with which it was connected were taken away. The pure concept of substance is the concept of a thing that is able to exist on its own, something whose existence is compatible with loneliness. Kant says here that matter does not conform to this pure concept of substance. Phenomenal substance does not conform to the pure concept of a substance, but it serves the task of a substance as far as we are concerned, because of its permanence, or abidingness. The notion of its being a 'comparative substance' is expressed with the metaphor of the 'abiding picture' (*beharrliches Bild*): matter is a mere picture of substance which can serve as a picture because of its abidingness. Matter is an image of an absolute subject, and despite its shortcomings, it is the best available to us, given that we must have a subject that can be given to the senses.

Substance as such is not to be found in matter or in the appearances. This is stated explicitly just after Kant's definition of a merely comparative substance, written close to the period of the *Critique*:

A phenomenon that is a substratum for other phenomena is thereby not a substance, or only a substance comparatively speaking. In the appearances we cannot be acquainted with something as substance. (*R* 5312)[17]

Knowledge of appearances does not give us any way of being acquainted with something *as substance*. This is precisely what is being asserted in the passage from the Amphiboly considered in the last chapter.

Matter is *substantia phaenomenon*. I search for that which belongs to it intrinsically in all parts of the space which it occupies, and in all the actions it performs, and these of course can only be appearances to outer sense. So I have nothing that is absolutely intrinsic, but only what is comparatively intrinsic, and that is itself again constituted by external relations. It is silly to suppose that matter has an absolute intrinsic nature of the sort conceived by pure understanding, for matter is not an object of pure understanding. On the other hand, the transcendental object which may be the ground of this appearance that we call matter is a mere something. (A277/B333)

Kant says that 'it is silly to suppose that matter has an absolute intrinsic nature of the sort conceived by pure understanding'. Matter does not conform to the pure concept of substance, for it lacks intrinsic properties.

He goes on to say that although it is silly to expect matter to have an intrinsic nature, as if it were something that conformed to the pure concept of a substance, there is a temptation to think what is given to us in experience must conform to the pure concept. The temptation should be resisted:

I must not say the following: 'A thing cannot be represented through bare concepts without an absolutely intrinsic nature. Therefore it is true of *both* things in themselves (to which these concepts apply), *and* the intuition of those things, that they possess nothing extrinsic ungrounded in something absolutely intrinsic'. (A284/B340, italics added)[18]

We must not infer that the pure concept of substance, which applies to things in themselves, also applies to the intuition of those things, i.e. to phenomenal substance. Hence we must not infer that since the pure concept of substance requires the presence of intrinsic properties, things in themselves and phenomenal substance *both* have intrinsic properties. The pure concept does

[17] Ak. xviii. 150, M 1777–80.

[18] My translation differs significantly from Kemp Smith's; 'so kann ich nicht sagen: weil, ohne ein Schlechthininneres, kein Ding durch bloße Begriffe vorgestellt werden kann, so sei auch in den Dingen selbst, die unter diesen Begriffen enthalten sind, und ihrer Anschauung nichts Äußeres, dem nicht etwas Schlechthininnerliches zum Grunde läge' (A284/B340).

apply to things in themselves, but not to the intuition of those things, i.e. phenomenal substance; things in themselves have an absolute intrinsic nature, but phenomenal substance does not.

There are striking similarities between these passages from the *Critique*, and the passages from outside the *Critique* just considered. Kant says repeatedly that matter is substance only 'comparatively speaking'; in the Amphiboly he says that we are acquainted with properties that are only 'comparatively intrinsic'. In the earlier cited passages Kant speaks of 'substance' of which matter is 'the phenomenon'; in the *Critique* he speaks of the transcendental object which is 'the ground' of 'this appearance that we call matter'. That ground is 'something of which we should not understand what it is, even if someone were in a position to tell us'; it is the 'substratum [of matter] which cannot be known' (A359). In short, the contrast between matter and substance in Kant's other writing is present in the *Critique* as the contrast between matter and things in themselves.

The reason that we cannot be acquainted in the appearances with something as substance is that we can be acquainted only with forces. Although forces can constitute matter, forces are not substances. The passages which follow make it evident that Kant thinks we are acquainted with force, not substance, and they show why he thinks that force and substance are not the same. The first, from the Amphiboly, has already been encountered. The others show how it is to be understood.

We are acquainted with substance in space only through forces which are active in this and that space, either drawing other objects (attraction) or preventing their penetration (repulsion and impenetrability). We are not acquainted with any other properties constituting the concept of the substance which appears in space and which we call matter. (A265/B321)

We are acquainted with the substantial only through that which endures . . . All that we are acquainted with of substance is force, fundamental force. (*R* 4824)[19]

In the end, however, we find everything in the object to be accidents. The first subject is something that makes the accidents possible . . . It is something with which I am acquainted through the enduring accident of impenetrability and also . . . attraction. We judge the reality of the accidents through the sensation of an object. The reality of the accidents is distinct from the reality of the [first] subject. (*R* 4412)[20]

---

[19] Ak. xvii. 739, A 1776–7.

[20] Ak. xvii. 537, M 1772. Kant sometimes denies that force is an accident, and says instead that it is a relation, but most generally it seems to be viewed as a relational accident, or property. Compare the idea of substance as something that 'first makes the extrinsic properties possible' in the Amphiboly, A283/B339.

All three of the above make the point that we can be acquainted with substance only through forces. The first appears to treat the following concepts as coextensive: matter, substance appearing in space, properties of repulsion and impenetrability. This identification of what Kant describes as properties (forces) with phenomenal substance makes sense on the present interpretation of phenomenal substance: something that can be treated as a substance, that is ultimately a property of something else. The second and third of the above identify that which *endures* as *force*: we are acquainted with substance through that which endures, and that which endures is force. This supports Guyer's suggestion about the connections between force, action, and substance raised in A204/B249, where Kant speaks of force, or action, as the adequate criterion in experience of substantiality.[21] The third passage refers to the 'enduring accident of impenetrability'.[22] It says that force is an accident, or property, of a substance. We have seen already that Kant says that matter 'consists entirely of relations': that matter is constituted by the forces of attraction and impenetrability. Here the same idea that matter is force is taken to imply that 'we find everything in the object to be accidents'. The conclusions are not so very different if Kant thinks that there is a sense in which forces are both relations and accidents: that they are relational properties.

In conclusion, substance in the First Analogy sense is a *phaenomenon substantiatum:* a property, that is treated as if it were a substance. In the realm of appearance we are acquainted only with forces, and forces are not substances but properties, relational properties, of substances unknown in themselves. Since matter, or the forces that constitute matter, is the substratum of other phenomena, matter is a non-substance that occupies the role of a substance for us. It is a 'picture' of an absolute substance, that, in virtue of its endurance, fills that role very well.

We can see, then, that Kant's commitment to phenomenal substance does not undermine the Distinction he holds. We can see how he can consistently believe that phenomenal substance is in the realm of appearance, while substance is not in the realm of appearance. Moreover, we can see how Kant might believe that despite our ignorance of substance, we are required to believe in its existence. This brings us back to a topic raised at the beginning of this chapter.

---

[21] It also supports Guyer's suggestion that Kant's views on the endurance of force imply a principle about the conservation of energy rather than of matter as traditionally conceived. Guyer, *Kant and the Claims*, 233.

[22] This is implicit in the *Critique* in other passages too: the enduring is, according to the First Analogy, 'the real in appearance' (A182/B225), and the real in appearance is, according to the Anticipations of Perception, force (A168/B210 ff.), which again favours Guyer's suggestion that substance is 'enduring action' or force.

5. *Note on the Inference to Substance*

Kant says that the first subject, or substance, is what makes the accidents possible (*R* 4412). If there were no substance, there would be no accidents. This requirement that there be a bearer, or subject, for accidents, resembles the requirement raised at the beginning of Chapter 2 that there be a bearer, or subject, for relations: that 'concepts of relation presuppose things which are absolutely [independently] given, and without these are impossible' (A284/B340). Indeed if the 'accidents' in question are relational properties, it may be that the requirement of a bearer of 'accidents' amounts to the same thing as the requirement of a bearer of relations. Just as Kant said that the bearer of relations must be thought of as having some independent existence, some 'intrinsic nature which is free from all external relations' (A274/B330), so he says, in similar vein, that the 'reality' of the first subject is distinct from the 'reality' of the accidents of impenetrability and attraction.

It is not enough that we are able to *treat* these latter accidents or relations *as if* they were substances. We are always able to treat any non-substance as if it were a substance, a *phaenomenon substantiatum*, if we need to.

I can say of anything and everything that it is a substance, in so far as I distinguish it from mere predicates and properties. (A349)

Everything can be thought as either a subject or a predicate, but not everything can exist as a subject. (*R* 5858)[23]

It is not enough to be able to think of something as if it were a subject: we are required to think that something *exists* as a subject.

Since logical subjects can always be predicates, we are required by laws of reason to think a last subject. This is substance. (*R* 4052)

The concept of substance is a *terminating concept*. (*R* 4039)[24]

Matter can be thought as a subject, but it cannot exist as a subject: not because it is dependent on our minds, but because it is adjectival in its character. Confronted in experience with predicates, or properties, or relations, we are required to think that they have bearers that have some independent existence. Confronted in experience with forces, even enduring forces, we are required, given (in Kant's opinion) the relational character of forces, to think they belong to something else. If one knows that the thing one takes

---

[23] Ak. xviii. 370, M 1780–1.

[24] Ak. xvii. 398–9, A 1769–70; Ak. xvii. 394, A 1769–70. Guyer comments on the use of substance as a terminating concept, *Kant and the Claims*, 234–5.

for a substance is mere *phaenomenon substantiatum*, one must infer the existence of something else. Hence there must be substances, things that conform to the pure category of substance, that are absolute subjects, capable
of independent existence. As substances that conform to the pure category,
they have an intrinsic nature that is free from all external relations: they have
intrinsic properties (A274/B330). As bearers of relational accidents they
have a reality that is distinct from those accidents (*R* 4412). Their relational
properties, forces, endure, affect us, and appear to us in space. There is further support here for the explanation given in the previous chapter of why
Kant thinks it so obvious that the notion of appearance logically implies a
thing in itself: that appearance implies a something that appears. If matter
is 'constituted entirely of relations', if it is nothing but relational 'accidents',
then matter in turn must have a bearer, a substance that, unlike matter, is an
'absolute subject'. And this is why Kant says that 'matter is mere external
appearance, the substratum of which cannot be known through any predicate that we can assign to it' (A359). Kant would not see this as an illegitimate use of the pure concept, since, while asserting the existence of a
substratum, it also denies that we thereby determine a thing 'through distinctive and intrinsic predicates' (A565/B593). Without having access to the
properties that 'belong to the thing whose role is to be a first subject'
(A147/B186), we cannot use the pure concept in a manner that enables us
to determine an object. A similar thought may also be present in the following (admittedly cryptic) passage.

Substantiality and its opposite: mere relation. [Substantiality] is not to be seen . . .
because the predicates are lacking. (*R* 4493)[25]

We cannot 'see' substantiality because the appropriate predicates, intrinsic
predicates, are lacking.

The alternative meaning of the notion of 'external appearance' recurs in
the passages we consider here. Kant says (A359) that matter is an 'external
appearance' of a substratum. By external appearance Kant does not mean
that matter is a construction of sensations in the spatial array provided by
outer sense. If he did, then Bennett's accusations of illegitimate conflation
of sensations with properties of substances would be quite justified. 'External', here, does not in the first instance concern space, nor, here, does Kant
even mean to emphasize that matter is outside *us*, although it is. 'External',
both here and in these other passages, is to be understood relative not

---

[25] Ak. xvii. 572, M 1773. Substance is one of three 'terminating concepts' in the discussion. I have extracted the part about substance because it seems to have much in common
with the other passages cited.

primarily to *us* but to the *substance* or substratum. This usage of 'external appearance' occurs in the quatrain of *Reflexionen* considered in Section 4:

All external appearances are *phaenomena substantiata*, for we treat them as substances. (*R* 4494)

Bodies, that is to say, external appearances, are *phaenomena substantiata*, that is to say, enduring substrata of other phenomena. (*R* 4495)

Bodies are *phaenomena substantiata* . . . because they are external appearances, in which the first subject is absent. (*R* 4699)

In [the field of] appearance one can certainly come upon comparative substance, and *phaenomena substantiata*. But one cannot come upon the substances themselves. (*R* 4830)

Bodies are external (extrinsic) to a substance, a first subject. Matter is force, and force is an 'external' property, an extrinsic or relational property, of a substance, whose intrinsic properties, on Kant's view, are unknown. To say that matter is external *appearance* is to add that it is constituted by forces that are presented *to us*, and with which we can become acquainted.

6. *Concluding Remarks and New Business*

Kant believes that there are things in themselves, that is to say, substances. They have intrinsic properties, and we do not know what those properties are. I have attempted, in this chapter, to show how it is possible to ascribe to Kant these views and at the same time recognize his commitment to the phenomenal substance of the First Analogy. In the process I have offered more support for the Distinction, and for the thesis of Humility, since most of the passages considered identify substance with the unknowable thing in itself, ascribe to substance unknowable intrinsic properties, contrast substance with its relations and relational accidents, and identify those relational properties as forces. Moreover, these passages show that Kant uses 'phenomena' to refer, not to sense data, as a phenomenalist might use the term; nor to observable events or regularities, as a philosopher of science might use it; but rather to *things that are not substances*. That, in the quoted passages, is primarily what the notion means. Kant contrasts substance with phenomenon. He contrasts substance with 'its opposite: mere relation' (*R* 4493). He says, in the *Critique*, that 'the understanding calls an object in a relation mere phenomenon' (B307). The concept of a phenomenon is not a concept that, in the first instance, has to do with how things look. Nor does it, in the first instance, carry any implication of ideality. On the contrary, Kant describes relational accidents as having a *reality* that is distinct from the reality of the subject (*R* 4412). What this means exactly will be a question for later: but for the moment the point to emphasize is that 'relational accidents' are both phenomenal, and real.

Allison said that there is conception of substance that is 'more or less common to the Western philosophical tradition'. It has two sides: substance as a bearer of attributes that cannot itself be borne by anything else, and substance as an enduring substratum of change. Allison said that Kant is obviously an heir to this tradition. If the argument of this chapter is correct, then Kant is not an heir but an exception to this tradition. To be sure, phenomenal substance is a substratum of change, and a bearer of attributes. But that can be true of mere *phaenomena substantiata*, love, and battles, rainbows, and raindrops. To be sure, phenomenal substance is, unlike these, an all-enduring substratum of change. That indeed makes it empirically serviceable, and enables it to fulfil the task of substance in appearance. It is no first subject, though, but a property borne by something else, the 'substratum of matter'.

Enough has been said, I hope, to remove the potential stumbling block posed by phenomenal substance. It is time now to turn to the question raised at the end of the last chapter, the problem raised by Strawson. Why is it that Kant believes that our ignorance of things in themselves, our ignorance of their intrinsic properties, follows from the fact that we are receptive creatures? So far we have seen many expressions of Kant's Distinction, and many expressions of Humility, but Kant's reasons for the latter are still mysterious. We have also seen that some of the clearest expressions of Humility are to be found in the Amphiboly of the Concepts of Reflection. There is something about this fact which deserves serious attention. In writing the Amphiboly Kant's chief aim is to show why *Leibniz is wrong*. Now, it is unlikely to be a coincidence that some of Kant's clearest expressions of Humility occur in the context of his discussion of Leibnizian philosophy. Perhaps it is even something of a clue. Perhaps there is a link between Kant's attitude to Leibniz and his belief in our ignorance of things as they are in themselves. Perhaps, then, we should consider Kant's reasons for thinking that Leibniz is wrong, if we would like to discover his reasons for Humility.

4

Leibniz and Kant

1. *Introduction*

Kant's expression of Humility is linked with a critique of Leibniz, and this critique assumes a particular interpretation of the Leibnizian philosophy;[1] so if we are to understand Kant's critique we must first see what, in Kant's opinion, Leibniz is doing. The primary task of this chapter is to sketch an interpretation of Leibniz which is in accord with Kant's own interpretation, in order then to raise the question of its connections with Kantian Humility.[2] Points of similarity between Kant and Leibniz will emerge, and also points of difference. The most obvious differences concern knowledge—how much we have, and how we get it. The Leibnizian philosophy is extraordinarily ambitious, without an ounce of epistemic humility. Its ambition is unhampered by a denial of causal interaction, and a corresponding absence of epistemic receptivity. However, the focus in this chapter will be, not on differences, but on similarities, real or alleged, between these two philosophers.

One point of similarity is a distinction in Leibniz between appearances and things in themselves which has much in common with the Distinction

---

[1] I use two translations of Leibniz's works: *Leibniz: Philosophical Papers and Letters*, trans. L. Loemker, 2nd edn. (Dordrecht: Reidel, 1969), and *Leibniz: Philosophical Essays*, trans. R. Ariew and D. Garber (Indianapolis, Ind.: Hackett, 1989); and occasionally borrow translations from Benson Mates, *The Philosophy of Leibniz: Metaphysics and Language* (New York: Oxford University Press, 1986), who provides a useful 'gallery' of texts on the topic of relations (222–6). The original-language sources of works cited are chiefly *Leibniz: Die Philosophischen Schriften*, ed. C. I. Gerhardt (abbreviated 'Gerhardt'); *Leibniz: Mathematische Schriften*, ed. Gerhardt (abbreviated 'Gerhardt M'); and *Opuscules et fragments inédits de Leibniz*, ed. Louis Couturat (abbreviated 'Couturat'). See Bibliography for full details.

[2] The interpretation offered is independently defensible, I believe, though it would be beyond the scope of this chapter to defend it in detail here. It is in broad agreement with, and has benefited from the work of, a number of different commentators, especially Nicholas Rescher, *The Philosophy of Leibniz* (Englewood Cliffs, N.J.: Prentice-Hall, 1967); Mates, *Philosophy of Leibniz*; Fabrizio Mondadori, 'Solipsistic Perception in a World of Monads', in Michael Hooker, ed., *Leibniz: Critical and Interpretive Essays* (Manchester: Manchester University Press, 1982), 21–44; Catherine Wilson, *Leibniz's Metaphysics* (Princeton, N.J.: Princeton University Press, 1989); and G. H. R. Parkinson, *Logic and Reality in Leibniz's Metaphysics* (Oxford: Oxford University Press, 1965). Particular debts and disagreements with these and other critics will be noted in due course, especially on the topic of the reducibility of relations.

I attribute to Kant. Indeed Kant's own view, with the sharp division between matter and substance described in the previous chapter, makes better sense when seen against its Leibnizian backdrop. A further point of similarity has been suggested by some commentators: that Kant endorses a Leibnizian view about the reducibility, or perhaps unreality, of relations. This further point of similarity has been taken to have implications for knowledge: a suggestion which, if true, would be of considerable interest. For while Leibniz himself is less than humble in epistemological ambition, if these critics are correct, then Kant is led to Humility, or something like it, because of his loyalty to a Leibnizian view about relations. Despite the interest of this suggestion, it is, I shall argue, mistaken. These commentators think that Humility has something to do with Kant's opinion about the reducibility of relations, and that is indeed so—but for a reason opposed to the one they offer. Kant advocates Humility not because he thinks that Leibniz is right about relations, but because he thinks Leibniz is wrong. That is why his expression of Humility is linked with a critique, and not an endorsement, of Leibnizian philosophy. This conclusion will take some argument, and I hope to establish it over the course of the immediately ensuing chapters.

The earlier caveats about the notion of a phenomenon apply as much to a consideration of Leibniz as they do to Kant, and for the same sorts of reasons. Leibniz endorses a philosophical distinction that divides phenomena from things in themselves, and this is something he shares with many philosophers, ranging from Kant back to Plato. Here again we have the same choice between a primarily epistemological and a primarily metaphysical way of understanding a distinction of this kind. We can think that 'phenomenon' may be a label for things as they look to us, through the murky lens of sense perception. We can think that the label suggests the manifest image of the world, something to be contrasted with things as they really are, independently of our sense perception. This epistemological distinction is not quite what these metaphysicians had in mind, however, any more than it is what Kant had in mind. It is true that the realm of things that we can sense seems to coincide with the realm of phenomena for Leibniz, as for Plato before him. And it is true that we are likely to find the two realms referred to in terms of how we know them: the sensible and the intelligible. But the fundamental distinction between phenomena and things in themselves is a distinction between things that are ontologically deficient, and things that are not: it divides the insubstantial from the substantial. Thus Plato divides the realm of Forms from the realm of concrete particulars. He has a view about how we get to know each. Forms can be grasped through the intellect; particulars can be grasped through the senses. But these latter epistemological facts are not what grounds his distinction. Phenomena are deficient; but they are not deficient because they are delivered to us through the senses. Rather, the senses are deficient because they deliver us only phenomena.

Leibniz's distinction is likewise, I think, fundamentally metaphysical,[3] and he goes so far as to compare his own opinion with that of Plato. Bodies are phenomena, he says. '[B]ody itself cannot be conceived independently of other things,' and thus 'bodies *do not deserve the name substances*; this seems to have been Plato's view when he remarked that they are transitory beings that never subsist longer than a moment.'[4] His distinction is not primarily between things as we sense them, and things as they are, but between substances and things that are not substances—regardless of how we happen to sense them. In everyday life we might think of physical things, like parrots and people, as substantial, real, basic; but things like flocks and football teams as less so. If in everyday life we think that way, we are thinking of parrots and people as things in themselves, flocks and football teams as phenomena, or at best as *phaenomena substantiata*. Leibniz uses a distinction between the substantial and the non-substantial to map a different terrain. Souls—monads, simple substances—are things in themselves, and bodies are phenomena. Souls are substances, bodies are not substances. There is something that the Leibnizian view has in common with everyday thinking, though. Bodies are to souls, for Leibniz, as football teams are to people, in everyday thinking.

> An aggregate of substances is what I call a *substantiatum*, like an army of men, or a flock of birds, and such are all bodies.[5]

2. *Kant's Version of Leibniz*

If Leibniz believes that 'bodies do not deserve the name substances', then his belief is guided by a particular conception of what a substance is. The

---

[3] It is also possible to have a more traditionally 'phenomenalistic' interpretation of Leibniz, as suggested, for example, by Robert Adams, who says that phenomena are primarily intentional objects of perceptual awareness (Adams, 'Phenomenalism and Corporeal Substance in Leibniz', in Peter French, Theodore Uehling, and Howard Wettstein, eds., *Midwest Studies in Philosophy*, viii (Minneapolis: University of Minnesota Press, 1983), 217–57). This is partly a difference of emphasis. Monads have a dual function in Leibniz's philosophy, as foundational constituents of the world, and as percipients, which in turn yields two ways of understanding phenomena, as the 'results' of these foundations, or the perceptions of these percipients. For the two roles see Catherine Wilson, *Leibniz's Metaphysics*, 196, and Montgomery Furth, 'Monadology', in Harry Frankfurt, ed., *Leibniz* (New York: Doubleday, 1972), 99–136.

[4] 'Conversation of Philarète and Ariste' (1712, revised 1715), Gerhardt vi. 585, 586, Ariew and Garber 262 (italics added). It is not ephemerality so much as dependence that disqualifies a thing from being a substance.

[5] From an undated essay, Couturat 13, Ariew and Garber 200 n. 249.

argument for monadology takes its starting-point from what Kant calls the pure concept of a substance, and from the corresponding distinction between two classes of properties a substance may have.[6]

Leibniz's monadology has its sole basis in the distinction between the intrinsic and the extrinsic, which he presented purely in relation to the understanding. Substances in general must have some intrinsic nature, which is therefore free from all external relations, and therefore also from composition . . . But what is intrinsic to the state of a substance cannot consist in place, shape, contact, or motion, since these properties are all external relations. We can therefore attribute to substances no intrinsic state except for that which we determine inwardly in our own sense, namely, the state of representations. Thus are the monads completed. They are supposed to serve as the raw material for the whole universe, despite having no active force, except for that consisting in representations (which, strictly speaking, are active only within the monads). That is why [Leibniz's] principle of the possible reciprocal community of substances had to be a pre-established harmony, and not a physical influence. For when everything is merely intrinsic . . . the state of . . . one substance cannot stand in any active connection whatsoever with the state of another. (A274/B330)

Leibniz first assumed things (monads), with an inner power of representation, in order afterwards to found on these their external relations and the community of their states . . . The mere relation of substances was then the ground through which space was possible as a consequence; and the mere connection of [a substance's] own properties with each other was then the ground through which time was possible as a consequence. (A267/B323).

Leibniz took the appearances for things in themselves. (A264/B320)

He assumed that we intuit things as they are, although in confused representation. (A268/B323)

The appearance was, for him, the presentation of the thing in itself. (A270/B326)

[Leibniz held] that our entire sensibility is nothing but a confused representation of things, that contains solely what belongs to the things in themselves, but with a crowding together of characteristics and partial representations, so that we cannot consciously distinguish the things from one another. (A43/B60)

These passages are from Kant's critique of Leibniz in the Amphiboly of the Concepts of Reflection, except for the last, which is from the Aesthetic. I want to consider their implications for the way Leibniz at once *distinguished* phenomena from things in themselves, yet at the same time 'took' the phenomena for things in themselves, according to Kant.

---

[6] This argument for monadology attributed to Leibniz by Kant is the subject of an excellent (though I think partly mistaken) analysis by van Cleve, 'Inner States and Outer Relations'.

Guided by the pure concept of substance, and by the distinction between intrinsic and extrinsic properties, Leibniz assumes that substances must have some intrinsic properties independent of any relations they bear to other things. Physical properties of place, shape, contact, or motion are not intrinsic properties, but 'external relations' of substances. However, substances must have some intrinsic properties: things capable of existing in the absence of relations to other things must have properties to match. According to Leibniz, the only possible candidates for such properties are inner representations: and thus the substances of his ontology are monads (A274/B330). On this description, Leibniz's division between phenomena and things in themselves involves a division between relational and intrinsic properties of substances. (We may leave aside, for the moment, Leibniz's conclusion about what exactly those intrinsic properties are supposed to be.) Phenomenal properties are physical properties, and are relational properties. Properties of things in themselves are to be contrasted with those of phenomena, they are not physical, and they are intrinsic properties of substances. Leibniz seems to endorse a distinction that—at least in these last respects—resembles Kant's.

A further aspect to Kant's understanding of Leibniz also emerges in these passages. Leibniz *takes the appearances for things as they are in themselves* (A240/B320). Note that on a phenomenalistic conception of Kant's distinction between appearances and things in themselves, this suggestion is puzzling. Bennett goes so far as to say that it is, at first sight, 'intolerably puzzling'.[7] It seems to ascribe to Leibniz the ludicrous view that phenomena are epistemically inaccessible, as things in themselves are for the Kant of the *Critique*. But it is evident, I think, what Kant has in mind. There are two very clear ways in which Leibniz does indeed take the appearances for things in themselves, and they go hand in hand.

Leibniz takes the appearances for things in themselves, because he *reduces* phenomena to things in themselves. Substances with their intrinsic properties are 'supposed to serve as the raw material for the whole universe', says Kant. On the Leibnizian account, there is a sense in which 'everything is merely intrinsic' (A274/B330), and hence a sense in which appearances are nothing over and above things in themselves. The monads and their intrinsic properties are 'grounds', or 'foundations', or 'raw material' for external relations, and the external relations of monads are nothing over and above the intrinsic properties of monads. The physical world is the world of appearance, constituted by the external relations of substances, yet relations are nothing over and above the intrinsic properties of monads. So appearances are nothing over and above things in themselves. As birds are constituents

---

[7] Bennett, *Kant's Dialectic*, 55.

or raw material for a flock, soldiers raw material for an army, so monads are raw material for the whole universe. Kant picks up this kind of metaphor at a later date, saying that according to the Leibnizian view,

There is . . . no other difference between a thing as phenomenon and the representation of the noumenon which underlies it than between a crowd of men which I see at a great distance and the same men when I am so close that I can count the individuals. It is only, [the Leibnizian] says, that we could never come so close to it. (*On a Discovery*, 1790)[8]

Just as a crowd is nothing over and above the men, so the phenomenal realm is nothing over and above the realm of monads. Kant says that monads are 'supposed to serve as the raw material for the whole universe, despite having *no active force*'. In place of an active force that would enable one substance to act upon another substance, there is a pre-established harmony of intrinsic states. The external relations of monads—the quasi-causal relations of reciprocal community operating between substances—are 'grounded' upon the intrinsic properties of the substances. These external relations in turn form the 'ground' whose 'consequence' is space (A267/B323). The dynamical and spatial features of the world are thus founded upon the intrinsic properties of monads. Spatial relations are reduced to dynamical relations, and the latter in turn are reduced to harmonies, or patterns of similarities and differences, among the intrinsic properties of substances. Given the nature of Leibniz's distinction between phenomena and things in themselves, in 'taking' phenomena for things in themselves, Leibniz takes the physical realm to be nothing over and above the monadic, and he takes relational properties to be nothing over and above intrinsic properties. He at once reduces phenomena, reduces bodies, and reduces relations.

Kant's observation that Leibniz takes the appearances for things in themselves has an epistemological dimension as well. In addition to their foundational role as 'raw material' of the universe, monads are also *percipients* who perceive the world of which they are themselves constituents. Leibniz takes the appearances for things in themselves, because he believes we have perceptual *knowledge* of things as they are in themselves. If Leibniz takes the appearances for things in themselves, then he believes that things in themselves are perceived through the senses. According to Kant, Leibniz believes that we can know 'through sensibility', albeit confusedly, the nature of things in themselves (A44/B62). Leibniz assumes that we intuit things

---

[8] Ak. viii. 208, Allison 124–5. The 'Leibnizian' in question is Eberhard, and Kant is careful here to distinguish this interpretation of Leibniz from a somewhat different, and more charitable, interpretation, as we shall see in Chapter 9.

as they are, although confusedly (A268/B323). The appearance is, for him, the presentation of the thing in itself (A270/B326). Leibniz thinks that the representations in our sensibility 'contain solely what belongs to the things in themselves' (A43/B60). Here we have a clear statement about what, in Kant's opinion, Leibniz believes is given to sensibility: nothing but properties that belong to things in themselves—nothing but the intrinsic properties of monads, albeit perceived in a crowded and distorted way.

Three major strands of Leibniz's philosophy have emerged in these brief reflections on Kant's interpretation of it: first, a *distinction* in Leibniz between phenomena and things in themselves, resting upon a distinction between intrinsic and relational properties of substances; second, a *reduction* of phenomena to things in themselves, resting upon a reduction of relational properties to intrinsic; third, a claim to *sensory knowledge* of things as they are in themselves. Let us consider these three one at a time.

3. *A Distinction between Phenomena and Things in Themselves*

Things in themselves are substances, and it is part of the pure concept of substance that a substance can exist independently of its relations to other things. Leibniz interprets that independence in a distinctive way. 'Each substance is like a world apart, independent of all other things, except for God.'[9] One aspect of the independence is causal. The monads are windowless: each is a microcosm, in complete causal isolation from the others. 'Speaking with metaphysical rigour, there is no real influence of one created substance on another.'[10] That is why Kant says that according to Leibniz there is no relation of physical influence or 'active connection' between monads (A274/B330). A further aspect of the independence is metaphysical: monads, unlike bodies, do not depend on other things for their existence. Leibniz says that 'bodies do not deserve the name substances', and that a true substance is not a physical thing. If (*per impossibile*) a substance were a body, it would have spatial parts. But nothing that has parts can be a true substance: for something that has parts depends on its parts for its existence, and is thus not an independent being. That is why 'body itself cannot be conceived independently of other things'.[11]

[G]iven that a body is a whole, it depends upon other bodies of which it is composed and which make up its parts. Only *monads*, that is, simple or indivisible substances, are truly independent of any other concrete created thing.[12]

---

[9] 'Discourse on Metaphysics' (1686), Gerhardt iv. 439, Ariew and Garber 47.
[10] 'A New System of Nature' (1695), Gerhardt iv. 483, Ariew and Garber 143.
[11] 'Conversation', Gerhardt vi. 585, Ariew and Garber 262.
[12] Ibid., Gerhardt vi. 585-6, Ariew and Garber 262.

A substance is the kind of thing that can exist on its own: the kind of thing whose existence is compatible with loneliness—compatible with the absence of any other distinct object. That notion of independence is interpreted in a particular way, and in a way analogous to that we saw at work in Kant's description of spatial properties as 'mere relations' (Chapter 2). Dependence on a proper part is dependence on a distinct thing, even if not a wholly distinct thing. If a thing depends on some distinct object, even if that object is not wholly distinct, then the thing is not a substance, according to Leibniz. So, on this view, a physical thing cannot be a substance.

Substances have properties: Leibniz says, 'Monads must have some qualities, otherwise they would not even be beings.'[13] This is perhaps the background to Kant's statement that 'substances in general must have some intrinsic nature' (A274/B330). If a substance is the kind of thing that can exist on its own, if it can exist and be lonely, then it must have properties compatible with loneliness, intrinsic properties. The stakes as to what can count as an intrinsic property have now been raised so high that no physical property can count as an intrinsic property. The conclusion Leibniz draws is, as Kant says, that since the properties cannot be physical, they must in some sense be mental.

The phenomenal world is the physical world, and this brings us to a distinctive contribution made by Leibniz to physics rather than to metaphysics. Leibniz is credited with being the author of the first dynamical theory of matter, a theory that makes force the fundamental physical property,[14] and Kant's own dynamical theory has its basic roots here. Leibniz declares in 'A Specimen of Dynamics' (1695) that 'force is something absolutely real in substances . . . while space, time, and motion, are, to a certain extent, beings of reason, and are true or real, not *per se*, but only to the extent that they involve . . . the force in created substances'.[15] Force is described as 'inherent in every corporeal substance *per se*'.[16] In proclaiming force as the fundamental property of matter, Leibniz rejects the other chief candidates for that role: Cartesian extension and Newtonian mass. Extension and mass are not primitive, he says, but rather to be explained in terms of the action of a force resisting the approach of other things and thereby filling space—as Kant was later to agree. Leibniz argued against the Cartesians that force was

---

[13] 'Monadology' (1714), Gerhardt vi. 608, Ariew and Garber 214.

[14] See e.g. Pierre Costabel, 'Newton's and Leibniz' Dynamics', in R. Palter, ed., *The Annus Mirabilis of Sir Isaac Newton* (Cambridge, Mass.: MIT Press, 1970); Irving Polonoff, *Force, Cosmos, Monads and Other Themes of Kant's Early Thought* (Bonn: Kant-Studien, Ergänzungsheft No. 107, 1973).

[15] 'Specimen of Dynamics' (1695), Gerhardt M vii. 247, Ariew and Garber 130. More accurately, Leibniz says that space, time and motion are real to the extent that they involve *either* 'the divine attributes' *or* the force in created substances.

[16] Ibid., Gerhardt M vii. 236, Ariew and Garber 119.

a distinct reality, not reducible to 'quantity of motion', and his arguments for the conservation of *vis viva* or 'living force' are among the earliest statements of the principle of the conservation of kinetic energy.

However, Leibniz's statement that 'force is something absolutely real in substances' must be interpreted in a particular way. Forces are not regarded as intrinsic properties of physical substances, as Newton conceived of mass, and Descartes conceived of extension. Kant is right to say that Leibniz thinks of physical forces as relations—or relational properties—of monadic substances. This does not clearly emerge in 'A Specimen of Dynamics', but it emerges in his correspondence with de Volder. Leibniz's theory of force had left de Volder dissatisfied. De Volder complained, 'I have always considered forces as being like an external denomination'—a relational property.[17] Is that compatible with its being 'absolutely real' and 'inherent in every corporeal substance'? In his reply to de Volder Leibniz says that physical force is *derivative*. There is such a thing as 'primitive' force, and it is an intrinsic property, but, as de Volder comments and Leibniz admits, it is hardly physical. It is 'like the "I"', it is 'perception and appetite'.[18] In short, it is the kind of property that a soul, a monad, and not a physical thing, can have. Where then does this leave corporeal force, as derivative force? Derivative predicates, according to Leibniz, are such that they '*only add relations to the reality of the attribute*'.[19] That is why Kant characterizes the Leibnizian view as holding that the dynamical properties of substances, such as reciprocal community, are 'external relations' of monads (A274/B330). Dynamical properties, in so far as they are physical, are relational properties. Physical forces thus belong to the phenomenal realm. Leibniz says, 'I also put corporeal forces where I put bodies, namely, among the phenomena, if they are understood as adding something over and above simple substances or their modifications.'[20] Leibniz has a relational conception of the physical world: to understand what a body is is to understand how it is related to other things. A body is something that resists the approach of other bodies, and thereby fills a space. All physical properties are relational properties, and in so far as any property is intrinsic, it is a property not of a body, but of an incorporeal substance.[21] Bodies are composed of parts that stand in

---

[17] As quoted by Leibniz in a letter to de Volder, 30 June 1704, Gerhardt ii. 270, Ariew and Garber 180.

[18] Letter to de Volder, 20 June 1703, Gerhardt ii. 251, Ariew and Garber 176; letter to de Volder, 1704 or 1705, Gerhardt ii. 275, Ariew and Garber 181.

[19] 'Conversation' (emphasis added), Ariew and Garber 259 n. 315 (citing an earlier draft of the work, in A. Robinet, *Malebranche et Leibniz: Relations personnelles* (Paris: J. Vrin, 1955)).

[20] Letter to de Volder, 1704 or 1705, Gerhardt ii. 276, Ariew and Garber 182.

[21] I am not doing justice here to Leibniz's attempts to find a coherent doctrine of corporeal substance which attributes to bodies an organic unity, so that they thereby become more than mere aggregates, though I do not see this doctrine as ultimately consistent with the monadology.

dynamical relations to each other, parts that cohere with each other, or repel each other. The parts stand in spatial relations to other parts. Those parts will in turn consist of parts similarly related, as one descends the infinite labyrinth of the continuum. But a body is constituted by, not just physical parts bearing certain relations to each other, but at the most fundamental level, monadic substances bearing certain relations to each other. Bodies are dependent in two ways: they are dependent on their (bodily) parts; and they are dependent on their monadic foundations. Bodies are founded on monads, not in the way that wholes are founded on their parts, but in the way that things of one ontological domain may be founded on things of quite a different domain. We shall have more to say about this shortly.

There is evidently common ground between the Kantian and Leibnizian conceptions of matter, and accordingly with their conceptions of the distinction between phenomena and things in themselves. First, matter is constituted by forces. This Leibnizian conception of matter is implicit in Kant's discussion of action and force as the criterion of material substance in the Second Analogy (A204/B249), discussed in the preceding chapter. Second, forces are construed, whether rightly or wrongly, as relations, or relational properties. Third, matter endures. Leibniz says that 'Corporeal substance can neither arise nor perish except through creation or annihilation. For when corporeal substance once endures, it will always endure, since there is no reason for any difference.'[22] Fourth, and most importantly, matter is something that we call a substance, and regard as a substance, that is really a phenomenon of substances. As Leibniz says, he puts corporeal forces where he puts bodies, 'namely, among the phenomena'. Corporeal substance is a *phaenomenon substantiatum:* something we treat as a substance that does not, as Leibniz says, 'deserve the name'.[23] Corporeal substance has a kind of inferior citizenship, a 'droit de bourgeoisie'.[24] Things in themselves are substances possessing intrinsic properties. Matter is something that does not really 'deserve the name' of substance (Leibniz), something that is a mere 'picture' of a substance, a merely 'comparative' subject (Kant). The properties of the physical, phenomenal world are relational.

However, Leibniz says more than this. Having distinguished phenomena from things in themselves in a way that has much in common with Kant, he then 'takes' the phenomena for things in themselves, saying that the former are nothing over and above the latter. This brings us to the question of how

---

[22] 'Primary Truths' (1686), Couturat 523, Ariew and Garber 34, italics deleted.

[23] Leibniz refers to aggregates as *substantiata* in a number of places; see also, for example, his notes for a letter to des Bosses, 5 February 1712, Gerhardt ii. 439, Ariew and Garber 200.

[24] Matter is thus described in a letter to Arnauld, 30 Apr. 1687, Gerhardt ii. 102, Ariew and Garber 90.

the phenomena are founded upon things in themselves, according to Leibniz.

4. *A Reduction of Phenomena to Things in Themselves*

Leibniz believes not only that monads have intrinsic properties, but that in some sense that have *only* intrinsic properties: that, as Kant puts it, 'everything is merely intrinsic' (A274/B330). This is not incompatible with his belief that the phenomenal realm is constituted by the relations of substances, if Leibniz at the same time takes the phenomena for things in themselves: takes relations and relational properties to be reducible to intrinsic properties, and takes the physical realm to be reducible to the monadic.

How are we to understand this reduction? Kant says that according to Leibniz, since everything is merely intrinsic, the monads form the raw material, or foundation (*Grundstoff*), for everything else that exists (A274/B330). This suggests one aspect of the reduction. For any beings other than monads, there must be monads to serve as the foundation for those beings. Kant also describes the foundations as 'grounds' (*Gründe*) for which the other beings are 'consequents' (*Folgen*) (A267/B323). This suggests a further aspect of the reduction: the intrinsic properties of monads are such that they *entail* the facts about the other beings.

In contemporary philosophical parlance, Kant's idea is that any beings other than monads must *supervene* on monads and their intrinsic properties. Derivative things supervene on foundational things when they satisfy the two features suggested in Kant's description: whenever there are derivative things that are a certain way, the foundational things must be some way or another; and how the foundational things are must entail how the derivative things are. This means that there will be no difference in the derivative things unless there is a difference in the foundational things. In an article which has become the *locus classicus* for the topic of supervenience, Jaegwon Kim defines the notion more precisely (restricting our attention to classes of properties) as follows:

A class of properties A supervenes on a class of properties B if and only if, necessarily, for every object x and for every property F in A, if x has F, then there exists a property G in B such that x has G; and necessarily, for every object y, if y has G then y has F.[25]

---

[25] Jaegwon Kim, 'Concepts of Supervenience', *Philosophy and Phenomenological Research* **45** (1984), 153–76. This is the definition for what he calls *strong* supervenience (165), which is the only sort of supervenience we shall be concerned with here and in the chapters to come.

Apply this general idea to the cases at hand. Suppose that the physical world supervenes on the monadic. Then if the physical world is a certain way, the monadic world must be some way or another; and the way the monadic world is must entail the way the physical world is. Suppose that relations supervene on the intrinsic properties of monads. Then for any relation, there must be some intrinsic properties amongst the monads; and those intrinsic properties must entail the relation.

Let us turn then to Leibniz, to assess the accuracy of Kant's version of him. The idea that bodies supervene on monads, and that relations supervene on intrinsic properties, can be seen as a consequence of—or as one aspect of—Leibniz's dizzying mirror thesis, according to which everything in the universe mirrors, or expresses, everything else. In the first instance, there is a mirroring of all monads in each monad, ordained by pre-established harmony:

[T]his mutual connection or accommodation of all created things to each other and of each to all the rest causes each simple substance to have relations which express all the others and consequently to be a perpetual living mirror of the universe . . . This universal harmony . . . results in every substance expressing exactly all the others . . .[26]

This mirroring yields relations of similarity and difference amongst the monads which in turn form the foundation for the realm of physical things: the physical world mirrors the world of monads.

[C]ompound beings are in symbolic agreement with the simple.

The souls follow their laws . . . and the bodies follow theirs, which consist in the laws of motion; nevertheless these two beings of entirely different kind meet together and correspond to each other like two clocks perfectly regulated to the same time.[27]

This correspondence between the two realms means that the physical realm *expresses* the realm of monads. Leibniz's notion of expression is broad:

One thing expresses another, in my usage, when there is a constant and regular relation between what can be said about one and about the other.[28]

One thing is said to express another if it has properties that correspond to the properties of the thing expressed . . . There are various kinds of expression; for example, the model of a machine expresses the machine itself, the projective delineation on a plane expresses a solid, speech expresses thoughts and truths, characters express

---

[26] 'Monadology', Gerhardt vi. 616, Loemker 648.
[27] Ibid., Gerhardt vi. 617, Loemker 649; 'Consideration on Vital Principles' (1705), Gerhardt vi. 540–1, Loemker 587.
[28] Letter to Arnauld, 9 Oct. 1687, Gerhardt ii. 112, Loemker 339.

numbers, and an algebraic equation expresses a circle or some other figure. What is common to all these expressions is that we can pass from a consideration of the properties of the expression to a consideration of the properties expressed. Hence it is clearly not necessary for that which expresses to be similar to the thing expressed, if only a certain analogy is maintained between the properties.[29]

If the laws of bodies and the laws of souls correspond to each other like two perfectly regulated clocks, then the laws of bodies express the laws of souls—and the laws of souls express the laws of bodies. However, there is an asymmetry here which the mere notion of expression or correspondence fails to capture. The bodies depend on the monads, but the monads do not depend on the bodies. The bodies are nothing over and above the monads.

De Volder complained that this means that Leibniz seems to 'eliminate bodies completely'. Leibniz seems to 'place them in appearances, and to substitute for things only forces, not even corporeal forces, but perception and appetite'.[30] Leibniz denied it. He replied, 'I don't really eliminate body, but *reduce it to what it is.*'[31] He says, in a marginal comment on Berkeley's *Principles*,

we don't have to say that matter is Nothing; it suffices to say that it is a phenomenon, like a rainbow, and that it is not a substance but a result of substances.[32]

Bodies are results of monads, but monads are not results of bodies. Bodies are phenomena: they are not substances, but a result of substances.

The reduction of bodies to monads, as Leibniz describes it, seems then to have the following features. There is a correspondence between the properties of bodies and the properties of monads; the realm of monads expresses the realm of bodies, and the realm of bodies expresses the realm of monads; and there is an asymmetry about the correspondence, so that the properties of bodies are the 'results' of the properties of monads, in such a way that bodies are said to be 'reduced' to monads. This is indeed well captured in the idea that bodies *supervene* on monads, which suggests that Kant's account of Leibniz—on the above interpretation—is accurate enough. One can, as Leibniz puts it, 'pass from a consideration of the properties of the expression to a consideration of the properties of the properties

[29] 'What is an Idea?' (1678), Gerhardt vii. 263–4, translation by Mates, *Philosophy of Leibniz*, 38.

[30] de Volder's words, as quoted by Leibniz in his letter to de Volder, 1704 or 1705, Gerhardt ii. 275, Ariew and Garber 181.

[31] Letter to de Volder, 1704 or 1705 (italics added), Gerhardt ii. 275, Ariew and Garber 181.

[32] Mates, *Philosophy of Leibniz*, 199, citing W. Kabitz, *Sitzungsberichte der Preussischen Akademie der Wissenschaften, Phil. Hist. Klasse* 24 (1932), 636; and A. Robinet, 'Leibniz: Lecture du treatise de Berkeley,' *Études de philosophie* (1983), 217–23.

expressed'. Since the properties of monads entail the properties of bodies, one can pass from a consideration of the properties of monads to the properties of bodies. And since supervenience implies that there is no difference in the properties of bodies without a difference in the properties of monads, one can pass from a consideration of the properties of bodies to a consideration of the properties of monads, to the following limited extent: where there is a difference in the bodies, one may infer that there is a difference in the properties of things in themselves. Supervenience can be viewed, then, as one particular kind of expression, or mirroring.

Kant is right to think that the doctrine of the reduction of bodies to monads is linked to that of the reduction of relations to intrinsic properties: Leibniz says that

in the universe, place and position . . . are only relations, resulting from other things . . . Considering the matter more accurately, I saw that they are only mere results, which themselves do not constitute any intrinsic denomination, and thus are only relations which need a fundament from the predicament of quality or an intrinsic accidental denomination.[33]

Relations, like bodies, are described as 'results', which 'need a fundament' in intrinsic properties. Spatial properties are here described as 'only relations', and dynamical properties, physical forces, are described in the same way. If physical properties are relational, then the reduction of bodies and the reduction of relations go together: the supervenience of bodies on monads, and the supervenience of relations on intrinsic properties, are aspects of the same reduction. As we saw earlier, Kant ascribes to Leibniz a two-tier reduction: of spatial relations to dynamical relations, and then of dynamical relations to intrinsic properties (A267/B323). And Leibniz does indeed take spatial and temporal properties to be less real than dynamical properties: space and time are real 'not *per se*, but only to the extent that they involve . . . the force in created substances'.[34] Dynamical properties in turn supervene on the intrinsic properties of monads, physical force being merely 'derivative' force, force that derives from the non-physical 'primitive force' which is an intrinsic property of the monad.

Leibniz's reduction of phenomena to things in themselves has thus led us to his reduction of relations to intrinsic properties. This means it has led us to a topic of considerable dispute amongst Leibniz scholars, and hence considerable well-founded hesitation on the part of any rational newcomer to the field. I attribute to Leibniz a thesis about reducibility which I take to be broadly consistent with Kant's own opinion about Leibniz, and with the

[33] Couturat 9, translation from Mates, *Philosophy of Leibniz*, 223.
[34] 'Specimen of Dynamics', Gerhardt M vii. 247, Ariew and Garber 130.

opinions of a number of recent commentators, though perhaps it is not quite to be found in its entirety in any single one of them.[35]

On this interpretation, the reducibility of the physical world—the reducibility of the spatial and dynamical relations to which Kant draws attention—is a consequence of the reducibility of relations in general. So let us turn, then, to the motivation for Leibniz's more general thesis about the reducibility of relations. Leibniz thinks that to exist is to be either a substance or a property of a substance, and since relations are not substances, the only candidate solution is that they are properties. But this creates difficulties. Suppose that David is the father of Solomon. To whom should we ascribe the property in question? David bears the relation 'is father of' to Solomon. David has the relational property of being father-of-Solomon. Solomon bears the relation 'is son of' to David. Solomon has the relational property of being son-of-David. There are two subjects or substances involved here. So there is a temptation to treat the relation as a property attributable to both. 'Fatherhood' has, so to speak, one leg in David, and another in Solomon. That is how Leibniz describes the matter in his fifth letter to Clarke. If we were to think of relations as properties, or accidents,

we should have an accident in two subjects, with one leg in one and the other in the other; which is contrary to the notion of accidents. Therefore, we must say that this

[35] In brief, I am in agreement with van Cleve, who attributes a supervenience thesis to Leibniz in 'Inner States and Outer Relations'; and I have learnt much from Mates, Rescher, and Parkinson. I follow the majority of commentators in attributing to Leibniz some sort of reducibility thesis, but Ishiguro and Hintikka are notable exceptions to this consensus. In taking reducibility *not* to be a thesis about the logical equivalence of relational and non-relational propositions, I disagree with Russell, and agree with van Cleve, Mates, and Rescher. Mates and Rescher see reducibility as requiring merely a one-way entailment from intrinsic properties to relational, rather than the logical equivalence required by Russell. A one-way entailment interpretation is weaker than the supervenience interpretation favoured by van Cleve and myself, since it amounts to just the second conjunct of a supervenience thesis about relations. Buroker sees Leibnizian reducibility as involving the 'logical priority' of non-relational properties over relational. This is surely too weak for Leibniz, even for Buroker's own interpretative purposes: as Kant says, a substance must have intrinsic properties, but need not have relational—a fact which is sufficient for the 'logical priority' of the intrinsic but implies nothing about the reducibility of relations. I see the well-foundedness of phenomena and the founding of the relational in the intrinsic as closely connected themes. In this I agree with Kant, Rescher, and Mondadori, but not with Adams. See Adams, 'Phenomenalism'; Buroker, *Space and Incongruence*, 34; van Cleve, 'Inner States and Outer Relations'; Mates, *Philosophy of Leibniz*; Parkinson, *Logic and Reality in Leibniz's Metaphysics*; Mondadori, 'Solipsistic Perception'; Rescher, *Philosophy of Leibniz*; Jaakko Hintikka, 'Leibniz on Plenitude, Relations, and the "Reign of Law"'; and Hidé Ishiguro, 'Leibniz's Theory of the Ideality of Relations', both in Harry Frankfurt, ed., *Leibniz* (New York: Doubleday, 1972); Ishiguro, *Leibniz's Philosophy of Logic and Language* (London: Duckworth, 1972); and Bertrand Russell, *A Critical Exposition of the Philosophy of Leibniz*, 2nd edn. (London: George Allen & Unwin, 1937).

relation . . . is indeed out of the subjects; but being neither a substance nor an accident, it must be a mere ideal thing, the consideration of which is nevertheless useful.[36]

It is impossible, according to Leibniz, to have 'an accident in two subjects'. In so far as a relation is conceived of as if it were really in two subjects, it is a 'mere ideal thing'. But the relation none the less has a firm basis in reality, for it must have 'foundations' in the things to which it is attributed.

[T]here are no purely extrinsic denominations, denominations which have absolutely no foundation in the very thing denominated. For it is necessary that the notion of the subject denominated contain the notion of the predicate. And consequently, whenever the denomination of a thing is changed, there must be a variation in the thing in itself.[37]

My judgment about relations is that paternity in David is one thing, sonship in Solomon another, but that the relation common to both is a merely mental thing whose basis is the modifications of the individuals.[38]

The relations must have a basis, a foundation, in the intrinsic modifications of the related individuals.[39]

How such a notion of reducibility might apply to David and Solomon is not easy to see, but there are simpler cases to hand. Assume for the sake of argument (and contrary to Kant and Leibniz) that height is an intrinsic property. The relation expressed in the proposition 'Simmias is taller than Socrates' (to borrow Plato's example) is then reducible not because the proposition is logically equivalent to the conjunction of, say, the propositions 'Simmias is six feet tall' and 'Socrates is five feet tall' (which it is not).[40] It is reducible because it supervenes on the intrinsic properties of Simmias and Socrates: for the relation to hold, Simmias and Socrates must have certain intrinsic properties; and those intrinsic properties must be such that they entail the relation. And that is an accurate description of the case. Both requirements are met. For the relation to hold, Simmias and Socrates must

---

[36] From the letters to Clarke, 1715–16, Gerhardt vii. 401, Ariew and Garber 339.

[37] 'Primary Truths' (1686), Couturat 520, Ariew and Garber 32.

[38] Letter to des Bosses, 21 Apr. 1714, Gerhardt ii. 486, Loemker 609, emphasis added.

[39] It is not sufficient for reducibility that a relational proposition be implied by a proposition that has only one-place predicates. Relational properties (e.g. is-a-father, and even is-a-father-of-Solomon) can be represented as one-place predicates, but they are not for that reason reducible. If they were, fatherhood would be reducible because David is father-of-Solomon, and that implies that he is father of Solomon. (The proposition having the *Fa* form implies the proposition having the *aRb* form.) But this would be a cheat, and in any case is not what Leibniz means, as Mates argues convincingly, *Philosophy of Leibniz*, 214–15. The reduction must be, not to one-place predicates, but to intrinsic properties.

[40] See Plato's *Phaedo*, trans. Hugh Tredennick, *The Collected Dialogues of Plato*, ed. Edith Hamilton and Huntington Cairns (Princeton, N.J.: Princeton University Press, 1961), 102.

be such that they have certain heights; and those heights must entail the relation. Simmias' being six feet tall and Socrates' being five feet tall is enough for the 'taller than' relation to hold, and therefore enough for the corresponding relational property 'taller than Socrates' to be attributable to Simmias. It is impossible for Simmias to be six feet tall, Socrates five, and for Simmias to fail to be taller than Socrates. The fact that Simmias is taller than Socrates is nothing over and above the fact that Simmias is six feet tall, and Socrates is five feet tall.

Just as the notion of supervenience provides a good way to understand Leibniz's reduction of bodies to monads, so it provides a good way to understand his doctrine of the reducibility of relations, along the lines just suggested. Many of Leibniz's remarks about relations make it seem clear that the reducibility he has in mind can be captured in the idea that relations supervene on intrinsic properties. Relations are described as mere 'results', where the results are a kind of non-causal dependence. It is perhaps worth noting—though we cannot put too much weight on this—that Leibniz even seems to use the label of 'supervenience' to describe the kind of results they are.[41] He also says, 'A relation, since it results from a state of things, never comes into being or disappears unless some change is made in its fundament.'[42] Here we have something close to the slogan for supervenience: no difference in the supervenient things without difference in the foundational things; no change in relation without change in its fundament. The same point is made in the passage from 'Primary Truths' quoted a moment ago: 'whenever the [extrinsic] denomination of a thing is changed, there must be a variation in the thing in itself.' The 'taller than' relation which Simmias bears to Socrates would never come into being or disappear unless some change were made in its fundament: in the intrinsic properties of Simmias and Socrates. The relation comes into being when, for example, Simmias grows; it would disappear if Socrates should have a belated growth spurt; it did disappear when Socrates ceased to exist, after the unfortunate verdict of the Athenian court.

In the above example we have a relation that supervenes on the intrinsic

---

[41] 'Relation is an accident which is in multiple subjects; it is what results without any change made in the subjects but *supervenes* from them', emphasis added. Quoted in Ishiguro, *Leibniz's Philosophy*, 71 n. 3, citing Bodemann 74. 'Relatio est accidens quod est in pluribus subjectis estque resultans tantum seu nulla mutatione facta ab iis supervenit.' I am unsure how to interpret the idea that relation results 'without any change made in the subjects', which seems at first sight to conflict with the passage quoted immediately hereafter. Perhaps the idea is that the relation can arise even when no change is made in one of the subjects, as when Socrates, without change 'in himself' becomes shorter than Simmias, when Simmias grows.

[42] Grua 547, translation from Mates, *Philosophy of Leibniz*, 223.

properties of the relata, taken *collectively*. The relation in question supervenes on the intrinsic properties of Socrates *and* Simmias, taken together. It may be that Leibniz holds that all relational properties and relations are reducible in this way: that all are reducible to the intrinsic properties of their relata, taken together—in other words, that they are what I shall call *bilaterally reducible*. Restricting our attention to two-place relations, for simplicity's sake, let us say that a relation is bilaterally reducible just in case it bilaterally supervenes on its relata, taken collectively. We can apply Kim's definition of supervenience to yield an approximation for—

> *Bilateral supervenience for relations*:
>
> A class of relations A bilaterally supervenes on a class of intrinsic properties B if and only if, necessarily, for every pair of objects x and y, and every relation R in A, if xRy, then there exist intrinsic properties G and H in B such that x has G, and y has H; and necessarily, for every pair of objects w and z, if w has G and z has H, then wRz.

In the discussions ahead I will be talking chiefly about reducibility for relational properties rather than relations. But we can say likewise that a relational property is bilaterally reducible just in case it supervenes on the intrinsic properties of its bearer and of some salient other thing.[43] Approximately, applying Kim again, we can have—

> *Bilateral supervenience for relational properties*:
>
> A class of relational properties A bilaterally supervenes on a class of intrinsic properties B if and only if, necessarily, for every object x, and every relational property F in A, if x is F, then there exists a y, and there exist intrinsic properties G and H in B, such that x has G, and y has H; and necessarily, for every pair of objects w and z, if w has G and z has H, then w has F.

Some relations and relational properties clearly are bilaterally reducible.

---

[43] Kim's definition seems to be restricted to cases of one-place properties supervening on other one-place properties of the same object; my applications of Kim's definition attempt to give an approximation for more than one-place properties supervening on one-place properties of more than one object. My notions of bilateral and unilateral reducibility are adapted from Keith Campbell's discussion of what he calls bilateral and unilateral relations, *Abstract Particulars* (Oxford: Blackwell, 1990). The only place I have found something like this distinction applied to the task of Leibniz exegesis is in Parkinson, *Logic and Reality in Leibniz's Metaphysics*, 45 and 147, with the labels 'weak' (bilateral) and 'strong' (unilateral) reducibility, though it seems to be in the context of a Russellian logical equivalence interpretation of reducibility. For simplicity I have a definition of bilateral reducibility, but strictly one needs a more general notion of *multilateral* reducibility which, unlike my definitions, would deal with n-place relations for n greater than two.

The relation of being *taller than* someone else seems to be bilaterally reducible, and so does the relational property of being *taller than Simmias*. Many relations and relational properties, on the other hand, do not seem to be bilaterally reducible: if Simmias is three feet away from Socrates, that relation ('three feet away from') and its corresponding relational property ('three-feet-away-from-Socrates') do not seem to supervene on the intrinsic properties of Simmias and Socrates taken together. But it may well be plausible, all the same, to ascribe to Leibniz the prima facie highly improbable view that *all* relations and relational properties are bilaterally reducible.

Sometimes, though, it seems that Leibniz may have a rather different reducibility thesis in mind. Sometimes Leibniz appears to believe that the facts about one thing considered *on its own* are sufficient to entail all the relational facts about it.

The complete or perfect notion of an individual substance contains all of its predicates, past, present, and future.[44]

[T]here are no purely extrinsic denominations, denominations which have absolutely no foundation in the very thing denominated. For it is necessary that the notion of the subject denominated contain the notion of the predicate.[45]

Indeed, this appears to follow from the Leibnizian mirror thesis, according to which facts about one monad 'express' all the facts about the other monads, and hence all the relational facts about the first monad.

[T]he concept of an individual substance includes all its events and all its denominations, even those which are commonly called extrinsic, that is, those which pertain to it only by virtue of the general connection of things and from the fact that it expresses the whole universe in its own way.[46]

The concept of an individual thing is said in these passages to entail all the predicates, including the relational predicates, of that very thing. Moving from predicates to properties, the idea suggested in such passages is that the relations and relational properties of a thing supervene on the intrinsic properties of that very thing.

On this second interpretation, to put the point more generally, the relations and relational properties of things supervene on the intrinsic properties of things, considered not collectively but *distributively*. We need to consider, not both terms of the relation together, but either one of them. This would be a notion of what I shall call *unilateral reducibility*. A relation

---

[44] 'Primary Truths', Couturat 520, Ariew and Garber 32.

[45] Ibid.

[46] Letter to Arnauld, July 1686, Gerhardt ii. 56, Loemker 337. Parkinson argues that Leibnizian reducibility is supposed to follow from the thesis that each monad expresses all the others, *Logic and Reality in Leibniz's Metaphysics*, 147.

is unilaterally reducible just in case it unilaterally supervenes on the intrinsic properties of the relata, taken distributively; and a relational property is unilaterally reducible just in case it unilaterally supervenes on the intrinsic properties of its bearer—roughly as follows:

Unilateral supervenience for relations:

A class of relations A unilaterally supervenes on a class of intrinsic properties B if and only if, necessarily, for every pair of objects x and y, and every relation R in A, if xRy, then there exist intrinsic properties G and H in B such that x has G and y has H; and necessarily, for every object w, if w has G, then there exists a z such that wRz, and if w has H then there exists a z such that zRw.

Unilateral supervenience for relational properties:

A class of relational properties A unilaterally supervenes on a class of intrinsic properties B if and only if, necessarily, for every object x, and every relational property F in A, if x is F, then there exists an intrinsic property G in B such that x has G; and necessarily, for every object w, if w has G, then w has F.

We saw that if Simmias is taller than Socrates, then the relation ('taller than'), and the relational property ('taller-than-Socrates') are bilaterally reducible, since they supervene on the intrinsic properties of Simmias *and* Socrates. If they were to be unilaterally reducible, by contrast, one would need to be able to tell, from looking at the intrinsic properties of Simmias *alone*, that Simmias is taller than Socrates. One would need to be able to tell, from looking at the intrinsic properties of Socrates *alone*, that Simmias is taller than Socrates. Or more accurately, since the point is not epistemological but metaphysical, the intrinsic properties of Simmias alone would be sufficient to determine that Simmias was taller than Socrates; and likewise for Socrates. The suggestion, for this example, is ludicrous. This relation and relational property are not, on the face of it, unilaterally reducible, since they do not supervene on the intrinsic properties of Simmias on his own, or of Socrates on his own. Note that if they *were* unilaterally reducible they would *a fortiori* be bilaterally reducible: if they were to supervene on the intrinsic properties of Simmias alone, then *a fortiori* they would supervene on the intrinsic properties of Simmias *and* Socrates. Unilateral reducibility is a stronger thesis than bilateral reducibility: unilateral reducibility implies bilateral reducibility, but not vice versa. Failure of unilateral reducibility does not imply failure of bilateral reducibility, as we see from the example: the 'taller than' relation is not unilaterally reducible, but is nevertheless bilaterally reducible. I'm afraid I cannot produce an illustrative example of any relation or relational property which is plausibly unilaterally reducible.

Perhaps this is because there are none, but let us postpone consideration of this question until the next chapter. It may well be plausible, all the same, to ascribe to Leibniz the prima facie even more improbable view that all relations and relational properties are unilaterally reducible.

It is not entirely clear at first sight which of these two reducibility theses to attribute to Leibniz: it may be that Leibniz holds each, at different times, or it may be that he conflates them, as indeed some of his commentators seem to. Nicholas Rescher attributes bilateral and unilateral reducibility theses to Leibniz without apparently noticing their distinctness; James Royse attributes a unilateral reducibility thesis to Leibniz and then appears to consider various bilateral theses as candidate elucidations of it (which they cannot be). Some commentators, such as Mates, do not seem to note the unilateral thesis at all. It may be, of course, that Leibniz himself holds both theses without conflating them: since the unilateral thesis implies the bilateral (but not vice versa), if he holds the first he is entitled to hold the second. I shall follow Parkinson in supposing that Leibniz consistently holds both reducibility theses.[47] This will assume some importance in the next chapter, but what matters most for our immediate task is that Leibniz held a reducibility thesis of this general form:

Reducibility:

All the relations between things, and the relational properties of things, are reducible to—i.e. supervene on—the intrinsic properties of their relata.

I have left this description ambiguous between the unilateral and bilateral possibilities, since it will sometimes be convenient to ignore these complications and have a simple, all-purpose thesis in mind.

If all relations supervene on the intrinsic properties of substances, then the dynamical and spatial relations that form the physical world are noth-

---

[47] Nicholas Rescher, in *Philosophy of Leibniz*, gives the two interpretations on 71 and 76 respectively; James Royse, in 'Leibniz and the Reducibility of Relations to Properties', *Studia Leibnitiana* 12, No. 2 (1980), 179–204, attributes a unilateral reducibility thesis to Leibniz on p. 181, gives what appear to be various bilateral theses as elucidations thereof from p. 184 onwards; see also Mates, *Philosophy of Leibniz*, 217–19. Parkinson, who unlike these favours a Russellian equivalence interpretation of reducibility, suggests that when Leibniz says there are no purely extrinsic denominations, he means both (a) when one asserts that *A* bears a relation to *B*, the asserted proposition is 'reducible to subject-predicate propositions whose subjects are *A* and *B* respectively' and also (b) in order to assert a relational proposition about *A* and *B*, 'it is in principle enough to know the [non-relational] predicates of *A* alone or the predicates of *B* alone' (*Logic and Reality in Leibniz's Metaphysics*, 45). This makes something like the unilateral vs. bilateral distinction—though the (b) option is described in a needlessly epistemological way, and seems to involve a merely one-way entailment from intrinsic properties to relations, at odds with the Russellian interpretation elsewhere favoured by Parkinson.

ing over and above the intrinsic properties of substances—in the same way that the fact of Simmias being taller than Socrates is nothing over and above facts about the two individual heights. We need not attend here to the details of how Leibniz hoped to make plausible the claim that dynamical and spatial relations—let alone all relations—are reducible in this way. For now we can simply pause and note the implications. Given the distinction between phenomena and things in themselves that Kant and Leibniz seem to have in common, Leibniz's view about the reducibility of relations must mean that *phenomena* are nothing over and above things in themselves. That is one of the two reasons why Kant is right in saying that Leibniz 'took the appearances for things in themselves' (A264/B330).

5. *Knowledge, via Phenomena, of Things in Themselves*

There is another sense in which Leibniz took the appearances for things in themselves, as we noted in Section 2. Leibniz not only takes phenomena to be *reducible* to things in themselves, but he also believes that things in themselves *are perceived through the senses*. Leibniz believes that we can know 'through sensibility', albeit confusedly, the nature of things in themselves (A44/B62). This is certainly how Kant interprets him. Recall the passages we considered earlier:

[Leibniz] assumed that we *intuit things as they are*, although in confused representation. (A268/B323, emphasis added)

[T]he appearance was, for him, the representation of *the thing in itself*. (A270/B326, emphasis added)

[Leibniz held] that our entire sensibility is nothing but a confused representation of things, that contains *solely what belongs to the things in themselves*, but with a crowding together of characteristics and partial representations, so that we cannot consciously distinguish the things from one another. (A43/B60, emphasis added)

Leibniz, on Kant's interpretation, believes that sensibility provides one route to knowledge of things in themselves, because sensibility contains solely what belongs to things in themselves: sensibility represents the intrinsic properties of monads, although it represents them in a confused or distorted manner.

While sensibility provides one route to knowledge of things as they are in themselves, pure understanding provides another, and better, route:

The celebrated Leibniz . . . believed . . . that he was acquainted with the intrinsic constitution of things by comparing all objects merely with the understanding and with the isolated formal concepts of its thought. (A270/B326)

The role of the senses, on Kant's interpretation, is to confuse the representations given by the understanding, the difference between understanding and sensibility being just a difference in the degree of confusion of their representations. Perhaps this oversimplifies Leibniz, who seems to have thought that knowledge could be obscure, confused, and inadequate (each of these terms meaning something different) for reasons that have little to do with the senses.[48] Nevertheless, on Kant's interpretation of Leibniz, the role of the senses is to know confusedly the nature of things as they are in themselves. The objects of both sensibility and understanding are things in themselves. That, according to Kant, is the mistake: knowledge of things as they are in themselves can be given neither through sensibility, nor through the understanding. The understanding cannot grasp the 'intrinsic constitution' of things as they are in themselves, nor do appearances represent things as they are in themselves (A276/B332). Both routes to things in themselves are blocked.

How we know, and how much we know, are thus questions to which Kant and Leibniz give very different answers. Russell remarks on the contrast.

Leibniz's theory of perception is rendered peculiar by the fact that he denies any action of outside things upon the percipient. His theory may be regarded as the antithesis of Kant's. Kant thought that things in themselves are causes . . . of presentations, but cannot be known by means of presentations. Leibniz, on the contrary, denied the causal relation, but admitted the knowledge.[49]

In Leibniz's philosophy, by contrast to Kant's, there is neither epistemic Receptivity nor epistemic Humility.

Strictly speaking, if Leibniz believes that a perceiving substance is not affected by something else, then on Kant's understanding of what sensibility is, that substance does not in fact perceive or sense anything. It is definitive of sensibility, according to Kant, that it is receptive, i.e. affected by objects. That, I think, is part of the reason why Kant sees Leibniz as not acknowledging sensibility, but rather as assimilating it to intellect (A271/B327). We can also see why, given Kant's own philosophical background, the thesis of Receptivity is by no means obvious and trivial: for while Leibniz allows two sorts of knowledge, intellectual and sensible, *neither* of the two is really receptive, since neither requires our being affected by objects.

[48] See 'Meditations on Knowledge, Truth and Ideas' (1684), Gerhardt iv. 422-3, Ariew and Garber 23-4. I am grateful to Margaret Wilson for drawing this to my attention. Kant's interpretation gives the impression that, for Leibniz, there would be clear knowledge and no confusion at all were it not for the senses. This Platonic-sounding interpretation seems not to do justice to Leibniz's view that for finite creatures like ourselves there can be no clear or complete knowledge even through concepts alone.

[49] Russell, *Critical Exposition*, 133.

Let us consider whether Kant is right in attributing to Leibniz the view that we are acquainted, through perception, with things in themselves. We can begin by noting that Leibniz's mirror thesis has implications not only for the grounding of phenomena on monadic foundations, but also for knowledge, indeed knowledge of both kinds. Leibniz says that 'expression takes place everywhere'—everything mirrors everything else. And when we move to consider the role of monads as knowers and percipients, rather than as foundational constituents, this mirroring and expression assumes great epistemological significance. Perception and intellectual knowledge are species of which expression is the genus:

One thing expresses another, in my usage, when there is a constant and regular relation between what can be said about one and about the other. It is in this way that a projection in perspective expresses a geometrical figure. Expression is . . . a genus of which natural perception . . . and intellectual knowledge are species . . . Now this expression takes place everywhere, because every substance sympathizes with all the others, and receives a proportional change corresponding to the slightest change which occurs in the whole world.[50]

What is required for both perception and intellectual knowledge is expression, a mirroring of the intrinsic properties of all other monads in perception and intellection. The object of perception, and of intellection, is nothing short of the entire universe of monads:

This mutual connection or accommodation of all created things to each other and of each to all the rest causes each simple substance . . . to be a perpetual living mirror of the universe.

It is not in the object but in the modification of their knowledge that the monads are limited.[51]

The object of a monad's knowledge is entirely unlimited. Each monad expresses and thereby has knowledge of all the other monads.

While perception and intellectual knowledge both 'express' the properties of monads, perceptual knowledge involves bodies in a way that intellectual knowledge does not. The monad perceptually represents the universe of substances as a physical world, and it represents its own body most clearly of all. The expression of the monadic world in the physical world explored in Section 4 has implications for sensory knowledge. Consider how the passage about the 'agreement' of bodies and monads continues:

[C]ompound beings are in symbolic agreement with the simple. For everything is a plenum, so that all matter is bound together, and every motion in this plenum has

[50] Letter to Arnauld, 9 Oct. 1687, Gerhardt ii. 112, Loemker 339.
[51] 'Monadology', Gerhardt vi. 616, 617, Loemker 648, 649, emphasis added.

some effect upon distant bodies in proportion to their distance . . . As a result, every body responds to everything which happens in the universe, so that he who sees all could read in each everything that happens everywhere . . . But a soul can read within itself only what it represents distinctly; it cannot all at once develop all that is enfolded within it, for this reaches to infinity. Thus, although each created monad represents the whole universe, it represents more distinctly the body which is particularly affected by it . . . And as this body expresses the whole universe by the connection between all matter in the plenum, the soul also represents the whole universe in representing the body.[52]

Just as each monad mirrors every other monad, so each body mirrors every other body. The account of perception that is thought to follow from this is difficult to grasp, but it seems to go something like this. The object of perception is, in the first instance, one's own particular body. Then, because one's own body mirrors the entire physical universe of bodies, one perceives the realm of compound bodies in space and time. But in perceiving physical bodies, the perceiving monad perceives things as they are in themselves. The phenomena that are physical bodies are well-founded, and their foundations are in their monadic constituents. By perceiving one's own body, one perceives the entire physical universe; by perceiving the physical universe one perceives the entire realm of monads. Perceptual knowledge of things in themselves is mediated by the physical, phenomenal realm. The properties of one's own body—itself constituted by monads—reflect the properties of all other bodies, and thereby reflect the properties of all the monads which are their foundations. The harmony or 'expression' of which Leibniz speaks is manifested here in very many different ways: in the similarities amongst the constituent monads—i.e. in the ultimate object of knowledge; in the 'correspondence' between the realm of bodies and their constituent monads—i.e. in the supervenience of bodies on monads; and in the conformity between the perceiving monad and what the monad perceives—i.e. in knowledge itself.

On this account of perception, the perception of things in themselves depends on the fact that bodies are well-founded phenomena: it depends on the fact that the realm of bodies supervenes on the realm of monads. The supervenience of bodies on monads is in turn a consequence of the more general thesis of the supervenience of relations on intrinsic properties. On this understanding, the perception of things in themselves, the well-foundedness of phenomena, and the reducibility of relations are all closely interconnected in Leibniz's philosophy.[53] The mirror metaphor is a meta-

---

[52] Ibid., Gerhardt vi. 617, Loemker 649.

[53] I find Rescher and Mondadori persuasive on this. I am also indebted to Rescher for making clear the two ways in which harmony is manifested in perception. See Mondadori, 'Solipsistic Perception'; Rescher, *Philosophy of Leibniz*, 86–7. The 'objective aspect' of well-

phor for all of them. A perceiving monad mirrors the universe of bodies; bodies, as well-founded phenomena, mirror the monads; the dynamical and spatial relations of the physical world mirror the similarity relations of the intrinsic properties of their monadic constituents; the perceiving monad mirrors the universe of monads.

We can see, finally, that Leibniz's claim that the phenomenal world provides only an *imperfect* mirror of the monadic world—so that there is something distorted and partial about the perception of the monadic world via the phenomenal—is a feature which makes good sense on the interpretation suggested here. If the physical, phenomenal world supervenes on the monadic world, then it does indeed express properties of the monadic world—but in a limited and imperfect way. One can pass from a consideration of the properties of physical things to a consideration of the properties of monadic things—but only to a limited extent. If physical things supervene on monadic things, then one can know that there is no difference in the former without a difference in the latter. So where there is a perceived difference in the bodies, one may infer that there is a corresponding difference in monadic things. This yields knowledge through perception, but only imperfect knowledge, of some features of things in themselves.

I do not pretend wholly to understand these Leibnizian views, but perhaps I have said enough to clarify Kant's opinion of them. Kant said that Leibniz 'took the appearances for things in themselves', meaning both that Leibniz *reduces* phenomena to things in themselves, and that Leibniz believes we can have knowledge of things in themselves through the *senses*, since appearances 'represent things in themselves'. What is crucial to grasp here is the connection between these two ways in which Leibniz took the phenomena for things in themselves. Things in themselves can be known through perception precisely because phenomena are nothing over and above things in themselves. The sensory knowledge, via phenomena, of things in themselves depends on the reduction of phenomena to things in themselves. In short: it seems that the stark absence of epistemic Humility, in Leibniz, depends on Reducibility.

6. *Kant and Leibniz on Relations*

If the foregoing interpretation is correct, there is a resemblance between Leibniz and Kant: Leibniz's distinction between phenomena and things in

foundedness is, Rescher says, to be found in the similarities of intrinsic properties of monads. For an opposing view, see Adams, 'Phenomenalism', who has something like a coherence view of well-foundedness.

themselves resembles Kant's Distinction, which suggests a certain Leibnizian heritage in Kant's philosophy. And there are two differences, both nicely
captured in Russell's remark that Leibniz denies the causal relation, but
admits the knowledge. We are not receptive creatures, yet we know everything, albeit confusedly. There is no Receptivity in Leibniz, and no Humility. We have also seen that Leibniz has a distinctive thesis about the reduction
of phenomena to things in themselves, resting on an even more distinctive
thesis about the reducibility of relations. Is this opinion about relations a
point of similarity or of difference?

A number of commentators, sensitive to Kant's Leibnizian heritage, have
said that Kant endorses a Leibnizian view about relations. They suggest that
this commitment may be what led him to idealism, and thereby to the view
that we have no knowledge of things in themselves. Guyer says that 'Kant
harboured a prejudice against the ultimate reality of relations'.[54] He quotes
Leibniz's view that a relation, in so far as it is considered to be in two things,
is a 'mere ideal thing'. The Leibnizian opinion of relations, according to
Guyer, views relations as unreal, and he says that Kant shares this opinion.
He attributes to Kant an argument for idealism based on the premise that
relations are not real, quoting a passage from the Aesthetic which we considered in Chapter 2, and which we can consider again—now with Guyer's
translation instead of mine.

Now a thing in itself cannot be cognized through mere relations; therefore it is well
to judge that since nothing can be given to us through outer sense except mere representations of relation, this can contain nothing but the relation of the object to
the subject in its representation, and not anything intrinsic which pertains to the
object itself. (B67)

According to Guyer, the first clause of the passage states the Leibnizian
assumption about the unreality of relations. When Kant says that 'a thing
in itself cannot be cognized through mere relations', he means, says Guyer,
that relations are not 'genuine existents', not 'ultimately real'. Since space
and time are nothing but systems of relations, space and time and the things
presented to us in space and time are not 'ultimately real' either. Here is
Guyer's response to Kant's argument, thus described.

Of course it would now be hard for us to take the metaphysical premise seriously.
After Frege and Russell succeeded in clarifying the logic of relations, a metaphysical prejudice against relations could certainly derive no comfort from their earlier
logical obscurity, and so this metaphysical argument could hardly be persuasive
today . . . Kant produces no metaphysical title to the claim that relations are not
real.[55]

---

[54] Guyer, *Kant and the Claims*, 351.   [55] Ibid. 352.

Guyer's discovery of a 'Leibnizian' Kant focuses on the ideality theme in Leibniz's doctrine of relations. This is not quite fair, I think, to Leibniz, who does not think that relations are simply ideal, but reducible. Leibniz's requirement of *foundations* for relations is missing in Guyer's account of him. But Guyer's suggestion is important all the same, for if Kant believes that sensibility yields knowledge only of relations, and relations are ideal, then this provides a quick route to idealism. As we have seen, Kant says that the phenomenal world consists 'entirely of relations'. If relations are ideal, and phenomena are constituted by relations, then we reach immediately the conclusion that phenomena are ideal, and, with that, the conclusion that we have no knowledge of things in themselves—understood as the conclusion that we have no knowledge of real things.

Jill Buroker focuses not on the ideality strand of the Leibnizian view, but on the reducibility strand. She believes that Kant's response to the Leibnizian principle about the reducibility of relations has a vital role to play in his philosophical development.[56] According to Buroker, Kant endorsed the Leibnizian reducibility principle until the problem of incongruent counterparts forced him to abandon it for spatial relations and, ultimately, move to the view that space is ideal. Even then he continued to endorse the reducibility principle for relations between things in themselves. And James van Cleve follows Buroker in attributing to Kant the premise that 'all relations among things in themselves are reducible to nonrelational characters (qualities) of the relata'.[57]

If these critics are right, we have a second point of common ground between Kant and Leibniz. Kant endorses a Leibnizian view about relations (Guyer), or at any rate thinks that a Leibnizian reducibility principle holds for things in themselves (Buroker).[58] Moreover, if these critics are right, Kant's Leibnizian sympathies have an important role to play in the development of his mature position, leading him to idealism and a conclusion about humility—not indeed Humility as I have described it, but humility

---

[56] See Buroker, *Space and Incongruence*.

[57] van Cleve, 'Incongruent Counterparts', 37.

[58] Note, however, that despite their apparent similarities these two 'Leibnizian' interpretations of Kant are wildly at odds with one another. Guyer takes the Leibnizian view to be that relations are 'ideal', therefore 'not ultimately real', and concludes on Kant's behalf that spatial relations are 'not ultimately real'. Guyer says, in other words, that a Leibnizian view about space leads Kant to think space is ideal. Buroker takes the Leibnizian view to be that relations are reducible, attributes to Kant the view that relations among things in themselves are reducible, that spatial relations are (*contrary* to Leibniz) irreducible, and concludes on Kant's behalf that spatial relations are not properties of things in themselves, and that they are therefore ideal. Buroker says, in other words, that a non-Leibnizian view about space, combined with a Leibnizian view about things in themselves, leads Kant to think space is ideal. It cannot be that both are right. In fact, neither are, as I hope to show in what follows.

construed as ignorance of real things. Both commentators cite Kant's early writings in support of their interpretations. Guyer finds the (allegedly) Leibnizian premise that 'relations are not real' in one of the earliest of Kant's philosophical works. He says of the argument he attributes to Kant in the Aesthetic (B67) that 'Kant had long held the general form of this argument'. He says that in the *New Exposition*, written in 1755, Kant offers a very poor argument premised on the same dubious assumption that relations are not 'genuine characteristics', 'not ultimately real'.[59]

These commentators suggest that Kant's beliefs about the reducibility of relations can explain why Kant thinks we have no knowledge of things in themselves. They suggest that these beliefs can be discovered in Kant's early works, and that they were held consistently over his intellectual career. I am in full agreement with these suggestions. But the agreement stops there. Kant's own interpretation of Leibniz, as considered in the present chapter, should be enough to give us grounds for considerable suspicion. Kant says that Leibniz takes the phenomena for things in themselves. But this is not mere exegesis of Leibniz—this is *complaint*. The Leibnizian reduction of phenomena to things in themselves—with its reduction of physical relations to the intrinsic properties of monads—is a target of Kant's *critique*. And if Leibniz thinks that knowledge, via phenomena, of things in themselves is based on that reduction of phenomena to things in themselves, then Kant's complaint against Leibnizian reduction will be one with his complaint against Leibnizian ambition. Far from accepting the opinion of Leibniz on relations, Kant decisively rejects it, and in the end it is the rejection, not the acceptance, that leads Kant to Humility. In the next two chapters I shall try to show why, and Kant's early works, Guyer's contempt for them notwithstanding, provide an excellent place to begin.

[59] Guyer, *Kant and the Claims*, 352.

5

Kant's Rejection of Reducibility

1. *An Early Distinction between Phenomena and Things in Themselves*

Many of Kant's earliest works display a preoccupation with the metaphysics of substance and relations, where substance is understood in a broadly Leibnizian manner, as something which conforms to what Kant was later to call the 'pure concept' of substance, and relation is understood primarily in causal, dynamical terms.

In Kant's first work, *Thoughts on the True Estimation of Living Forces* (1747), we find a clear expression of the fundamental conception of substance as an independent being, and of the distinction between a substance as it is in itself, and a substance as it is in relation to other things.

> Either a substance is in a connection and relation with things external it, or it is not. Since any independent being contains the complete source of all the properties it has within itself, it is not necessary to its existence that it stand in connection with other things. Hence substances can exist and nevertheless have no external relation toward others at all, they can exist and stand in no real connection with others.[1]

There is an insistent contrast here between how a thing is in isolation, and how it is in relation to other things. There is an argument which begins with the notion of a substance as something capable of existing by itself, and an assumption that it has properties compatible with its existing by itself, intrinsic properties. Since a substance is an independent being, it possesses intrinsic properties within itself; so it is not necessary to its existence that it stand in any relations to other things. If a thing's relations were necessarily to follow from its mere existence and its intrinsic properties, that thing would not be a substance, but a being dependent on other things for its existence. Kant rightly concludes that the relations of a substance are not implied by its mere existence, and that a substance cannot have relational properties as essential properties. He concludes that it is possible for substances to exist,

---

[1] *Living Forces* (1747), Ak. i. 21. Polonoff attributes a modal error to Kant in this passage: the inference from possibly *p* to necessarily *p*—possibly a substance exists without having relations to other things, therefore necessarily a substance exists without having relations to other things. Polonoff, *Force, Cosmos, Monads and Other Themes of Kant's Early Thought*, 47. But there seems to be no such error.

but exist *nowhere*. Kant holds, at this stage, the partly Leibnizian view that space is constituted by—supervenes upon—the dynamical relations between substances. (He does not, as we shall see, hold the wholly Leibnizian view that space supervenes ultimately upon the intrinsic properties of substances.) In the absence of these dynamical relations a substance exists, but exists nowhere.

The *Physical Monadology* (1756) draws an equally sharp contrast between substances and their forces, and develops the theory of force into a sophisticated matter theory. Substance is defined as something which 'can exist separately' from other substances, having 'an existence of its own sufficient unto itself' (Props. I and V). Kant calls these substances physical monads, physical in the sense that they are substances whose forces constitute matter. This is compatible with such monads having additional properties that are non-physical, and with the possibility of some monads having no physical properties at all—as when a substance exists alone, and thereby exists nowhere. But a monad that has dynamical relations with other monads can be called a physical monad.[2] Before we turn to the text, whose resonance with certain passages in the *Critique* is highly illuminating, let me offer a quick sketch of the general project.

Kant proposes a dynamical theory of matter, a kind of field theory (similar in many respects to the theory of Boscovich), which is a precursor to that of the *Metaphysical Foundations of Natural Science*. He proposes it in order to solve the problem that was later to occupy him in the Second Antinomy. Matter must have simple, indivisible, constituents, for otherwise it could not be constructed at all; but space itself is infinitely divisible (Props. II and III). The former metaphysical truth can be reconciled with the latter truth of geometry when one distinguishes the field of a substance's activity from the substance itself. By analogy (though the analogy is not quite Kant's), just as a planet is the source of the gravitational field that surrounds it, and is yet distinct from the field of its activity, so a monad is distinct from the field of forces radiating from it. The planet's gravitational field is not a substance, since it would not exist on its own, and the same applies, *mutatis mutandis*, to forces of monads. The gravitational field of the planet can be thought of as a property of the planet, and likewise the forces can be thought of as properties of the monad. The forces are to be thought of as relations, or relational properties: first because they are causal powers of the substance

---

[2] 'The purpose of my account is only to treat of the class of simple substances which are the primitive parts of bodies . . . I shall use the following terms as if they were synonymous: simple substances, monads, elements of matter, and primitive parts of body.' *Physical Monadology* (1755), footnote to Prop. I, Ak. i. 477, Beck 117–18.

to relate to other things, and secondly because they are in a sense 'external' to the substance, located at a place where, strictly, the monad is not. By analogy, the gravitational field of a planet can be thought of as consisting of causal powers enabling the planet to relate to other things in certain ways; and as being in a sense 'external' to the planet, located in places where the planet is not. Shrink the planet in imagination, so that it becomes a mere unextended point; add to it a force of repulsion; multiply so that there are infinitely many of them; and we have something like Kant's physical monads. Any strangeness here may have to do with the fact that Kant is inventing field theory within the constraints of a metaphysics of substance and accident. The problem of how properties can exist 'external' to their substances is a problem that was to exercise the pioneers of field theory, Hans Oersted and Michael Faraday, and Kant is already aware of it: the most 'weighty' difficulty of his theory, he concedes, is that it 'externalizes' the properties of a substance. He responds to this difficulty by saying that the properties in question are relations, and relations are always in some sense 'external' to a substance, since they relate one substance to another different from itself (Note to Prop. VII).

Monads are unextended centres of fields of force. The force field is divisible, but the monads themselves are not. The physical world cannot arise from the mere existence of substances, but only from their forces, of which there are two, attraction and repulsion. A substance determines its space 'by the field (*ambitus*) of its activity, whereby it hinders things on both sides of it from any further mutual approach' (Prop. VI). This force of impenetrability is finite at any distance from the monad, but infinite at the centre, following an inverse cube law. Both forces are needed for the constitution of matter. Driven by the forces of repulsion alone, the monads would scatter themselves to infinity. Attraction is needed for the constitution of matter, and attraction is Newtonian gravitation, following an inverse square law. As a result of the differing laws governing the two forces, there is in effect a physical corpuscle whose 'surface' is the set of points at which the effect of one force is cancelled out by the effect of the other. This, Kant thinks, supplies the solution to the problem of the divisibility of matter. The physical world is the virtual and not the actual presence of monads. We would not think that, in dividing the physical world wherein God acts, we are dividing God himself (Prop. VII). Nor should we think that, in dividing fields of force, the sphere of the activity of substances, we are dividing the substances that act. A kitten pouncing on a dancing light beam does not thereby catch the flashlight. The girl cutting her birthday cake does not thereby divide substance. Matter is divisible; substance is indivisible. Matter is not substance.

The main argument is of great interest, drawing a sharp contrast between the intrinsic and extrinsic properties of substances, and bearing a striking similarity to passages in the *Critique*.[3]

Proposition VII. Whatever is intrinsic to substance, i.e. the substantial itself, is not properly defined by space. The substance itself is the subject of extrinsic properties [forces], and those extrinsic properties are something properly to be sought in space. But, you say, substance is there in this little space, and present everywhere within it; therefore if one divides space, does not one divide substance? I answer: space is the field of the external presence [force] of the element (monad). If one divides space, what is divided is the extensive magnitude of the external presence [force] of the monad. But besides external presence, i.e. the relational properties of the substance, there are other intrinsic properties, without which the relational properties [forces] would not exist, because there would be no subject in which they inhered. But the intrinsic properties are not in space, precisely because they are intrinsic. Nor by the division of extrinsic properties are these intrinsic properties divided, any more than the subject itself, i.e. the substance, is divided . . . In the field of activity of a substance you will not find a number of things, of which one could exist separated and isolated from another. For what is present in one region of space adjacent to what is present in another cannot be separated as if it existed in itself, since both presences are nothing more than extrinsic properties of one and the same substance, and accidents do not exist without their substances.

Proposition VIII. The force by which the simple element of a body fills its space is the same as that which others call impenetrability.[4]

There is a familiar division here between intrinsic and extrinsic properties, the latter being also described as 'external presences', 'relational determinations', and 'forces'. Space is filled by forces, not by solid atoms. Forces are not substances. It is explicitly stated that a force is an accident, and that it does not fulfil the necessary condition for being a substance: for a force cannot exist 'separated and isolated'. Force does not conform to the pure concept of a substance, because it cannot exist on its own.

   Kant says that space is the field of activity of substances, and that it is impossible to find in this field of activity anything but force: it is impossible to find something in space that is capable of existing on its own. He imagines a challenge: isn't the monadic substance in space, and hence divisible? And he replies: no. Substance is not to be found in space: for the intrinsic

---

[3] L. W. Beck draws attention to the similarity with passages in the Amphiboly, in Beck 134 n. 10, and so too does Alison Laywine in her excellent study, *Kant's Early Metaphysics and the Origins of the Critical Philosophy*, North American Kant Society Studies in Philosophy, vol. iii (Atascadero, Calif.: Ridgeview, 1993), 157 n. 13. Laywine and I agree that Kant's inference to intrinsic properties in the *Physical Monadology* indicates a commitment at this time to a Leibnizian conception of substance, and that these intrinsic properties are not subject to physical laws.

[4] Ak. i. 481–2, Beck 122–4.

properties of substance are not to be found in space. Space provides a structure only for the 'external presence', the relational properties, of a substance, not for its intrinsic properties. He presents as a self-evident truth the following remarkable claim: 'The intrinsic properties are not in space, precisely because they are intrinsic.' This claim makes sense on a Leibnizian understanding of what counts as an intrinsic property. We have already seen that Kant and Leibniz alike can be understood as understanding the idea of a 'distinct' object to mean a non-identical—even if not *wholly* distinct— object, in which case a part of a thing counts as distinct from it, and part-dependent spatial properties will count as extrinsic. Leibniz says: 'given that a body is a whole, it depends upon other bodies of which it is composed and which make up its parts' and accordingly 'only monads . . . are truly independent'.[5] Kant says in the *Critique*, 'Corporeal things are never anything but relations only, at least of their parts external to one another' (A339/A283). There is great similarity between this discussion of matter and substance in the *Physical Monadology*, and passages in the Amphiboly.

Matter is *substantia phaenomenon*. I search for that which belongs to it intrinsically in all parts of the space which it occupies, and in all the actions it performs . . . I have nothing that is absolutely intrinsic, but only what is comparatively intrinsic, and that is itself again constituted by external relations . . . The transcendental object which may be the ground of this appearance that we call matter is a mere something. (A277/B333)

The *Physical Monadology* provides us with a clear account of the physical theory whose consequence is that phenomenal substance is a merely comparative substance, a *phaenomenon substantiatum*. Matter is force, and force is 'external presence'. Force is not substance, but a relational property of substance.

There is something more to note from the *Physical Monadology*, and that is the inference to the substance as bearer of intrinsic properties.

But besides external presence, i.e. relational properties of the substance, there are other intrinsic properties, without which the relational properties [forces] would not exist, because there would be no subject in which they inhered.[6]

Jill Buroker takes this to be, not simply an inference to the existence of intrinsic properties, but rather a commitment to a Leibnizian thesis about the reducibility of relations. She says,

Kant evidently imagines a direct correlation between metaphysical substances, which have only 'internal' properties, and physical substances in space, which are composed of 'external' properties. Thus he incorporates at least part of the

---

[5] 'Conversation', Ariew and Garber 262.   [6] Ak. i. 481, Beck 123.

Leibnizian theory of relations in his view that the external or physical (relational) properties of things depend on their internal (non-relational) properties.[7]

Lewis White Beck appears to share Buroker's view, for he says, of the *Physical Monadology*, 'at this time Kant accepted the Leibnizian account of space as only a *phaenomenon bene fundatum*'.[8] If space is a *phaenomenon bene fundatum*, a well-founded phenomenon, then it supervenes, ultimately, on the intrinsic properties of monads.

These views are mistaken. Buroker's suggestion is based on Kant's statement that 'besides external presence, i.e. relational properties of the substance, there are other, intrinsic properties'. But Kant's requirement that there be 'intrinsic properties' is not the Leibnizian reducibility requirement, as the remainder of the passage shows. The relational properties would not exist if the intrinsic properties did not exist—'because there would be *no subject in which they inhered*' (emphasis added). Relational properties require substances, and substances require some intrinsic properties or other: that is the extent of the dependence. These are the same general requirements already encountered in the *Critique*:

Concepts of relation presuppose things which are absolutely [i.e. independently] given, and without these are impossible. (A284/B340)

Substances in general must have some intrinsic nature, which is therefore free from all outer relations . . . (A274/B330)

The requirement that substances must have some intrinsic nature is not the requirement that relations must supervene on intrinsic properties. It is a far weaker requirement. The requirement that substances must have some intrinsic nature follows simply from the independence requirement on substance. A substance may be independent whether or not relations are reducible to intrinsic properties. There is every reason to think that Kant

---

[7] Buroker, *Space and Incongruence*, 42. Despite the disagreements I have with Buroker in interpreting early Kant, her basic argument for Kant's belief in the irreducibility of spatial relations is persuasive and I have benefited much from her impressive study, which at the very least fulfils admirably the task of drawing attention to Kant's interest in the reducibility issue. My main complaint is that she underestimates the importance of this issue as applied to causal properties, as opposed to spatial properties. She too addresses Kant's criticisms of Leibniz in the Amphiboly (86–7), viewing them as containing a compressed version of Kant's incongruent counterparts argument about space. But, as we have already seen, there is more at stake in the Amphiboly than spatial relations. I attend very little to Kant's views about space, the reason being that I believe Kant would endorse Humility no matter what his beliefs about space. Buroker pays the *New Exposition* almost no attention in her book—which is somewhat surprising for a commentator who sees Kant's attitude to the Leibnizian reducibility principle as the key to his philosophical development.

[8] This is in the Introduction to *Physical Monadology*, in Beck 12.

would fiercely reject the view Buroker attributes to him—as we shall see when we turn our attention to the *New Exposition* (1755).

One of the major aims of this early work is to present a pair of new principles which Kant promises will be 'rich in consequences'. Those who see Kant's early works as a mere foil to the jewel of the *Critique* will find this promise hollow, but it is not.[9] The arguments in it do not seem to spring from the mind of a slumbering dogmatist, but from the mind of one already acutely aware of the weaknesses in his own metaphysical tradition: in particular, its weakness in the metaphysics of relations, and of causal powers. Kant's promise was fulfilled, though perhaps not in the way he at this time anticipated. The two principles, and the arguments for them, help to tell us something about why, ultimately, their author was driven to deny that we have knowledge of things as they are in themselves: why, in other words, he was driven to Humility. But in this chapter our interest in the two principles will be in their immediate consequences for two questions: about whether *knowledge is receptive*; and whether *relations are reducible*.

The arguments for both principles are made against the backdrop of the kind of distinction between phenomena and things in themselves to be found in Leibniz, in Kant's other early works, and in the later Kant. The argument for the first, the Principle of Succession, contains most importantly an implicit argument for a thesis denied by Leibniz, but crucial to Kant's own philosophy—the thesis of Receptivity. This argument is discussed in Section 2. The argument for the second principle, the Principle of Co-existence, explicitly rejects the Leibnizian principle of the reducibility of relations: against Leibniz, Kant argues that relations and relational properties are not reducible to the intrinsic properties of substances. This is the topic of Section 3. The argument yields a fourth Kantian thesis: Irreducibility. This thesis holds the key to understanding why Kant is driven to Humility, or so I believe, though the task of explaining how is reserved for the next chapter. The argument for Irreducibility is sophisticated and reasonably persuasive, at least on one interpretation, and Sections 4 to 7 are devoted to its analysis.

---

[9] For some somewhat dismissive attitudes to these early works, see for example L. W. Beck and John Reuscher, in their introductions to *Physical Monadology* and *New Exposition* respectively, in Beck. A refreshing exception is Alison Laywine's detailed discussion of the *New Exposition* in *Kant's Early Metaphysics*, ch. 2. I am fortunate to have been able to have helpful conversations on these topics with Laywine in 1989; she and I share an interest in Kant's two metaphysical principles, though not, I think, for quite the same reasons. Michael Friedman, too, provides a more sympathetic account of the *New Exposition* in his Introduction to *Kant and the Exact Sciences* (Cambridge, Mass: Harvard University Press, 1992). Both of these authors draw interesting connections between Kant's metaphysical principles and principles of Newtonian mechanics in ways I do not pursue here.

2. *The Principle of Succession, and Receptivity*

Proposition XII. Substances are capable of change only to the extent that they are connected with other substances, their reciprocal dependence determining their mutual changes of state. Thus if a simple substance is cut off from every external connection and left by itself in isolation, it is obviously *per se* immutable. Furthermore, even when a substance interacts with other substances, if this relation is not altered, no change (including that of internal condition) can occur in it. Consequently in a world devoid of all motion (as a matter of fact, motion is the phenomenon of change in the connection of things) not the least trace of succession is to be found even in the internal condition of the substances. From this it follows that when the interconnection among substances is completely eliminated, succession and time in like manner take their leave.[10]

As in Kant's other works, the conception of a true substance is of something that is capable of existing 'cut off from every external connection and left by itself in isolation'. This is substance conforming to the pure concept of substance discussed in the *Critique*: the 'absolute subject' of which Kant speaks in the Dialectic, which remains even when one takes away all relations to other things, the thing that can exist on its own (A525/B553). The argument turns on the contrast which preoccupies Kant in his other early works, between what a substance is like when it exists in isolation from other things, and what a substance is like when it stands in relation to other things. Whether or not it stands in relation to other things, it has a certain intrinsic state. But that intrinsic state, according to Kant's argument, will change only if the substance stands in relations (*changing* relations) to other substances. The relations of which Kant writes are relations of 'connection' and 'interaction', causal relations of 'reciprocal dependence' (*dependentia reciproca*), the causal community of Kant's Third Analogy in the *Critique*. This nexus of causal relations constitutes the physical realm (motion being a 'phenomenon' of change in the causal nexus). If the causal nexus is abolished, time is abolished: without a changing nexus of relations there is no change and hence no time.

His argument proceeds by a thought experiment:

Suppose some simple substance were to exist in isolation from any connection with other substances. I contend that it would be impossible for its intrinsic state to be altered. For since those intrinsic properties of the substance which already belong to it are fixed by internal reasons, to the exclusion of the opposite properties, if you want some different property to follow one that is already present, you must posit some different reason. But since the opposite of this new reason is intrinsic to the substance and (by the supposition) no external reason is added, it is patently obvious that the new property cannot be introduced into this thing.[11]

[10] Ak. i. 410, Beck 96.   [11] Ak. i. 410, Beck 96–7.

Kant says that properties intrinsic to a substance cannot on their own give rise to new and different properties of that substance. The intrinsic properties of a thing are determinate: for every possible property, the substance either has that property, or its negation. If a substance has some property F, then there is a 'reason' for its having F and not not-F. Since, *ex hypothesi*, the substance is in isolation from all others, that 'reason' is some other property intrinsic to the substance. Suppose we consider the possibility of the substance undergoing change, and acquiring a new property, not-F. The substance already has intrinsic to it a 'reason' for its being F and not not-F. The change therefore cannot be the result of properties intrinsic to the substance. So change is impossible, where the substance exists alone. Kant describes this as an 'easy and infallible chain of reasons'. It is not easy, and presents many causes for philosophical disquiet. The assumption that for every intrinsic property there is another intrinsic property that is the 'reason' for the first seems to imply an infinite regress. And what of the apparent counterexamples? An alarm clock can be set (at its creation if need be) to ring at six, with no outside interference. Perhaps this is no objection: since a clock is no simple substance, its internal changes are the result of changing relations between its parts. But there is something odd too about its ringing at six, if the time is nothing independent of its own changes. I leave these causes for disquiet, for the chief interest of the argument is elsewhere.

There is common ground with Leibniz: the basic distinction, the supervenient dependence of time on change within a substance, and of motion on change in dynamical relations between substances. But there is heresy in the Principle itself: monads are not windowless, but open to the influence of other created beings. Kant says that his Principle 'overturns the very foundations of the Leibnizian pre-established harmony' since the pattern of changing events in different substances can only be the result of their causal interaction. Had Leibniz been right about the windowlessness of monads, we would be as changeless as our Creator, and the many-coloured harmony of the infinite choir would be a single sustained chord.

Kant begins to fulfil his promise of 'rich consequences' by showing that, armed with the Principle of Succession, he can refute idealism, and prove that a mind must be associated with some definite body if it is to be blessed with changing thoughts.[12] As a matter of empirical fact we have a changing succession of ideas. This change would be impossible unless we were in real

---

[12] And also, for good measure, prove the immutability of God. Since God is not in a relation of mutual causal dependence with any other substance, by the Principle of Succession, he can undergo no change. One wonders whether God is therefore incapable of thought; though here we perhaps approach the divine mysteries of creative intuition.

causal nexus with other things. This nexus of causes, of external relations, of forces, is identical with the realm of physical bodies in motion. Hence our changing succession of ideas is the result of commerce with physical bodies. So idealism is false.[13] Moreover, since thought requires a succession of internal states, if spirits are to think then they need 'some kind of corporeal organism'; the human mind is thus 'tied to matter in the performance of the internal functions of thought'. Note what this argument reveals about Kant's conception of the mental and the physical. A mind is a monadic substance, the kind of thing that is independent; but it is not as Descartes thought a mind must be. The mind would not be thinking at all if it were to exist in isolation from other things. There is a leap from the conclusion that one's mind must be interacting with something other than itself, to the conclusion that it must be interacting with some definite body. (Why could not our changing mental states be the effects of some incorporeal substance: God, or angels, or telepathic human minds?) The leap, though, is no *non sequitur* on a Leibnizian premise about what a body is: 'external connection'—connection of a substance with something else —is sufficient for there being something physical. A body is something like a 'flock' of substances, a group of substances related to each other causally—or at any rate (for Leibniz) harmoniously. If I am a substance, and I am in 'real connection' with some other substance, then there exists a group of substances related in a certain way: so there is something physical.[14]

What is most significant, however, is that the Principle of Succession implies that, contrary to Leibniz, knowledge must be *receptive*. A substance cannot have thoughts unless it is affected by another substance. Kant here writes of the capacity of one substance to be affected by another, and of the representations formed in a substance as a result of being affected by another. He writes, in other words, about what he will later call receptivity and sensibility: 'The receptivity of our mind, its power of receiving representations in so far as it is affected in any way, is called sensibility' (A51/B75). If a substance cannot have thoughts unless it is affected by

---

[13] For an excellent discussion of Kant's Refutations of Idealism, comparing the critical versions with others before and after, see Guyer, *Kant and the Claims*, Pt. IV.

[14] I call the principle about body being constituted by a plurality of related substances a Leibnizian doctrine, but there is a sense in which Kant has turned the Leibnizian philosophy on its head. Leibniz said: changing relations between substances depend (superveniently) on changing intrinsic properties within substances. Kant says: changing intrinsic properties within substances depend (causally) on changing relations between substances. Despite the different kinds of dependence, it is a striking reversal that has consequences for the reducibility of relations. If the changing intrinsic properties of a substance depend causally on a changing relation with other things, as implied by the Principle of Succession, then that changing causal relation cannot depend superveniently on the changing intrinsic properties of the substances. This implicit rejection of reducibility is made explicit in Kant's second principle.

another substance, and cannot have knowledge without having thoughts, then we cannot have knowledge unless we are *affected*. Human knowledge is necessarily receptive.

The rationalist argument of Kant's earliest Refutation of Idealism thus has a germ of empiricism at its core. I say that the germ is there, and implied by the Principle of Succession. I do not say that Kant is as yet fully aware of it.

3. *The Principle of Coexistence, and Irreducibility*

With his second principle, Kant overturns the foundations of a further Leibnizian thesis: he argues that relations are not reducible to intrinsic properties. That is the consequence of his second metaphysical principle. Since we shall, in a moment, be attending to the argument closely, and since opinions about the argument vary widely, it will be worth quoting some of the text in detail.

Proposition XIII. Finite substances are, through their solitary existence, unrelated, and are evidently not connected by interaction, except in so far as they are maintained by the principle of their common existence (namely the divine intellect) in a pattern of mutual relations.

Demonstration: Single substances, of which neither is the cause of the existence of the other, have a separate existence, i.e. an existence that is absolutely intelligible without all the others. Therefore if the existence simpliciter of a substance is posited, there is nothing in that which proves the existence of other substances different from itself. Indeed, since relation is a determination that looks toward something else (i.e. it will not be intelligible in a being viewed entirely by itself), the relation and its determining reason cannot be understood through the existence of the substance as posited in itself. If, therefore, nothing more is added to this existence, there would be no relation among beings and clearly no mutual interaction. Therefore, in so far as single substances have an existence independent of other substances, there is no place for their mutual connection . . ., and it must be granted that their relation depends on a common cause, namely God.

[From the sixth Application] A substance never has the power through its own intrinsic properties to determine others different from itself, as has been proven.

[From the first Application] The mutual relation of substances requires a conceptual plan in a corresponding creative thought of the divine intellect. This thought is plainly arbitrary on God's part and can therefore be omitted or not omitted at His own pleasure.[15]

---

[15] Ak. i. 412–13, 415, 414, Beck 100–4. Note that Reuscher's translation in Beck makes an error in the scope of the negation in the passage quoted above from the sixth Application,

The principle earns its title from Kant's belief that substances do not coexist—do not exist as things in the same world—unless they interact in a pattern of mutual causal relations. In this respect it is a precursor to Kant's Principle of Community in the Third Analogy of the *Critique*.

This, then, is the argument which Guyer dismisses. He finds it hard to take seriously, and speaks of its 'metaphysical prejudice' and 'logical obscurity'.[16] He takes the passage quoted to present an entirely question-begging argument for the 'Leibnizian' thesis of the unreality of relations. Kant assumes, according to Guyer, that the only 'genuine characteristics' of a substance are characteristics the substance would have in isolation from other things, and he thereby from the outset prevents relations from counting as genuine or real characteristics. Contrary to Guyer, however, Kant does not equivocate between 'genuine characteristics' and intrinsic properties. He does not say that relational determinations are not real.

It is clear, at least in broad outline, what Kant does say. While he does not say that relational determinations are unreal, he does say that they are not intrinsic. He says that the relational determinations of substances cannot be understood through the existence, simpliciter, of substances. He says in his Demonstration that if nothing is added to the existence of substances there would be no relation among beings. He says in the sixth Application that a substance never has the power through its own intrinsic properties to determine others different from itself. He says in the first Application that, for relations among substances to exist, something must be added through an act of God, and that this act is 'obviously arbitrary' and 'can be omitted or not omitted at His own pleasure'. The gist of Kant's argument, at any rate, seems clear. Kant is arguing against the Leibnizian reducibility thesis.[17]

Beck 104. (The original has this: 'Verum quia quaelibet substantia non per ea, quae ipsi interne competunt, potestatem habet alias a se diversas determinandi (per demonstrata).') Thanks to Margaret Wilson for help in confirming the above translation.

. [16] *Kant and the Claims*, 352. Other commentators seem equally unenthusiastic. Vleeschauwer says that this argument, like all arguments of the *New Exposition*, is conducted 'in a confused manner'. See Herman J. de Vleeschauwer, *The Development of Kantian Thought*, trans. A. R. Duncan (London: Thomas Nelson 1962), 24 (originally published as *L'Évolution de la pensée kantienne* (Paris: Presses Universitaires de France, 1939)).

[17] Although this interpretation of the *New Exposition* disagrees with Guyer and Buroker, it is in some agreement with Friedman and Laywine, who see Kant as arguing against Leibniz for real relations of interaction. The implications of this for the reducibility issue I do not, however, find entirely clear in these authors. Friedman says that 'For Kant, by contrast [with Leibniz], relations of interaction between substances are in no way ideal: a universal principle of mutual interaction is a distinct reality over and above the mere existence of substances (requiring a distinguishable divine action going beyond the creation of the existence of substances simpliciter)'. However, in apparent tension with this he writes: 'space . . . is derivative from or constituted by the underlying non-spatial reality of simple substances',

Leibniz thought that the relational determinations of substances supervene on the substances. He thought that the relational determinations mirror or express the intrinsic properties of substances. For Leibniz, the mere exist- ence of substances—with their intrinsic properties—entails the existence of relations of community among the substances. For Leibniz there is a sense in which the relational determinations of substances can indeed be under- stood through the mere existence of substances. In creating the realm of substances, God creates the realm of relations among substances: there is no need for God to 'add' anything else. Kant's argument rejects all this. Kant argues, in short, for

> *Irreducibility*: The relations and relational properties of substances are not reducible to the intrinsic properties of substances.

Here we have our fourth Kantian thesis.

We have the pieces in place, now, to explain how Kant's views about rela- tions, and his rejection of Leibniz, might lead to the conclusion that we have no knowledge of things in themselves. But I shall postpone putting the pieces together until the next chapter. In the meanwhile, the argument for Irreducibility deserves closer attention than my brief outline has given it, and the remainder of this chapter will be devoted to its analysis.

4. *Analysis of the Argument for Irreducibility: Preliminaries*

Kant's thesis of Irreducibility, as described above, is ambiguous in a num- ber of different ways, three of which need to be considered before we even begin.

First, there is a scope ambiguity. Is Kant supposed to mean 'all relations are not reducible', i.e. 'no relations are reducible'; or is he supposed to mean 'not all relations are reducible'? The interpretations I shall offer construe him in the first, more ambitious, way.

Second, there is an ambiguity in the notion of reducibility itself, even where that reducibility is construed as supervenience. Reducibility, as we saw in the preceding chapter, may be bilateral or unilateral. Which of the two it is will depend on whether we give a distributive or collective reading to the final occurrence of the plural 'substances' in the statement of Irre-

---

which looks like a reducibility doctrine according to which space is ultimately constituted by the intrinsic properties of simple substances. Perhaps he means only that space is constituted by the dynamical properties of simple substances, leaving aside the further question about the constitution of the dynamical properties by the intrinsic. See Friedman, *Kant and the Exact Sciences*, especially 8, 26; Laywine, *Kant's Early Metaphyics*, especially ch. 2.

ducibility above. Kant may mean that for any given substance, its relational properties do not supervene on its intrinsic properties, i.e. are not unilaterally reducible; or he may mean that for all substances, their relational properties do not supervene on their intrinsic properties taken collectively, i.e. are not bilaterally reducible.

Third, there is ambiguity in the notion of a relation and a relational property. In Kant's terms a relational property is a *determinatio respectiva*: 'a determination that looks toward something else', something 'not intelligible in a being viewed entirely by itself' (*in ente absolute spectato haud intelligibilem*). As in the *Critique*, he makes no very clear distinction between relations and relational properties, or between quite different sorts of relational property. In this he seems to be in good company, in his philosophical tradition, and perhaps also our own. We saw in Chapter 2 that Baumgarten defines relations in a manner which uses an assortment of notions as synonymous: relations, external determinations, properties that are outer, relative, extrinsic, respective, or 'looking towards something else'.[18] I shall tend to conduct discussion in terms of relational properties, but even then there is an important distinction to be made between two rather different sorts of relational property.

Kant speaks of the *determinatio respectiva* in two different ways. He speaks of it in the Demonstration as a determination of a substance that 'proves the existence of other substances'. In the sixth Application he speaks of it as a power (*potestas*) a substance has to determine others different from itself. These two ways of speaking map a distinction between two different kinds of relational property: ordinary relational properties (as I shall call them), and powers, or dispositional relational properties. (I shall use the terms 'power' and 'disposition' synonymously.) If Helen is *loved*, then she has an ordinary relational property. If Helen is loved, that implies the existence of somebody else, who has some relation to Helen. (Let us for the sake of the example stipulatively exclude the possibility of self-love.) If Helen is loved, she has a property which, in Kant's terms, 'proves the existence of' something else. Helen is loved if and only if somebody loves her. She has the ordinary relational property of being loved if and only if she bears an actual relation to a lover. If she is *lovable*, she has a dispositional relational property. Helen is lovable if and only if someone would love her in certain circumstances. (Compare the pairs married/eligible, dissolved/soluble, moving/mobile.)[19] The thing about dispositional properties is that, unlike

---

[18] Baumgarten, *Metaphysica*, § 37 (1757), Ak. xvii. 35.

[19] To make the examples work, let us stipulate (in these wicked times) that one is still eligible even when married, just as something is still soluble when dissolved and still mobile when moving.

ordinary relational properties, they have a counterfactual aspect: they imply what relations *would* exist if something else were to exist (and other conditions were fulfilled). I noted in Chapter 2 that powers, or dispositions, are relational in their concepts: but that this is not enough to show that they are extrinsic properties. Opinions may differ as to whether powers or dispositions are extrinsic properties. At least on the face of it, they are not properties which prove the existence of something else: they are not properties which require the *actual* existence of something else. Helen, all on her own, may still be lovable. A bachelor, all on his own, may be eligible; a sugar lump, all on its own, may be soluble. We shall return to this in a moment.

The distinction between ordinary relational properties and powers might make us wonder whether Kant is concerned with the question of how substances stand in certain *actual* relations with other *actually* existing substances, and thus possess what I have called ordinary relational properties; or with the question of how substances have the *power* of standing in relations with substances which may or may not actually exist.

While Kant's argument is conducted at a formidable level of abstraction, so that the argument and its conclusion appear to be about relations and relational properties in general, it emerges later on that what he has in mind are forces: causal relations of reciprocal community. Kant conceives of relations between substances in dynamical terms. He says, in *Living Forces*,

All connection and relation amongst existing substances is due to the reciprocal actions of their forces exerted against each other.[20]

In the *New Exposition* he has particular interest in the forces of Newtonian gravitational attraction:

The determinations of substances look toward each other, i.e. substances that are different from one another act reciprocally . . . [I]f the external phenomenon of universal action and reaction . . . is that of mutual approach, it is . . . *Newtonian attraction*.[21]

The fact Kant has force in mind does not settle the question just considered: for as we saw in Chapter 2, the notion of a force can pick out a variety of features of the world, sometimes being the notion of a *power* to act on other things in a certain way; and sometimes being the notion of *acting* on other things in a certain way. All the same, if concrete illustrations are needed for the abstract argument of the Demonstration, we can draw on Kant's interest in the powers and relations associated with Newtonian attraction.

---

[20] *Living Forces*, Ak. i. 21.
[21] Ak. i. 415, Beck 103–4.

Having distinguished these ambiguities, we are in a position to consider, one at a time, two versions of the argument. More are possible, but these are the two I find most promising.

5. *Irreducibility Argument I*

1. No ordinary relational properties of a thing are reducible to the intrinsic properties of that thing.
2. Therefore none are unilaterally reducible.
3. Therefore none are bilaterally reducible.
4. Therefore ordinary relational properties must be superadded by God.

We begin by considering Steps 1 and 2. Kant says that a substance is an independent thing, that it has a 'separate existence, i.e. an existence that is absolutely intelligible without all the others'. We can interpret this to mean that a substance could exist (with its intrinsic properties) all on its own: it could exist and be lonely. But a substance cannot possess an ordinary relational property, and exist all on its own. We can interpret Kant's description of a property that 'looks toward something else' as a description of a property that implies the existence of something other than the bearer, i.e. an ordinary relational property. Kant implicitly suggests that there is something about a substance's having a relational property that 'proves the existence of other substances different from itself'. If Helen is loved, then there exists someone who loves her. If John is married, then there exists someone to whom he is married. If one substance attracts another, then there exists another attracted substance. No ordinary relational properties of a substance are implied by the mere existence of the substance, with its intrinsic properties. They must therefore, Kant concludes, be added to substances by God, in a separate and 'arbitrary' act of creation.

Thus described, the argument appears to be directed against the Leibnizian thesis of *unilateral reducibility*. Recall that Leibniz said,

there are no purely extrinsic denominations, denominations which have absolutely no foundation in the very thing denominated. For it is necessary that the notion of the subject denominated contain the notion of the predicate.[22]

If Kant is arguing the way we have here supposed, then he refutes this Leibnizian position effectively. Kant asks us to imagine the substance all on its own, and argues that there is nothing about the substance, thus considered, that implies the relational property.

---

[22] 'Primary Truths' (1686), Ariew and Garber 32, Couturat 520.

Steps 1 and 2 of this argument are philosophically impeccable. Kant would be right to say that no ordinary relational property is unilaterally reducible. A property is an ordinary relational property just in case it implies accompaniment: just in case it implies the existence of something distinct from its bearer.[23] An ordinary relational property is, so to speak, existentially committed. So an ordinary relational property cannot supervene on the intrinsic properties of its bearer. Helen's being loved cannot supervene on her intrinsic properties alone; Simmias' being taller than Socrates cannot supervene on his intrinsic properties alone; John's being married cannot supervene on his intrinsic properties alone; and so forth. Steps 1 and 2 of the *New Exposition* argument are, on this interpretation, in good shape.

What of Steps 3 and 4, though? On this interpretation, Kant concludes on the basis of the failure of unilateral reducibility that there must be a need for a special act of creation, over and above the creation of substances with their intrinsic properties. Would he be right to conclude this? The answer has to be, no. In order to establish 'relations among beings', God admittedly needs to do something in addition to creating the one substance. He needs to create at the very least another substance. But we have no reason, so far, for thinking that would not suffice. The relational property possessed by Simmias of being taller-than-Socrates is not unilaterally reducible: it does not supervene on the properties of Simmias considered on his own, not even on the intrinsic property of being six feet tall. Nevertheless, all God needs to do to endow Simmias with the relational property of being taller-than-Socrates is to create Socrates as well, and to make him five feet tall. God has no need for a special act of creation, endowing Simmias himself with a special mysterious something to make him taller. The relational property of being taller-than-Socrates supervenes on the intrinsic properties of both relata, taken collectively: it is bilaterally reducible. So the failure of unilateral reducibility does not imply the failure of bilateral reducibility. This has implications for Kant's argument here, for *bilaterally reducible relations do not require superadding acts of God*. Kant has proven that the *determinatio respectiva* is not unilaterally reducible, but he has not thereby proven the need for a special act of creation, over and above the creation of substances with their intrinsic properties.

Only the failure of bilateral reducibility would justify the need for superadding creative acts. That is the reason for my insertion of Step 3, which legitimates a move from 3 to 4, the conclusion about God's creation. Unfortunately this does not get us very far: it only shifts the problem to the move from Steps 2 and 3—the move from the failure of unilateral reducibility to

[23] Cf. also Bennett's definition of a relational property, in *Locke, Berkeley, Hume*, 253.

the failure of bilateral reducibility. One possibility is that Kant is confused: he has failed to distinguish unilateral from bilateral reducibility. Perhaps Kant thinks that, having shown that unilateral reducibility is false (Step 2), he has shown that bilateral reducibility is false (Step 3). One piece of evidence for this is that he seems to move, without explanation, from talk of a *single* substance, as in the Demonstration above, to talk of *many* substances. In the Clarification immediately following the Demonstration, it is evidently the bilateral and not the unilateral reducibility thesis that Kant has in mind:

> The co-existence of *the substances of the universe* is not sufficient for establishing a connection among them . . . [E]ven if, over and above substance *A*, God created *other substances B, D, E, to infinity*, their mutual dependence in regard to determinations would not immediately follow from the fact of their given existence.[24]

Here we have explicit attention to the question: what if God were to create many substances, with their intrinsic properties? Kant's answer is that this too would be insufficient to establish interactive relations between the substances. In other words, he appears to offer the rejection of *bilateral* reducibility as a 'clarification' of his rejection of *unilateral* reducibility in the Demonstration.

Perhaps we can do better than attribute to Kant a crude conflation. The Clarification can be interpreted as offering, not a conflation, but an *argument* which aims to justify the move from one substance to many. Let us see if we can reconstruct the argument afresh. Perhaps it goes like this. The relational properties of *A* are not reducible to the intrinsic properties of *A*, as proven in the Demonstration; the relational properties of *B* are not reducible to the intrinsic properties of *B*; the relational properties of *C* . . . etc. Therefore, the relational properties of *A, B, C* . . . to infinity, are not reducible to the intrinsic properties of *A, B, C* . . . to infinity. Therefore the relational properties of things are not reducible to the intrinsic properties of things. The relational determinations of substances do not 'immediately follow from the fact of their existences'.

This has a plausible look about it, even a valid look about it. Indeed it is a valid argument, on one disambiguation of its ambiguous conclusion—but not on the other. Kant's conclusion that relational properties do not 'immediately follow from . . . [the] existences' of substances—his conclusion that the relational properties of things are not reducible to the intrinsic properties of things—could mean either: for any given set of things, the relational properties of those things are not reducible to the intrinsic properties of those things, considered distributively; or, for any given set of things, the relational properties of those things are not reducible to the intrinsic prop-

---

[24] Ak. i. 413 (emphasis added), Beck 101.

erties of those things, considered collectively.[25] In other words, the conclusion of this freshly reconstructed argument is still exactly ambiguous between unilateral and bilateral reducibility. Only on the second would he be justified in inferring a special act of creation to establish the existence of relational properties. So the conflation has not been escaped.

The mistake, as it appears in Kant's argument, might look subtle. But it has the same general structure as the following argument. John is married to Jane. Bill is married to Betty. Therefore John and Bill are married to Jane and Betty. On the distributive reading, the conclusion is unexceptional, and the argument valid. On the collective reading, the conclusion is rather more interesting (four bigamists!), but the argument invalid.

In short, Kant has refuted the Leibnizian thesis of unilateral reducibility. But he has not refuted the Leibnizian thesis of bilateral reducibility. Only the latter refutation would justify a conclusion about the need for a special act of creation. It may be that we can nevertheless find in these passages an argument that will after all vindicate Kant's conclusion. Here is a second, and alternative, interpretation.

6. *Irreducibility Argument II*

1. No causal powers of a thing are reducible to the intrinsic properties of a thing or things.
2. Therefore none are unilaterally or bilaterally reducible.
3. Therefore the causal powers of a thing must be superadded by God.

As we have seen, there is reason for thinking that in his talk of relations, Kant may well have in mind the notion of a *causal power* (*potestas*). In his sixth Application, quoted in part at the beginning of Section 3, he says:

Indeed, a substance never has the power through its own intrinsic properties to determine others different from itself, as has been proven. It only has the power in so far as substances are held together in a nexus through the idea of an infinite being.[26]

Kant says that he has already proven that the intrinsic properties of a substance are not sufficient for its 'power'. This suggests that it is power he has been talking about all along, in the *determinatio respectiva* of his Demonstration.

---

[25] In Kant's words this ambiguity is present in the somewhat vague plural of 'e data ipsarum exsistentia'. The dependent determinations of substances do not immediately follow 'out of the given existence of them'.

[26] Ak. i. 415, Beck 104 (but see note 15).

What is a causal power? We noted that powers, or dispositional properties, do not seem, on the face of it, to be properties which 'prove the existence of something else'. However there are philosophers who have viewed causal powers as variants on ordinary relational properties. Jonathan Bennett, for example, says that a relational property implies the existence of something other than its bearer. He also says that the powers in Locke's philosophy, the secondary and (by implication) tertiary qualities, are dispositional and relational.[27] (Kant's example of attractive power would, in Locke's terms, be a tertiary quality.) So Bennett's view seems to imply that a world without human beings would be a world without colour, taste, smell. It seems to imply that gold would lack the property of being soluble in aqua regia in a world without aqua regia. It seems to imply that a substance would lack its attractive power in a world where there was nothing for it to attract. If Kant were to conceive of powers in Bennett's way, as variants of ordinary relational properties, then he would be correct to conclude that causal powers are not unilaterally reducible. But the argument for the irreducibility of causal power would then have just the merits and defects of our first interpretation.

If Bennett's approach to powers seems unattractive, then powers should be understood as different to ordinary relational properties: they should be understood in an existentially non-committal way. A power is a dispositional relational property that a thing can have even if the relevant relata (aqua regia, other bodies) do not exist, for powers have to do with how things *would* relate to other distinct things in certain, not necessarily actual, circumstances. Against this understanding of a power it might be objected that Kant says that a *determinatio respectiva* 'will not be intelligible in a being viewed entirely by itself', *in ente absolute spectato haud intelligibilis*. On the first interpretation, this was taken to mean: 'would not *exist* in a thing that existed entirely by itself'. This would make the *determinatio respectiva* an ordinary relational property. But there is an alternative reading. Kant could be making a *conceptual* point about powers. He could be saying that one cannot think of a substance possessing the relational property and at the same time think of nothing but the substance: the property will not be *intelligible* in a being *viewed* entirely by itself. One cannot think of a thing as having a certain power of attraction without thinking about how it would interact with other things if they were present: and this is a fact about our *concept* of the property. The concept of a power could in this sense be relational, without the property implying the actual existence of something else.

If we understand power in this non-committal way, a substance could have a causal power, and in particular the power of attracting another sub-

---

[27] Bennett defines relational properties in *Locke, Berkeley, Hume* 23, and says secondary qualities are relational in ch. 4.

stance, even if it were all on its own. For the following counterfactual would still be true of it. If there were another substance, suitably massive, and at a suitable distance, the first would attract it. If this is so, then a thing's causal power seems to be an intrinsic property of it. On the assumption that an intrinsic property is a property a thing can have on its own, a property compatible with loneliness, a power seems to be an intrinsic property—notwithstanding the fact that the *concept* of a power is relational, since it implies certain (counterfactual) relations to other things. On this understanding, powers are conceptually relational, but not extrinsic.

If we understand the notion of power in this way, then Kant's argument is off to a bad start. It has failed to establish even the first step. If the power of attraction is itself intrinsic, then of course it is reducible to intrinsic properties: it can supervene on itself. If a causal power is itself intrinsic, it is unilaterally reducible. If a causal power is itself intrinsic, all God has to do to endow a substance with a power is simply make the substance with its intrinsic properties. There will be no need whatsoever for God to engage in any creative acts over and above the creation of substances with their intrinsic properties. If causal powers are unilaterally reducible, they are *a fortiori* bilaterally reducible. So this conclusion is thoroughly at odds with what Kant wants to say.

Despite the bleak outlook for this argument so far, it seems to me that there might well be the makings of a promising argument here. We should pause to see where exactly the interpretation just given has gone off the rails. The first assumption was that *determinatio respectiva* should be taken to mean a causal power, *postestas*, *Kraft*, and this is a reasonably well-supported assumption. Kant says that the intrinsic properties of a substance are not sufficient for its power: 'a substance never has the power through its own intrinsic properties to determine others different from itself.' He says that the power of a substance to act on other things does not supervene on its intrinsic properties. The second assumption was that intrinsic properties are properties a thing can have on its own: properties compatible with loneliness. That is, I think, a reasonable way of understanding Kant's notion of intrinsicness: his notion of the internal determinations that a substance has even when it is quite solitary. But it is unlikely, to put it mildly, that Kant will have anything as precise as this understanding of intrinsicness in mind. Perhaps the notion of intrinsicness we have ascribed to Kant should be amended. On the interpretation we are considering, Kant believes that powers are extrinsic properties; and he believes that powers of substances are not reducible to their intrinsic properties. Is there a conception of intrinsicness that would make this true?[28]

---

[28] Lloyd Humberstone argues that there is no single intrinsic/relational distinction in philosophy, but rather a family of distinctions (see Humberstone, 'Intrinsic/Extrinsic').

The answer is, yes. Many philosophers share Kant's intuition that causal powers are extrinsic properties. What guides this intuition is a thought that things could be just as they are with respect to their intrinsic properties, yet different with respect to their causal powers—in particular, that if the laws of nature were different, things could have the same intrinsic properties, but different powers. In a world where the laws of nature were different, something could look green, despite having the very same intrinsic properties that brown things actually have. In a world where the laws of nature were different, things might not be soluble, despite having the very same intrinsic properties that soluble things actually have. In a world where the laws of nature were different, things might not have an attractive power, despite having the very same intrinsic properties that attractive things actually have. These modal intuitions rest on certain assumptions about the contingency of laws of nature, and the contingency of connections—if any—between intrinsic properties and causal powers. These modal intuitions suppose that causal powers do in a sense depend on something other than the way a thing is, in and of itself: that causal powers do depend on *something else*—but the *something else* is not simply the existence of some distinct object, but the existence of certain laws.

For Kant, these modal intuitions are expressed in thoughts about what God could or could not do. God could have created a world where the laws of gravity were different, or where there was no gravity at all, yet where substances had the same intrinsic properties they do in our world.

Newtonian attraction . . . is effected by the . . . connection of substances . . . [I]t is the first basic law of nature to which matter is subject and it continues permanently in force . . . only because God gives it His direct support.

A substance never has the power through its own intrinsic properties to determine others different from itself, as has been proven. It only has the power in so far as substances are held together in a nexus through the idea of an infinite being.

[This] creative thought . . . is obviously arbitrary on God's part and can therefore be omitted or not omitted at His pleasure.[29]

Laws of nature, for example those governing Newtonian attraction, are not necessary consequences of the intrinsic natures of substances. Laws of nature are the contingent result of divine action. The causal power a particular substance has, its power of attraction, for example, is therefore not something the substance has through its own intrinsic properties. Kant takes his argument to have shown that facts about intrinsic properties place no constraints at all on facts about causal powers. God superadds (*insuper accesserit*) to the monads powers of relating to each other, and this creative

[29] Ak. i. 414, 415, Beck 104, 102.

addition is entirely 'arbitrary', and can be omitted or not omitted at God's pleasure. God is free to add, or not to add, any powers he pleases. Intrinsic facts do not constrain relational facts in any way—otherwise God's creative act would not be unconstrained and arbitrary. This talk of the arbitrariness of God's action can be seen as a way of talking about the contingency of laws of nature, and hence of the contingency of causal powers.

If these modal intuitions are to be respected, then what is needed is a conception of intrinsicness according to which an intrinsic property is a property something can have, no matter what else exists—and no matter what the laws are. The simplest way to amend our conception of intrinsicness to take this into account would be to say that a property is intrinsic just in case something could have it in the absence of other things—and in the absence of laws. In short, a property is intrinsic just in case it is compatible with loneliness and lawlessness.[30]

We are supposing, on this final interpretation, that in considering whether causal powers are reducible to intrinsic properties, Kant instructs us to conduct a thought experiment: not simply the thought experiment of imagining what a substance would be like on its own, as we tried at first, but the thought experiment of imagining what God could do. Could God have made a world of substances with the very same intrinsic properties that substances have in our world, and yet have made the world with different laws— or no laws at all—governing the dynamical relations of substances? Kant says yes, and so, I think, would many contemporary metaphysicians—at any rate to a secular translation. But if the answer to this second question, about God, is yes, then the answer to the first question, about reducibility, is no. The powers of things do not supervene on the intrinsic properties of things. This will be so whether we consider things distributively or collectively, since what matters is not how many things, but what laws there are. In a world just like our own with respect to the intrinsic properties of substances, where God had not endowed substances with gravitational power, it would make no odds how many of the substances one took the trouble to consider. Causal powers, on this understanding, are not bilaterally reducible; *a fortiori* they are not unilaterally reducible (Step 2). Since they are not bilaterally reducible, they must be superadded (Step 3). Now we have an argument

---

[30] This is a simplification of a suggestion in Langton and Lewis, 'Defining "Intrinsic"', n. 12, itself an adaptation of a suggestion from Peter Vallentyne, 'Intrinsic Properties Defined', *Philosophical Studies* 88 (1997), 209–19. The above point could, it seems, be made equally well in terms of Lewis's own conception of intrinsicness, according to which intrinsic properties are those properties shared by all actual or possible duplicates. Duplicates are not guaranteed to share the same causal powers. James van Cleve also makes the point that dispositions are intrinsic on one, but not the other, of two conceptions of intrinsicness similar to those described above, in 'Putnam, Kant, and Secondary Qualities', App. 2.

which takes aim at both Leibnizian reducibility theses, and demolishes both.[31]

The comparison just drawn between Kant's modal intuitions about the contingency of causal powers, and similar intuitions in contemporary metaphysics is, I think, a fair one.[32] However, there is one very important difference. For Kant, forces and *not* intrinsic properties are taken to be the causally active features of the world. Indeed, he takes this to be established by the fact that forces are not reducible to intrinsic properties. He says it is never through its own intrinsic properties that a substance has the power to determine others different from itself. Intrinsic properties are required, not to provide the basis for forces or powers—for they cannot, in Kant's opinion, do that—but only for the very general reason that substances require some intrinsic properties or other. The substance must have intrinsic properties— otherwise there would be no subject in which the forces inhered (*Physical Monadology*, Prop. VII). By contrast, many metaphysicians of our own time take powers, construed as dispositions, to be causally impotent, and believe that the real causal work is always done by intrinsic properties—notwithstanding the fact that powers are not reducible to intrinsic properties. They think intrinsic properties are required for two reasons. First, there is the general requirement with which Kant would agree, that substances must have some intrinsic properties or other. Second, there is a particular requirement with which Kant would disagree, that substances which have dispositions must have intrinsic properties which form the (contingent) ground of the dispositions. For the moment I simply want to draw attention to this dif-

---

[31] Is this compatible with the claim also made by many contemporary metaphysicians that powers, or dispositions, do supervene on intrinsic properties, and hence are, in a sense, reducible? Yes. What is meant by this popular claim is that, *within any given world*, there can be no difference in powers without a difference in intrinsic properties. There can of course be cross-world differences in powers without corresponding differences in intrinsic properties. In Jaegwon Kim's terms, the popular thought is that powers *weakly* supervene on intrinsic properties, but they do not *strongly* supervene on intrinsic properties. We are concerned here only with strong supervenience. See van Cleve for a clear discussion of this issue, and a defence of the weak supervenience thesis for dispositions, in *Putnam, Kant, and Secondary Qualities* (Apps. 1 and 2).

[32] For some statements of what I take to be a contemporary orthodoxy about powers, see e.g. Frank Jackson, Robert Pargetter, and Elizabeth Prior, 'Three Theses about Dispositions,' *American Philosophical Quarterly* 19 (1982), 251–7; David Armstrong, *What is a Law of Nature?* (Cambridge: Cambridge University Press, 1983); James van Cleve, 'Putnam, Kant, and Secondary Qualities'; Elizabeth Prior, *Dispositions* (Aberdeen: Aberdeen University Press, 1985). For some contemporary opposition to the orthodoxy, see e.g. Sydney Shoemaker, 'Causality and Properties', in P. van Inwagen, ed., *Time and Cause* (Dordrecht: Reidel, 1980); Chris Swoyer, 'The Nature of Natural Laws', *Australasian Journal of Philosophy* 60 (1982), 203–23; Brian Ellis and Caroline Lierse, 'Dispositional Essentialism,' *Australasian Journal of Philosophy* 72 (1994), 27–45; C. B. Martin, 'Dispositions and Conditionals', *Philosophical Quarterly* 44 (1994), 1–8.

ference. The possible merits of Kant's view over our contemporary orthodoxy will be a topic of Chapter 8.

On this final interpretation, Kant is concerned with the source of causal
power, or force. He says that if 'nothing more is added to the existence of
the substance' with its intrinsic properties, there will no relationship or community among substances. God must 'superadd' the causal powers. Kant
emphasizes the arbitrariness of the special act of creation: the divine creative thought is 'obviously arbitrary on God's part, and can therefore be omitted or not omitted at his pleasure'. This I think gives us reason for saying
Kant has a doctrine of *superadded forces.* And we know that Leibniz would
have detested Kant's proposal, just as he detested a somewhat similar proposal he thought he noticed in Locke. 'If . . . God gave things *accidental
powers which were not rooted in their natures* and were therefore out of reach
of reason in general; that would be a back door through which to re-admit
"over-occult qualities" which no mind can understand.'[33] The conclusion
of Kant's *New Exposition* is that things do indeed have 'accidental powers . . .
not rooted in their natures'. They have powers to relate to other things, not
'through their own intrinsic properties', but through an arbitrary act of
God.[34]

7. *Concluding Remarks*

We now have two interpretations of Kant's argument. On neither of the
interpretations is the argument hopelessly confused, each has its appeal, and
there seems to be very little in the way of the irredeemable logical obscurity
and metaphysical prejudice Guyer found. The first interpretation takes the
determinatio respectiva to be an ordinary relational property, and on this
interpretation Kant successfully refutes the Leibnizian thesis of unilateral
reducibility, and has in addition a plausible-seeming argument against bilateral reducibility in the Clarification. The plausible-seeming argument

---

[33] Leibniz, *New Essays on Human Understanding* (1765), Gerhardt v. 363, Remnant and
Bennett 382.

[34] The argument, on this interpretation, works, but perhaps there is still something unsat-
isfying about it. On the final interpretation, the notion of intrinsicness is understood in terms
of certain modal facts, where the modal facts are understood through the notion of what God
could or could not have created; and the conclusion itself concerns what God could or could
not have created. The understanding of intrinsicness seems parasitic on the understanding
of certain modal facts, and vice versa. Perhaps this is a version of the circle lamented by
Lewis, who himself defines intrinsicness in terms of the modal facts of duplication, but in
turn defines duplication in terms of intrinsicness—the tight little circle of interdefinability
that led Lewis to explore Jaegwon Kim's idea in the first place, as a possible way out. See
Lewis, 'Extrinsic Properties'.

admittedly turns out to be fallacious, and this spells failure for Kant's con-clusion that relational properties must be superadded through a special cre-ative act.

The second interpretation takes the *determinatio respectiva* to be a causal power, and on this interpretation, and a broader understanding of intrin-sicness, Kant successfully refutes both Leibnizian reducibility theses: powers do not supervene on the intrinsic properties of things, and therefore must be superadded by God. Despite its success, one might have reserva-tions about this argument too, both philosophical and interpretive. One qualm might be that Kant never seems to consider the possibility of a sub-stance existing on its own, but with the *power* of relating causally to other substances. He tends to talk in the very same breath of a substance having a power, and of a substance *exercising* that power on other substances, almost as if he thought of these as presenting the very same philosophical problem.

We do not need to decide between these two interpretations, although I favour the second. What is not in doubt is that Kant rejects the Leibnizian reducibility thesis. What may not be quite so clear is how he rejects it, and whether his rejection is philosophically vindicated. Leibniz, as I understand him, and as Kant understands him, says that all relations and relational prop-erties are bilaterally reducible. Perhaps Kant does not reject Leibniz by say-ing in response that no relations or relational properties are bilaterally reducible (though his argument could conceivably be interpreted that way). Perhaps substances bear (bilaterally) reducible relations of similarity and difference toward each other, or of compossibility and incompossibility. Kant has given no persuasive argument against that, nor does he seem inter-ested in that issue. Pre-established harmony makes relations of causality into relations of similarity between substances: like clocks chiming the hour together, their similar successive states are no signs of real causal connec-tion between them. But such relations, Kant says, are not sufficient for exter-nal connection. In particular, causal powers and causal relations are not similarity relations: they do not supervene on the intrinsic properties of things. What is missing in the Leibnizian account, as Kant says later in the Amphiboly, is a real relation of physical influence (A274/B330). Causal powers and relations are not reducible. There is a real relation that connects substances together, 'a real action of substances that occurs among them, or interaction through truly efficient causes'.[35] On both of the two interpreta-tions of this argument that we have considered, Kant believes he has proven that relational properties are not reducible, and that they must therefore be superadded by God. On the first interpretation his belief is not vindicated; on the second it is vindicated. Kant believes that no matter how many sub-

---

[35] Ak. i. 415, Beck 105.

stances God cares to create, mere addition of substances with their intrinsic properties will never endow the substances with their relations, or powers to relate. That is why there is a need for a special creative act.

I see the argument for Irreducibility as more significant than its other commentators have done. And before we move on to consider why it might be so significant, it is perhaps worth observing that Kant himself presents his argument with a certain air of discovery. It would be unwise, of course, to suppose that a philosopher is a particularly good judge of the significance of his own arguments, and there is no doubt that the phenomenology of philosophical discovery is not always to be trusted. Still, the air of discovery is unmistakable, and, I think, noteworthy. Kant thinks he is the very first philosopher to have shown what he has shown:

It appears to me that I am the first to have furnished completely evident reasons in support of the view that the co-existence of the substances of the universe is not sufficient for establishing a connection among them.[36]

Whether or not the reasons are as 'completely evident' as Kant hoped, there is surely no mistaking the importance he himself attributed to his conclusion.

---

[36] Ak. i. 413, Beck 101.

6

Fitting the Pieces Together

1. *Assembly*

Kant thinks that the mere fact that we must be affected by things if we are to know them destines us to ignorance of things as they are in themselves. According to Strawson, he never explains why.[1] In this chapter I draw together (in this section) the pieces collected in previous chapters, in order to suggest a reason (Section 2). The remainder of the chapter aims to explain and defend this understanding of Kant's path to Humility.

The first of the pieces is the Distinction we have encountered in the later Kant, versions of which also appear in the Leibnizian philosophy (Chapter 4), and in the early Kant (Chapter 5).

> *Distinction*: Things in themselves are substances that have intrinsic properties; phenomena are relational properties of substances.

While the Distinction provides one point of similarity between Kant and Leibniz, it was suggested by some critics that Kant also endorses a Leibnizian view about relations, and these critics claimed to find support in Kant's early writings of 1755 and 1756. We have seen now how far from the truth this is. Kant does not endorse a Leibnizian principle about the reducibility of relations, at least in these early works, but rejects it. And this is the second piece.

> *Irreducibility*: The relations and relational properties of substances are not reducible to the intrinsic properties of substances.

The third of the pieces concerns knowledge. Kant says, in the *Critique*,

> the receptivity of our mind, its power of receiving representations in so far as it is in any way affected, is called sensibility . . . Our nature is so constituted that our intuition can never be other than sensible, that is, it contains only the way in which we are affected by objects. (A51/B75)

Kant argues, in the *New Exposition*, that a mind cannot possess changing states, and hence cannot think, unless it is affected by some other substance. His argument for the Principle of Succession is at the same time an argument for this thesis of the *Critique*:

---

[1] Strawson, *Bounds of Sense*, 250.

Receptivity: Human knowledge depends on sensibility, and sensibility is receptive: we can have knowledge of an object only in so far as it affects us.

With these three theses before us I would like, at this point, to pause.

2. *An Imaginative Exercise*

All three of these pieces are to be found in the *New Exposition*. All three are also present in the later Kant. But since that may be more controversial, let us remain for a moment with the early Kant, and imaginatively step into the shoes of a philosopher who believes only what has been established in the *New Exposition* (1755), helped a little by some borrowing from the *Physical Monadology* (1756).

There are substances, and relations. There are monads, with intrinsic properties, and these monadic substances are connected with one another in dynamical relations of reciprocal dependence. These relations unite substances into one world, a physical world, constituted by the dynamical relations of substances. Matter is constituted by forces of attraction and repulsion, attraction acting at a distance and uniting all coexisting substances into one world, repulsion filling space by hindering the approach of other things. However, these powers that enable substances to relate to one another are not, in Leibniz's phrase, 'rooted in their natures'.[2] The powers of substances, and the causal relations among them, are not reducible to their intrinsic properties, but result instead from a special and arbitrary act of creation: for 'a substance never has the power through its own intrinsic properties to determine others different from itself.'[3]

What, on this picture, can we know? The first thing to be said is that human minds are substances, and cannot have thoughts without being affected by some other substance, as the Principle of Succession shows. Human knowledge is receptive: we can have knowledge of a thing only in so far as we are affected by it. Now ask: what affects us? For, given the thesis of Receptivity, that is how we must find an answer to the question about what we can know.

Given the metaphysical assumptions of these early works, the immediate answer to the question, what affects a substance, must be *forces*, forces of attraction and repulsion that constitute the physical world, the vast universe of whirling galaxies that happens to include a small planet, in a modest solar system, inhabited by human creatures. The Principle of Succession

---

[2] Leibniz, *New Essays*, Gerhardt v. 363, Remnant and Bennett 382.
[3] *New Exposition*, Ak. i. 415.

tells us that only if we ourselves are part of a dynamical community of substances will we have any knowledge of other things. But since we are in fact members of such a community, inhabitants of a world, we can have knowledge of the world we live in. It is a world constituted by forces, and since these are 'relations', it is a world constituted by relations. The physical world is what affects us, and if, as Receptivity implies, we can in principle know what affects us, then we can know the physical world.

But there is more to the universe than this.

Besides external presence, i.e. relational properties of substance, there are other, intrinsic properties without which the relational properties would not exist, because there would be no subject in which they inhered.[4]

We have knowledge of the forces, the 'external presence' of substances. Can we know those substances as they are in themselves, i.e. can we have knowledge of the intrinsic properties of substances? That all depends. We can in principle have knowledge of whatever affects us: that is what Receptivity implies. So we can have knowledge of the intrinsic properties of substances only if they can affect us. Kant's reply to the question of whether we can be affected by the intrinsic properties of substances must be: no. For the intrinsic properties of substances are independent of the causal powers and dynamical relations that unite substances together in a world. The way things are intrinsically does not determine the way they are relationally. Relational properties do not supervene on the intrinsic properties of substances. Any *determinatio respectiva* possessed by a substance must be added to a substance by God in a special and arbitrary act of creation. If we can know only what affects us, then, on the assumptions of the *New Exposition*, it seems to follow that—as Kant says much later—'We are acquainted with substance in space only through forces . . . We are not acquainted with any other properties constituting the concept of the substance . . .' (A265/B321). Put together these three pieces, Receptivity, the Distinction, and Irreducibility, and they yield that distinctive thesis of the *Critique*.

> *Humility*: We have no knowledge of the intrinsic properties of substances.

In short, we have a candidate answer to Strawson's question. We have an argument for the 'fundamental and unargued complex premise of the *Critique*'.[5] If it is not through its own intrinsic properties that a substance has the power to determine things other than itself, then if we are affected by substances, it is not through the intrinsic properties of the substance that we are affected. And if we can know only what affects us, then we cannot

---

[4] *Physical Monadology*, Ak. i. 41, Beck 123.
[5] Strawson, *Bounds of Sense*, 250.

know the intrinsic properties of substances. Humility does follow from Receptivity, given Irreducibility.

This understanding of Kant needs more explanation and defence, and in the remainder of this chapter—indeed, in the remainder of the book, though less directly—I attempt to address these tasks. Kant's commitment to Irreducibility persists through the writing of the *Critique*, and is a crucial aspect of Kant's rejection of Leibniz, contrary to Guyer. Leibniz believed that the realm of relations offers a mirror for the realm of things in themselves. The epistemic Humility so evident in Kant, and so evidently absent in his predecessor, is in part a consequence of Kant's shattering of that Leibnizian mirror—as Section 3 aims to explain. Section 4 continues with this task by showing that the argument for Irreducibility is endorsed in a great variety of Kant's writings, from the *Inaugural Dissertation*, the *Critique*, the *Metaphysical Foundations*, and others, ranging in time from 1747 to 1804, and that it therefore seems to persist throughout Kant's philosophical lifetime. Many other features of Kant's philosophy change in the meanwhile, but this one seems to be constant.

3. *Kant, Leibniz, and a Mirror Broken*

That premises implicit in the *New Exposition* appear to imply Humility is surely an interesting result. It is remarkable that the conclusion for which the mature Kant is famous should be entailed by premises argued for in his earliest philosophical writing. But if the Kant of the *Critique* does not himself endorse those three premises, then the result may be remarkable, but unhelpful.

We saw in Chapter 2 that the Distinction and the thesis of Receptivity are both to be found in the mature Kantian philosophy—but there may be doubts about Irreducibility. Guyer, for example, claimed to find evidence of a Leibnizian view of relations not only in the *New Exposition*, but in the *Critique* itself.[6] He was mistaken about the former, as we saw, but what of the latter? If Guyer is right, it would be wrong to attribute an anti-Leibnizian thesis about relations to the mature Kant. We saw that Guyer cites in his support the following passage from the Aesthetic:

Now a thing in itself cannot be cognized through mere relations; therefore it is well to judge that since nothing can be given to us through outer sense except mere representations of relation, this can contain nothing but the relation of the object to the subject in its representation, and not anything intrinsic which pertains to the object itself. (B67, Guyer's translation, my italics added)

[6] Guyer, *Kant and the Claims*, 351–2.

According to Guyer, Kant means by that first (italicized) clause that relations are not real, but ideal.

This suggestion is, I think, as implausible here as it was in the *New Exposition*. Here is the passage in a little more detail, this time as I gave it in Chapter 2, Section 3:

Everything in our knowledge which belongs to intuition . . . contains nothing but mere relations, of locations in an intuition (extension), of change of location (motion), and of laws according to which this change is determined (moving forces). What presents itself in this or that location, or, beyond this change of location, what activities occur within the things themselves, is not given through these relations. *Now through mere relations one cannot be acquainted with a thing as it is in itself.* We may therefore conclude that since external sense gives us nothing but representations of mere relations, this sense can contain in its representation only the relation of an object upon the subject, and not the intrinsic properties that belong to the object as it is in itself. (B67, my translation, italics added)

If we are acquainted only with the relations, or relational properties of a thing, then we cannot thereby know that thing as it is in itself: we do not know the intrinsic properties of that thing. The passage asserts the thesis of Humility. The contrast in this passage is not between the ideal and the genuine, but, as in Kant's earliest works, between the relational and the intrinsic. The argument assumes the Distinction at work in the earlier writings—the contrast between *Verhältnisse*, relations, and on the other hand *das Innere*, the intrinsic (properties) that belong to the object as it is in itself. Compare it to the passage we have considered from the *Physical Monadology*.

Whatever is intrinsic to substance, i.e. the substantial itself, is not properly defined by space. The substance itself is the subject of extrinsic properties [forces], and those extrinsic properties are something properly to be sought in space . . . But besides external presence, i.e. relational properties of the substance, there are other intrinsic properties, without which the relational properties [forces] would not exist, because there would be no subject in which they inhered. But the intrinsic properties are not in space, precisely because they are intrinsic.

Where Kant speaks, in the *Physical Monadology*, of the 'external presence' of monads, he speaks in B67 of a thing 'presenting itself' in some location, in both cases the presence being described as a relation or relational property. In both passages he says that intrinsic properties (and 'activities occurring within the things themselves') are not in space, that they are not structured by space. The pictures given in the two passages are very much alike. Where the passage from the Aesthetic differs from the passage from the *Physical Monadology* is in the assertion of Humility: the statement that the intrinsic properties are unknown. A reason for Humility is hinted at, namely that we can have knowledge only through external *sense*, and therefore can know things in so far as they can affect us, or exert forces upon us (B67). We are thus able to represent the forces, but not the intrinsic properties that belong to the object as it is in itself. Kant's views about space may well have undergone major changes in the intervening periods, but the basic Distinction between the intrinsic and dynamical relational properties of substances remains quite intact. (I defer addressing these caveats about space to Chapter 10.) It seems that contrary to Guyer, the B67 passage fails to state a Leibnizian thesis about relations. Rather, it asserts Kant's Distinction, expresses Humility, and hints at Receptivity.

However, there is something more here. I want to suggest that this passage not only fails to state a Leibnizian thesis about relations, but, more importantly, it implies the *falsity* of a Leibnizian thesis about relations. The passage asserts the thesis of Irreducibility. To see why, we need to recall Kant's understanding of Leibniz.

Kant says that through mere relations we cannot be acquainted with a thing as it is in itself. If we know only the relational properties of a thing, then we have no acquaintance at all with the intrinsic properties of that thing. This does not express agreement with Leibniz, but *disagreement*. Leibniz believes just the reverse. Leibniz, as Kant understands him, believes that through the mere relational properties of a thing we *can* be acquainted—at least partly—with a thing as it is in itself. Leibniz *takes* the phenomena for things in themselves (A264/B320, A268/B323). The appearance is, for Leibniz, 'the presentation of the thing in itself' (A270/B326). Leibniz identifies the phenomena with certain relational properties of monads—and takes those relational properties to be nothing over and above the properties of things in themselves. Acquaintance with phenomena is acquaintance with the relational properties of monads: and since those relational properties supervene on the intrinsic properties of monads, acquaintance with phenomena yields acquaintance, albeit distorted and partial, of the intrinsic properties of monads. That is why Leibniz thought, according to Kant, that through sensibility we can know the nature of things in themselves (A44/B62)—and

that our entire sensibility is nothing but a confused representation of things, that contains *solely what belongs to the things in themselves*, but with a crowding together of characteristics and partial representations, so that we cannot consciously distinguish the things from one another. (A43/B60, italics added)

We saw in Chapter 4 that Leibniz's reduction of phenomena to things in themselves, resting on his reduction of relations to intrinsic properties, has epistemological implications. There can indeed be knowledge, via phenomena, of things in themselves. Given the nature of the distinction between phenomena and things in themselves, this means that there can indeed be knowledge via relations of a thing as it is in itself—directly contrary to Kant's argument of B67. If the relations of things express or mirror the intrinsic properties of things, then knowledge of relations will yield some sort of knowledge of the intrinsic properties of things. Supervenience guarantees that at the very least one knows there can be no changes in the relations without changes in things themselves: so changes in phenomena will be proof of changes among the intrinsic properties of monads.

Leibniz says that our sensory states express the bodies constituting the physical world, and thereby express the infinite universe of monads constituting the bodies. Just as we perceptually represent the innumerably many waves of the sea in an indistinct roar, so we perceptually represent the harmonious orderings of intrinsic properties of the monads as causality and space and body. The difference between phenomenon and thing in itself is like the difference between a crowd of men seen from afar, and the individual men who compose it. Recall Kant's description of the Leibnizian view:

There is . . . no other difference between a thing as phenomenon and the representation of the noumenon which underlies it than between a group of men which I see at a great distance and the same men when I am so close that I can count the individuals. It is only, [the Leibnizian] says, that we could never come so close to it. This, however, makes no difference in the thing, but only in the degree of our power of perception.[7]

The perception of things in themselves, the well-foundedness of phenomena, and the reducibility thesis, are closely interconnected. If phenomena are simply monads reducibly related in a certain way, and sensibility yields knowledge of phenomena, then sensibility yields some knowledge of things in themselves. If we are acquainted, through perception, with bodies, and bodies and monads both follow laws that 'correspond to each other like two clocks perfectly regulated to the same time', then knowledge of the laws of bodies will yield knowledge (if confused, indirect) of the laws that govern monads. If we are acquainted, through perception, with compound beings, and compound beings are in 'agreement with the simple', then we can have knowledge (confused, indirect) of the simple beings that constitute them. If perceptual states mirror a physical world constituted by dynamical and spatial relations, and those relations mirror the intrinsic properties of monads, then perceptual states mirror the intrinsic properties of monads.[8] So through acquaintance with mere relations one can indeed be acquainted with a thing as it is in itself.

---

[7] 'On a Discovery' (1790), Ak. viii. 208, Allison 124–5.

[8] 'Monadology', Loemker 649; 'Consideration on Vital Principles' (1705), Loemker 587.

Kant says that the Leibnizian 'makes no difference in the thing, but only in the degree of our power of perception'. Kant makes a difference in the thing. He makes a far sharper division than Leibniz did between substances with intrinsic properties, and the relations whereby those substances constitute the phenomenal world. If making a world was like making a crowd, all God would have to do is make many substances. But, as Kant argued, the difference between relational and intrinsic properties—in particular the irreducibility of the former to the latter—requires more of a world-making God. Because of the 'difference in the thing'—because phenomena are not to be taken for things in themselves—there must be a difference in the act of creation of the thing. The need for separate acts of creation argued for in the *New Exposition* reflects the difference in the thing: the difference between phenomena and things in themselves.

This difference Kant makes in the thing has consequences for the power of perception. For Leibniz, bodies mirror monads, and perception mirrors bodies: so perception can mirror monads. For Kant, a mirror is broken. Bodies do not mirror monads. The realm of bodies no longer mirrors the realm of monads like 'clocks perfectly regulated to the same time'. If perception mirrors bodies but bodies do not mirror the monadic realm, if perception mirrors the realm of relations, but relations do not mirror intrinsic properties of substances, then perception does not, even indirectly, mirror things as they are in themselves. Contrary to Leibniz, through the mere relations of things one cannot be acquainted with things as they are in themselves; and 'It is not that through sensibility we are acquainted in a *merely confused* way with the nature of things as they are in themselves; we are not acquainted with that nature in any way *at all*' (A44/B62, italics added).

In sum, it is not, as Guyer says, because Kant believes Leibniz is right about relations, but because he believes Leibniz is wrong, that he concludes that we have no knowledge of things as they are in themselves. Kant's argument of B67 is directly opposed to the Leibnizian doctrine about relations. And it constitutes excellent evidence that the argument for Irreducibility in the *New Exposition* is no fossil from Kant's early years: on the contrary, Kant endorses it within the *Critique* itself, in 1787.

4. *Later Signs of the Irreducibility Argument*

The argument of the *New Exposition* is the most careful and detailed Kantian argument for Irreducibility of which I am aware. One major reason for thinking that it is in the background of Kant's mature philosophy is that it makes good sense of some of the otherwise most problematic aspects of

Kant's philosophy. It provides an explanation, and justification, for the unargued premise of the *Critique*. It shows why Kant insists both that there exist things in themselves, and that we cannot know them as they are in themselves. It removes the problem of affection, as I argued in Chapter 1, and at the same time does justice to the metaphysical Kant who, in advocating Humility, believes that we are thereby missing out on something.

However, since the Irreducibility argument, as I have described it, comes from the period of alleged dogmatic slumber, lingering suspicions may remain that it was after all shaken off when Kant awoke. More may be needed than the demonstration just given that the argument is alive and well in the Aesthetic (B67). In this section I continue the task of alleviating these suspicions by suggesting that Kant endorses the *New Exposition* form of argument throughout most of his lifetime. I do not deny that much of Kant's philosophy changed radically over this period, and I shall have more to say about that in Chapter 10. This part, though, seems constant.

One first thing to say is that on the present interpretation, many passages in the *Critique* that express the thesis of Humility thereby express the thesis of Irreducibility. That was so for the B67 passage from the Aesthetic: Kant's denial that a thing can, through its mere relations, be known as it is in itself, is at once an assertion of Humility and a denial of Leibnizian reducibility. Something similar is true for other expressions of Humility. When Kant says, 'We are acquainted with substance in space only through forces', and 'all that we know in matter is merely relations' (A285/B341), he expresses a rejection of the Leibnizian view that acquaintance with forces and relations is *ipso facto* acquaintance (albeit partial) with the intrinsic properties of substances. When Kant says, that 'matter is mere external appearance, the substratum of which cannot be known through any predicate that we can assign to it' (A359), he expresses a rejection of the Leibnizian view that knowledge of external appearance *ipso facto* provides knowledge (albeit partial) of the monadic 'substratum' of the appearance. Just as the absence of Humility in Leibniz depends on a Leibnizian commitment to the reducibility of relations, so the expression of Humility in Kant depends on a Kantian commitment to Irreducibility.

There are passages where the commitment to Irreducibility is much more explicit than this, however, and they can be found in a great variety of works. I'm afraid I do not here attempt to do justice to the more general themes of these works, nor treat the topics I discuss with the degree of care and depth that they deserve. (Some of them will, however, be scrutinized in more detail later on.) My concern is simply to show a common thread running through all of them, namely the basic argument for Irreducibility; for they all seem to assert that the relations or relational properties of substances do not supervene on the existence of substances, with their intrinsic properties.

(i) *Inaugural Dissertation* (1770)

§ 11. Phenomena are strictly species of things, not ideas, and do not express the intrinsic and absolute quality of objects . . .

§ 16. What is the principle upon which this [interactive] relation of all substances itself rests, a relation which, when viewed intuitively, is called space? . . . how is it possible that several substances should be in mutual interaction? . . .

§ 17. Given a plurality of substances, a principle of possible interaction between them is not given by their existence alone. Something more is required from which their mutual relations are to be understood.[9]

Phenomena, contrary to Leibniz, 'do not express the intrinsic and absolute qualities' of substances (§ 11). However, it would not be correct to say that phenomena do not express *any* features of substances: for the interactive *relation* of substances with each other is, 'when viewed intuitively', space (§ 16). There is a certain isomorphism envisaged between the spatial relations of the sensible world and the dynamical relations among monadic substances. If the relations between substances are forces, then forces are what are 'viewed intuitively' in a system of spatial relations. The problem of the *New Exposition* presents itself again. How can there be relations of interaction among substances (§ 16)? The existence of substances (with their 'intrinsic and absolute qualities') is not sufficient for the possibility of causal interaction between them (§ 17).

Similar thoughts seem to be present in some of the *Reflexionen*, of which the following are a sample:

No mutual interaction is original. All are derivative and sustained by something else. (*R* 4438)

It is impossible for substances to be in mutual interaction without the mediation of some sustaining cause. (*R* 4539)

The actions [of bodies] and their forces concern only the phenomena of relations in general, without their intrinsic properties. (*R* 5429)[10]

Compressed and cryptic though these may be, the basic conclusion of the *New Exposition* argument for Irreducibility shines through.

(ii) The *Critique*: Amphiboly (A274/B330)

It is worth taking a further look at a passage we have already considered in some detail, which offers Kant's characterization of the Leibnizian philosophy:

---

[9] 'The Inaugural Dissertation', Ak. ii. 397, 407, Kerferd and Walford 61, 74–5.
[10] Ak. xvii. 546, M 1772; Ak. xvii. 587, M 1773; Ak. xviii. 179, M 1777–80.

Monads are supposed to serve as the raw material for the whole universe, despite having no active force (*tätige Kraft*), except for that consisting in representations (which, strictly speaking, are active only within the monads). That is why Leibniz's principle of the possible reciprocal community of substances had to be a pre-established harmony, and not a physical influence. For when everything is merely intrinsic . . . the state of one substance cannot stand in any active connection whatsoever with the state of another. (A274/B330)

The notion of force (*Kraft*) can be understood as the notion of power: and Kant's complaint in this passage is that the monads have no 'active power' that would enable them to stand in 'active connection' with other substances. He says that this is an inevitable consequence of a metaphysic where 'everything is merely intrinsic'. Now if causal powers were indeed to supervene on the intrinsic properties of substances, then the fact that 'everything is merely intrinsic' would be no barrier to the possibility of substances' possessing causal powers, and interacting causally with each other. So Kant's statement in this passage that the *absence* of causal power *follows* from the fact that everything is 'merely intrinsic' implies a commitment to the thesis of Irreducibility: a commitment to the thesis that causal powers, at least, fail to supervene on the intrinsic properties of monadic substances. So this passage, too, can be seen as offering a compressed version of the argument for Irreducibility from the *New Exposition*.

(iii) The *Critique*: Amphiboly (A263/B2319, A272/B328)

The Leibnizian reducibility thesis holds that spatial properties supervene on dynamical properties, and dynamical properties supervene on intrinsic properties. There can be no difference in the supervenient properties without a difference in the 'foundational' ones. Leibniz says that 'A relation, since it results from a state of things, never comes into being or disappears unless some change is made in its fundament'.[11] Kant's discussions of identity and difference in the Amphiboly show that he rejects this reducibility thesis, this time with respect to spatial properties rather than the causal properties just considered.

[Leibniz] compared the objects of the senses in so far as they are to be judged by the understanding to be identical or different . . . Certainly, if I were to know a drop of water as if it were a thing in itself, with all of its intrinsic properties, then if the concept of the one is identical with others, I cannot allow that the drop is distinct from the others. But if the drop is an appearance in space, it has its place not only in the understanding (under concepts) but also in the intuition of external sense (in space). And there the physical locations of things are quite indifferent to the

---

[11] Grua 547; Mates, *The Philosophy of Leibniz*, 223.

intrinsic properties of things. A location *b* can hold a thing which is exactly like another in a location *a* just as easily as if the things were intrinsically ever so different. (A272/B328, cf. also A263/B319)

If the Leibnizian thesis of reducibility were right, there could be no difference in spatial properties without—ultimately—a difference in intrinsic properties. Here Kant says: there can easily be a difference in spatial properties without there being a difference in intrinsic properties.[12] So he rejects the supervenience of spatial properties on intrinsic properties.

(iv) The *Critique*: Postulates of Empirical Thought

How are we to think it possible that, when several substances exist, from the existence of one, some reciprocal action on the existence of the others can follow? We think that because something is in the one there must also be something in the others which is not to be understood solely from their own existence alone. For that is what community requires. But among things that are each totally isolated (each isolated in its own subsistence) community is completely inconceivable . . . However we can make quite comprehensible the possibility of a community of substances—substances as *appearances*—when we represent them to ourselves in space, in external intuition. For this already contains in itself *a priori* formal external relations as conditions of the possibility of real external relations (action and reaction) and thus community. (B293–4)[13]

Kant begins with the general problem of the *New Exposition*. How is it possible, starting with the mere existence of a plurality of substances, for those substances to interact? The interactive relations of the substances do not follow from the mere fact that the substances exist. When one conceives of substances as independently subsisting beings, conforming to the pure concept of substance, the question of how such beings could acquire causal powers enabling them to interact with each other remains unanswered. The substances and their intrinsic properties are not sufficient to establish relations among them. That is the problem of Irreducibility. Kant's response this time is to focus on experience, and to abandon, as far as experience is concerned, the pure concept of substance 'as conceived through the understanding', i.e. substance as independent and self-subsistent. In its

---

[12] Jill Buroker has traced the significance of Kant's rejection of reducibility for spatial relations, though not for causal relations, in *Space and Incongruence*. She sees passages like this as containing a compressed version of Kant's arguments about incongruent counterparts.

[13] Kant also says here, 'That is why Leibniz had to make use of a Deity when he attributed community to the substances of the world, i.e. substances as thought through pure understanding.' The community which Leibniz thus achieved, however, was merely ideal, rather than the community of 'real external relations' Kant says is necessary.

place is something that does not conform to the pure concept of substance, i.e. substance as appearance. Kant says that external intuition contains in itself 'a priori formal external relations', namely space; and that these formal external relations make it possible for us to represent 'real external relations' of action and reaction, and thus community. Here, as in the *Inaugural Dissertation*, a kind of isomorphism is envisaged between space and force: space provides the formal relations which make it possible for us to represent real relations of reciprocal action and reaction. 'Substance' is now the name for whatever real thing it is that can be represented in the system of formal relations provided by space: and that real thing is no 'intrinsic and absolute quality', to borrow the phrase from the *Inaugural Dissertation*, but the 'real relation' of action and reaction—the real relation of force.

(v) The *Critique*: Third Analogy

All substances, in so far as they can be perceived to co-exist in space, are in thoroughgoing reciprocity . . . Now suppose that a plurality of substances as appearances were each completely isolated—so that none would act on the other, and would receive from the other no reciprocal influence. I say that the co-existence of these substances would be no object of possible perception, and that the existence of one of them could not lead through the way of empirical synthesis to the existence of the other . . . Each substance must therefore contain in itself the causality of certain properties in the others, and at the same time contain in itself the effects of the causality of others, that is, they must stand in dynamical community if their co-existence in a possible experience is to be known. Now, with respect to objects of experience, something is *necessary* if experience of the objects themselves would be impossible without it. Therefore it is necessary that substances in the [field of] appearance, in so far as they are coexistent, should stand in a thoroughgoing community of mutual interaction. (B 256, A212/B258–A213/B260)

Here we have the Critical successor to the Principle of Coexistence in the *New Exposition*. The argument bears some resemblance to the preceding passage from the Postulates of Empirical Thought. It is not easy to interpret, but it seems to proceed by *reductio*. Suppose (*per impossibile*) there were a plurality of substances as appearances each of which was completely isolated from the others. Such substances would not act upon each other, and would not be objects of possible perception. Hence they would not be substances as appearances, contrary to the hypothesis. Hence substances as appearances must not be isolated, but stand in dynamical community. What this has in common with the 1755 argument is the connection Kant seems to see between the metaphysical independence of substance—the isolation, or perhaps isolability, of one substance from another—and the absence of causal interaction between them. The argument seems to assert Irreducibility: that the mere existence of substances each of which is capable of existing by itself is not sufficient for interaction among them. And then Kant simply gives up on the problem, thus conceived. Abandoning the question of how a substance can be endowed with relations in order to form a world, Kant says that what is relevant as far as we are concerned is this: if we are to have experience of anything, then we must already be part of a world of causally interactive substances.

(vi) *Metaphysical Foundations of Natural Science* (1786)

Matter fills a space, not by its mere existence, but by a special moving force . . . Lambert and others called the space-filling property of matter its solidity (a rather ambiguous expression). They held that solidity must be assumed in everything that exists (substance), at least in the external sensible world. According to their way of thinking the presence of something real in space must by its very concept imply this resistance. They thought that a solid thing must, in accordance with the principle of contradiction, exclude the coexistence of anything else in the space in which it is present. But the principle of contradiction does not drive matter back! . . . Only when I attribute to a space-occupant a *force* to repel every external movable thing that approaches it, do I understand how a contradiction is involved when a space which a thing occupies is penetrated by another thing of the same kind.[14]

Here we have, in a very different context, a conclusion that draws on the argument for Irreducibility. From the mere existence of a thing, possessing certain hypothesized intrinsic properties such as *solidity*, no conclusions follow about how that thing will relate to other things. One cannot deduce from any premise about the mere existence of a thing, with its intrinsic properties, that it will repel anything that advances toward it. After all, says Kant—with what the translator informs us is an 'example of Kantian wit'—the principle of contradiction does not drive matter back.

This is an *ad hominem* argument directed against those who, unlike Kant, believe a physical substance can have intrinsic properties such as solidity. Suppose, as Lambert believes, that matter has the intrinsic property of solidity. Lambert, according to Kant, 'thought that a solid thing must, in accordance with the principle of contradiction, exclude the coexistence of anything else in the space in which it is present'. Lambert believed that certain facts about relations follow from certain facts about intrinsic properties—that facts about how things will causally relate to other things follow logically from facts about the intrinsic properties of things. Lambert believed that it is impossible for something to be solid without being impenetrable. He believed that the causal power of impenetrability supervenes on the intrinsic property of solidity. Kant says it does not. No facts about the

---

[14] *Metaphysical Foundations*, Ak. iv. 497–8, my translation, Ellington 42 (Ellington here remarks that this is an example of Kantian wit).

intrinsic properties of things will entail—in accordance with the principle of contradiction—facts about the causal powers of things. Contrary to Lambert, it is possible for something to be solid without being impenetrable. The causal power of impenetrability does not supervene on the intrinsic property of solidity. So here, in a very different context to the others so far considered, we find a version of the *New Exposition* argument for Irreducibility. Kant's response this time is to offer a further development of his competing dynamical theory of matter, which, unlike that of Lambert, makes *force*, not solidity, the fundamental feature of matter. This argument has interesting implications for Kant's views about primary qualities, and will receive more detailed attention in Chapter 8.

(vii) *What Real Progress has Metaphysics made in Germany since the Time of Leibniz and Wolff?* (Prize Essay for 1791, published 1804)

It is already in the [Leibnizian] concept of substances, that, if nothing is added to them, they must be represented as completely isolated. For one substance cannot have, in virtue of its subsistence, an inherent accident that is the cause of something in another substance, and even if others existed, the first could not in any way be dependent on them . . . If they should stand in community as substances of a world, this community can only be ideal and cannot be a real physical influence. The possibility of this latter interaction cannot be understood from the mere existence of the substances . . . But if, by contrast, one begins with the pure intuition of space, which lies a priori at the ground of all external relations . . . then all substances are thereby bound in relations that make physical influence possible.[15]

Here, at a late date, we seem to find again the anti-Leibnizian argument of the *New Exposition*. When we begin with the pure (Leibnizian) concept of substance, we begin with the concept of a thing capable of existing independently of other substances, and possessing intrinsic properties—properties it can have in the absence of other substances. Such substances must be thought to exist in complete causal isolation from each other—unless something is added to them. It cannot be that a substance has, just in virtue of its 'subsistence'—just in virtue of its existence as an independent intrinsic property bearer—a causal power. It cannot be that a substance has, just in virtue of its 'subsistence', an 'accident that is the cause of something in another substance'. The possibility of a real physical influence among substances cannot be understood as being a consequence of the mere existence of the substances.

At this stage, however, Kant's response is very different to his first response to the argument for Irreducibility. He gives up on the endeavour

---

[15] *What Real Progress?*, Ak. xx. 283–4.

of attempting to deduce the relations of things from their existence, their intrinsic properties, or even God's creative actions. It is enough to know that if we are to have any experience at all, it will be experience of a causally inter-active world, because our sensibility is such that we must be dynamically affected by things if we are to know them, and the form of our sensibility is such that we represent those real dynamical relations in a spatial form. The formal and a priori spatial relations are, so to speak, the blueprint that enables us to represent the real dynamical relations of a causally interactive world. But it is a blueprint that captures only relations: the intrinsic prop-erties of Leibnizian substances remain unknown. This passage too warrants more attention, which it will receive in Chapter 10.

In sum then, Strawson is right to say that Humility follows from Recep-tivity, according to Kant. It follows from our need to be affected that we can know only the causal powers of substances; and given that causal powers fail to supervene on the intrinsic properties of substances, it follows that we have no knowledge of the intrinsic properties. Humility follows from Receptiv-ity, given the assumption of Irreducibility. These arguments for Irre-ducibility throughout Kant's philosophical lifetime show a remarkable constancy. Their persistence shows that Kant continued to believe that it is never 'through its own intrinsic properties' that a substance has the power to affect another thing; he continued to believe that the causal powers of things do not supervene on their intrinsic properties. Kant thinks that things affect us. More to the point, he thinks that 'things in themselves' affect us: that is to say, things that have an intrinsic nature affect us. In doing so, Kant ascribes causal power to things that have an intrinsic nature. If causal powers belong to substances that have intrinsic properties, but it is 'not through its own intrinsic properties' that a substance has its causal powers, then although we are affected by things that have intrinsic properties, it is not through those intrinsic properties that we are affected. So a receptive crea-ture cannot have knowledge of the intrinsic properties of things. We can have no knowledge of things as they are in themselves.

7

A Comparison with Locke

1. *A Phenomenalist Reading of the Comparison*

In the *Prolegomena* Kant compares his own philosophy to that of Locke in a way that may appear to undermine the suggested interpretation of Kant.[1] Kant's Distinction, I have said, is not a traditional veil of appearance distinction that divides things as they look to us, from things as they are, independently of us. But by comparing his own view to Locke's distinction between primary and secondary qualities, Kant may seem to be implying the reverse.

Here is the passage I want to consider.

Idealism consists in the claim that there are none other than thinking beings; the other things which we believe we perceive in intuition are only representations in the thinking beings, to which in fact no object outside the latter corresponds. I say on the contrary: things are given to us as objects of our senses situated outside us, but of what they may be in themselves we know nothing; we only know their appearances, i.e. the representations that they effect in us when they affect our senses. Consequently I do indeed admit that there are bodies outside us, i.e. things which, although wholly unknown to us as to what they may be in themselves, we know through the representations which their influence on our sensibility provides for us, and to which we give the name of bodies. This word therefore merely means the appearance of that for us unknown but none the less real object. Can this be called idealism? It is the very opposite of it.

That it can be said of many of the predicates of outer things, without detriment to their real existence, that they belong not to these things in themselves but only to their appearances and have no existence of their own outside our representations, is something that was generally accepted and admitted long before LOCKE'S time, but more so afterwards. To these predicates belong heat, colour, taste, etc. But that I for weighty reasons also count as mere appearances, in addition to these, the remaining qualities of bodies which are called *primariae*, extension, place, and space in general with all that depends on it (impenetrability or materiality, shape, etc.) is

---

[1] Hilary Putnam comments on this comparison in *Reason, Truth and History* (Cambridge: Cambridge University Press, 1981), 59, and endorses the philosophical move he takes Kant to be making. Since the writing of this chapter, an excellent study of this comparison has come to my attention, namely James van Cleve's 'Putnam, Kant and Secondary Qualities'. Van Cleve's analysis overlaps in many ways with the project of this chapter, although our final conclusions are not the same, since he in the end endorses a phenomenalist interpretation of Kant.

something against which not the slightest ground of inadmissibility can be adduced. A man who will not allow colours to be attached to the object in itself as qualities, but only to the sense of sight as modifications, cannot be called an idealist for that; equally little can my doctrine be called idealistic merely because I find that more of, indeed all, the qualities that make up the intuition of a body belong merely to its appearance; for the existence of the thing that appears is not thereby cancelled, as with real idealism, but it is only shown that we cannot know it at all through the senses as it is in itself.[2]

The philosophical move Kant here describes seems to be precisely Berkeley's, namely that of placing the primary qualities on the same footing as the secondary. Kant appears to be saying: nobody minds the fact that the secondary qualities are merely ideas in us, so nobody should mind if (for good reasons) I go further and say that *all* the qualities, including those hitherto regarded as primary, are mere ideas in us. Kant does, of course, offer us some comfort. The passage, after all, is couched as a *defence* against idealist interpretations of the Kantian philosophy. This is not idealism at all, Kant says, 'it is the very opposite', since the independent existence of the object is not denied. But the comfort is cold comfort. We have, it seems, just Berkeley plus unknowable things in themselves. Kant seems to bring all the qualities to our side of the veil, but leave the veil intact, with things in themselves left behind it.

Whether this Berkeleian move has to yield the Berkeleian position will depend on what we take Locke's distinction to be. Berkeley's Locke—and I don't say Locke himself—was a phenomenalist about secondary qualities, in the manner I just assumed. Colours, tastes, and smells are merely ideas in us. If we begin with that, and then go on to say with Berkeley that shape and solidity have just the same status, then all are equally ideas in us, and we have a complete phenomenalism with regard to bodies. There is certainly a reading of Kant which makes this his position too. Early reviewers thought Kant was offering little more than Berkeley in disguise. Some recent commentators have agreed, and Colin Turbayne added that the disguise, though thin, was deliberately assumed.[3] Bennett, as we have seen, says that according to Kant, statements about phenomena are equivalent to statements about actual and possible sensory states.[4] On Berkeley's version of Locke's distinction, and on a phenomenalist reading of Kant, the *Prolegomena* analogy looks appropriate.

---

[2] *Prolegomena*, Ak. iv. 288–98, Lucas 45.

[3] Christian Garve, review of Kant's *Critique of Pure Reason* (with editorial changes by J. G. H. Feder), published in the *Göttinger Anzeigen von gelehrten Sachen*, Jan. 1782; Colin Turbayne, 'Kant's Refutation of Dogmatic Idealism', *Philosophical Quarterly* 5 (1955), 225–44. See Margaret Wilson, 'Kant and "the *Dogmatic* Idealism of Berkeley"', *Journal of the History of Philosophy* 9 (1971), 464–70.

[4] Bennett, *Kant's Analytic*, 22

It must be admitted that it also looks appropriate when seen in conjunction with Kant's refutation of sceptical idealism in the Fourth Paralogism. Here Kant explicitly attacks the familiar 'veil of appearance' doctrine attributed to many philosophers including Locke, but again he seems to replace a Lockean veil of appearance with yet another veil of appearance. According to sceptical idealists like Locke, outer objects are not immediately perceived, but their existence is inferred as the cause of given perceptions (A367 ff.). The inference across this gap is notoriously shaky, and this leaves our knowledge of outer objects in doubt. Kant's solution is to close the gap: 'In order to arrive at the reality of outer objects I have [no] need to resort to inference . . . For . . . the objects are nothing but representations, the immediate perception (consciousness) of which is at the same time a sufficient proof of their reality' (A371). Kant's solution seems to be the worst of all veil of appearance philosophies: Berkeley plus unknowable things in themselves. And this move does connect neatly with the comparison we are considering.[5] Berkeley's Locke thought the secondary qualities were merely representations in us; the primary qualities belonged to things themselves, and were causally responsible for the representations in us. Kant and Berkeley alike say: no. The primary qualities and the secondary are on an equal footing: nothing but appearances, nothing but representations in us. The most natural way to understand this is that Berkeley and Kant alike leave us with nothing but our ideas: they leave us with what we immediately perceive, with what is manifest to the senses, and—apart from an unknowable something—that is all.

2. *Problems, and a Contradiction*

There are good reasons for thinking this simple phenomenalist reading of Kant is mistaken. In this section I shall say why, and the following three sections are devoted to the task of finding an alternative to the mistaken phenomenalist reading.

One major reason for thinking the phenomenalist interpretation mistaken is that the phenomenal realm is not the realm of sensory ideas, and not even the realm of what is manifest to the senses. Kant cares less for the manifest image than for the scientific image—to borrow the labels that Wilfrid Sellars has made famous.[6] Quite the contrary: Kant endorses a strong scientific

---

[5] Notwithstanding Bennett's claim that the veil of appearance doctrine and the primary/secondary quality distinction have nothing to do with each other (Bennett, *Locke, Berkeley, Hume*, 112–23). Of course *his* version of the latter distinction has nothing to do with the former doctrine; but that's another story, which we will come to in Chapter 8.

[6] Wilfrid Sellars, *Science, Perception and Reality* (New York: Humanities Press, 1962).

realism, and he believes that a primary/secondary quality distinction holds *within* the phenomenal world.[7] Phenomenal objects do have the often unobservable properties that physics ascribes to them; and they do not have colours and tastes.

First, Kant is an empirical realist about the theoretical entities of science. The phenomenal world is populated with all manner of imperceptible forces, ether, caloric fluids, molecules, invisible magnetic matter, Newtonian *lamellae* or light particles.[8] Kant is not an instrumentalist about these unobservables, as some commentators might lead one to believe;[9] he thinks that such entities are empirically real, and not simply fictions useful for predicting the future course of observable events.

Kant's theory of force provides a prime example of his scientific realism. Matter, as we have seen, is thought to arise from a 'conflict' of forces: 'only an original attraction in conflict with an original repulsion can make possible a determinate degree of the filling of space, which is matter'.[10] These two fundamental forces are, by any standards, unobservable theoretical entities. There are some qualifications. Kant thinks the force of repulsion is sometimes perceivable: 'By means of the sense of feeling [repulsion] provides us with the size and shape of an extended thing . . . [It] reveals its existence to us by sense, whereby we perceive its impenetrability, namely by feeling.'[11] But it is a consequence of his theory that the force of repulsion occupies *all* of space, and thus occupies parts of space much too small to be perceptible. The force of repulsion is present in parts of space that we cannot perceive, and is thus sometimes to be inferred rather than observed. And the force of attraction is entirely a theoretical entity, since it is never directly observed at all, in Kant's view: 'Attraction . . . in itself can give us either no sensations at all, or at least no determinate object of sensation . . . Attraction is not felt but is only to be inferred.'[12] Kant sometimes writes as though he thinks direct observation and inference to the unobserved 'amount to the

---

[7] This has been convincingly argued by Margaret Wilson in 'The "Phenomenalisms" of Berkeley and Kant', in Allen Wood, ed., *Self and Nature in Kant's Philosophy* (Ithaca, N.Y.: Cornell University Press, 1984), 157–73. I myself argued that Kant must be understood as a scientific realist, and that such realism is incompatible with his transcendental idealism, in 'Kant and Scientific Realism', B.A. Honours thesis, Department of Traditional and Modern Philosophy, University of Sydney, 1985.

[8] For forces, ether, caloric fluids, see *Metaphysical Foundations*, Ak. iv. 496–535, Ellington 40–94; for magnetic matter, the *Critique* A226/B273; for Newton's *lamellae*, *On a Discovery*, Ak. viii. 205, Allison 122.

[9] e.g. Gottfried Martin, *Kant's Metaphysic and Theory of Science*, trans. P. Lucas (Manchester: Manchester University Press, 1955), 95, 137; Mary Hesse, *Forces and Fields* (London: Thomas Nelson, 1961), 171.

[10] *Metaphysical Foundations*, Ak. iv. 518, Ellington 69.

[11] Ibid., Ak. iv. 510, Ellington 58.

[12] Ibid., Ak. iv. 510, 513, Ellington 59, 62.

same thing': 'Knowledge of real forces . . . can only be given empirically—for example, of moving forces, or what amounts to the same thing, of certain successive appearances, as motions which indicate the presence of such forces' (A207/B252). This attitude is in keeping with his discussion of our knowledge of the existence of imperceptible magnetic matter, in the Postulates of Empirical Thought:

The knowledge of things as real does not, indeed, require immediate perception (and therefore sensation of which we are conscious) of the object whose existence is to be known. (A225/B272)

From the perception of the attracted iron filings we know of the existence of a magnetic matter pervading all bodies, although immediate perception of this stuff is impossible because of the constitution of our organs. For if our senses were finer, we would come upon a direct empirical intuition of it in an experience, in accordance with the laws of sensibility and the context of our perceptions. The grossness of our senses does not in any way decide the form of possible experience in general. Our knowledge of the existence of things reaches, then, as far as perception and its advance according to empirical laws can extend. (A226/B273)

Whether or not we can actually see or hear or touch something is quite irrelevant to whether it is empirically real, Kant evidently thinks. Some readers might be tempted to view the above passage as offering a typical phenomenalist response to the question of the existence of unobserved items: namely, the appeal to *possible* sensory states. Such readers might be tempted to cite a comparable passage from the Antinomies:

That there may be inhabitants of the moon, although no one has ever perceived them, must certainly be allowed. This, however, only means that in the possible advance of experience we may encounter them . . . To call an appearance a real thing prior to our perceiving it, either means that in the advance of experience we must meet with such a perception or it means nothing at all. (A493/B521)

This can readily be given a contemporary phenomenalist cast if we interpret Kant as saying that talk of an object's existence is meaningful in so far as it can be analysed in terms of certain counterfactual sensory states. Thus talk of moon-dwellers is meaningful, understood as equivalent to statements of the form: if we were to travel to the moon, we would have experiences of the moon-dweller-perceiving kind. Talk of magnetic matter is meaningful, understood as equivalent to statements of the form: if we were to have different sensory organs and encounter magnetic matter, we would have experiences of the magnetic-matter-perceiving kind (which would be what, I wonder?). However, this phenomenalist interpretation of Kant's attitude to unobservables is, I think, a mistake. Kant does not think that it is because we would have certain experiences that a thing counts as existing, and being a part of our world: rather, it is because the thing exists, and is already a part of our world, that we would have certain experiences of it.[13] The counterfactuals do not make the existence claim true: rather, the real existence makes the counterfactuals true.

One sign of Kant's realism about the hypothetical entities of science is his hostility towards scientific theories that cannot be interpreted in a realist manner. Newtonian atomism is such a theory, in his view. In positing particles of absolutely dense space (atoms) floating in absolutely empty space, the theory has two posits that are in principle unobservable ('neither . . . can be discovered and determined by any experiment'); and in having these posits, the theory gives

far too much freedom to the imagination to supply by fiction the lack of knowledge of nature. Absolute emptiness and absolute density are in the doctrine of nature . . . a barrier for the investigating reason, with the result that either fiction occupies the place of reason or else reason is lulled to sleep on the pillow of occult qualities.[14]

If Kant were an instrumentalist about science—if he were interested in a theory that was simply a useful predictive device—then he would not express objections of this kind to atomism. Why not, especially if one is idealist already, simply 'supply by fiction' an account of atoms which will render predictable the course of phenomenal representations? That would be a typical phenomenalist response to the theoretical entities of science. If to be is to be perceivable, then the imperceptible cannot be. If phenomenalism is true, then there is no room for existential commitment to the unobservables of science. Their role must be restricted to that of a useful predictive device—as Berkeley himself supposed, saying that '*force, gravity, attraction* and terms of this sort are useful for reasonings and reckonings about motion . . . but not for understanding the simple nature of motion itself'.[15] Kant's realism about unobservable entities does not sit well with a phenomenalist interpretation of his philosophy, since it assumes the (phenomenal) reality of things whose reality is not directly exhibited in perception, and hence the (phenomenal) reality of things which cannot—on a phenomenalist understanding—be phenomena.

---

[13] A phenomenalist interpretation of this kind is offered by Bennett, but I agree with those commentators who view Kant as an empirical realist about science: for example Gerd Buchdahl, *Metaphysics and the Philosophy of Science* (Oxford: Blackwell, 1969); Brittan, *Kant's Theory of Science*; and Allison, *Kant's Transcendental Idealism*. Kant's realism about unobservables will be discussed also in Chapter 9, where I suggest an additional reason for it, relating to Kant's conclusions about community in the Third Analogy.

[14] *Metaphysical Foundations*, Ak. iv. 533, 532, Ellington 92, 90. Kant's hostility to instrumentalism is well discussed in Brittan's chapter on 'The Anti-Reductive Kant', in *Kant's Theory of Science*.

[15] George Berkeley, *De Motu* § 17, trans. A. A. Luce, in *Berkeley's Philosophical Writings*, ed. David Armstrong (London: Collier Macmillan, 1965), 250–73.

There is a second aspect to this scientific realism which is equally alien to a phenomenalist understanding of Kant, and it is one to which Margaret Wilson draws attention.[16] Kant appears to maintain a primary and secondary quality distinction within the phenomenal realm. We have already seen that his empirical realism about science leads him to ascribe to phenomenal objects certain primary qualities: properties discoverable by science, some of which are unobservable. Kant's phenomenal world is the world of the *scientific image*: it possesses qualities that are not manifest. And, equally strikingly, it lacks (many of) the qualities that are manifest. The sensible qualities of colours and tastes are not to be ascribed to objects, even taking objects to be appearances.

Colours, taste . . . cannot rightly be regarded as properties of things, but only as alterations in the subject, which may, indeed, be different for different people. (A29/B45)

The taste of a wine does not belong to the wine's objective properties, not even if by the wine as an object we mean the wine as appearance, but to the special constitution of sense in the subject that tastes it. Colours are not properties of the bodies to whose intuition they are attached, but only modifications of the sense of sight, which is affected in a certain manner by light . . . Taste and colours . . . are connected with the appearances only as effects accidentally added by the particular constitution of the sense organs. (A28)

Kant believes that there are aspects of the physical world that are causally responsible for subjective sensations of colour, aspects that some later philosophers called the objective correlates of subjective sensations; and he believes it is those objective correlates, discoverable by physics, that really exist in the phenomenal world, and not the colours, which are mere 'modifications of the sense of sight'. Consider Kant's remark about the objective physical basis for colour: 'Newton's *lamellae*, of which the colored particles of bodies consist, have not yet been seen through a microscope. Nevertheless, the understanding . . . recognizes (or supposes) their existence.'[17] According to Kant, Newton's invisible *lamellae* are objects of experience, while colours are not.

There is a great contrast between Kant and Berkeley in this respect, as Wilson has emphasized. Kant's attitude to the phenomenal realm embodies exactly the kind of scientific rationalism that was abhorrent to Berkeley, with its hostility to the commonsense world of tart red cherries, purple skies, fragrant blooms, and wild sweet bird song.[18] Wilson concludes that Kant's

---

[16] Wilson, 'The "Phenomenalisms" of Berkeley and Kant'.
[17] *On a Discovery*, Ak. viii. 205; Allison 122.
[18] Wilson, 'The "Phenomenalisms" of Berkeley and Kant', 162.

notion of experience is recondite at best, and we can see that she is quite right. We have good reasons for thinking Kant cared for the scientific, not for the manifest, image. We therefore have good reasons for thinking that the phenomenalist interpretation of Kant is a failure.

If the phenomenalist interpretation in general is a failure, then so too is its particular application to the passage from the *Prolegomena*. Kant says that he turns the primary qualities into secondary qualities. Suppose the secondary qualities are the manifest qualities. Then Kant turns the primary qualities into the manifest qualities. But he does not—as shown by his scientific realism. The properties ascribed to phenomenal objects are very often *not* manifest at all; and the properties that *are* manifest, such as colour and taste, are not to be ascribed to phenomenal objects.

We have yet to find an explanation for Kant's comparison in the *Prolegomena*. What is worse is that we are now left with an apparent contradiction. According to Kant's scientific realism, phenomenal objects do not have colours and tastes. They have only the properties ascribed to them by science. In other words, *the properties of phenomenal objects are exclusively primary*. However, if Kant turns the primary qualities into secondary qualities, then *the properties of phenomenal objects are exclusively secondary*. We need to find some way of interpreting the Lockean distinction so that Kant is consistent. It would be good to find some respect in which it is true to assert each of these apparently contradictory claims.

3. *A Different Lockean Distinction*

On the first quick look at Locke's distinction, we interpreted the primary/secondary quality distinction as a distinction between the scientific and the manifest image. And we interpreted that distinction in a rather crude way, according to which the secondary 'manifest' qualities are mere sensory ideas in us, while the primary qualities are qualities independent of our sensory ideas. This, in terms of the discussion of Chapter 2, is Bennett's distinction (a), a distinction between sensory states and things independent of sensory states. And we have seen that we need to find an alternative. The alternative should, ideally, meet the following three desiderata. First, it must have good claim to the title of a Lockean primary/secondary quality distinction; second, it should enable us to resolve the apparent contradiction just noted; and third, it should enable us to see how the Kant who endorses the Distinction between phenomena and things in themselves fits in with the Kant who compares himself to Locke.

What has good claim, then, to the title of the primary/secondary quality distinction? There is little doubt that one of Locke's chief motives in

Book II, chapter 8 of his *Essay* is to drive a wedge between properties that are in some way perceiver-dependent, and properties that are not—properties to which human beings contribute in an idiosyncratic way, and properties to which we do not. He wants to distinguish manifest, subjective secondary qualities, from the primary qualities required by Boylean science. But that is not, I think, the only purpose he has in mind. He certainly says that primary qualities are qualities that are in bodies 'whether we perceive them or no'; but he also goes on to say that they are qualities that give us 'an *Idea* of the thing, *as it is in itself*'.[19] This may be viewed as just another way of saying the same thing; or it may suggest a quite different purpose.

What has been missing in the discussion so far is that distinctively Lockean notion of a *power*. A better interpretation of Locke will refuse to go Berkeley's way, refuse to identify secondary qualities with the 'ideas in us' and, with better textual basis, will identify them with the '*Powers* to produce various sensations in us . . . as Colours, Sounds, Tasts'.[20] Powers are typically contrasted with the '*real Original*, or *Primary Qualities*' of objects.[21] The class of powers is not identical with the class of secondary qualities, as they are traditionally conceived, for there are, in addition, qualities of 'a third sort', which we can call, in line with common practice, the tertiary qualities. (Sometimes Locke uses the 'secondary quality' label to cover both of these kinds of qualities.) The sun has a power to produce perceptions in me of light and warmth, a power which is to be counted among its secondary qualities. The sun has a power to produce changes in other things as well, a power to melt wax, and to blanch it, and those powers are to be counted among its tertiary qualities. They are 'equally Powers in the Sun . . . in the one case, so to alter the Bulk, Figure, Texture, or Motion of some of the insensible parts of my Eyes, or Hands, as thereby to produce in me the *Idea*

---

[19] Locke, *Essay*, II. viii. § 23, p. 140, second italics added.

[20] II. viii. § 10, p. 135, my italics. Peter Alexander has argued that names of colours are not names of secondary qualities, according to Locke: secondary qualities are the powers that correspond to (ideas of) colours, smells, tastes, etc; see 'The Names of Secondary Qualities', *Proceedings of the Aristotelian Society* 77 (1976–7), 203–20. I think that his arguments have some plausibility, but, as should be clear from what I have said already, I doubt there is one unique way of charting Locke's distinction. It seems to me that Locke is doing very many things at once, not all of which fit neatly together: he wants to distinguish sensations from properties of objects; perceiver-relative from perceiver-independent properties of objects; unscientific from scientific properties of objects; properties of macroscopic objects from properties of corpuscles; relational powers from intrinsic properties; nominal from real essences. It seems to me that all of these distinctions have something to do with Locke's somewhat fluid distinction between primary and secondary qualities, and I do not here take time to disentangle them all. All I need, for my purpose, is that the interpretation I shall offer maps one of the distinctions Locke has in mind in dividing primary qualities from secondary.

[21] II. viii. § 23, p. 141.

of Light or Heat; and in the other, so to alter the Bulk, Figure, Texture, or Motion of the insensible Parts of the Wax, as to make them fit to produce in me the distinct *Ideas* of White and Fluid'.[22]

In separating 'powers' from other qualities, Locke is drawing a different distinction to the one we imagined on our first interpretation. To begin with, the secondary qualities are not ideas in us at all, but are to be located somehow 'in the object' as powers in the object to affect our perceptual organs in a certain way. This is sufficient to show that Berkeley's simple reading of Locke is a mistake. But there is more. The secondary qualities are grouped with a class of qualities that apparently has nothing to do with perceivers at all. The secondary qualities are, strictly, a proper subset of the powers, and the distinction between powers and primary qualities, whatever it might be, is not a distinction between qualities that are perceiver-dependent, subjective, and qualities that are not. Powers, like primary qualities, are in an object 'whether we perceive them or no'; yet, Locke thinks, they are not in the object 'as it is in itself'. This means there is a sense in which a property can fail to be in a thing 'as it is in itself' for reasons other than its perceiver-dependence.

One might be tempted to think otherwise, and think that Berkeley is not too far off the mark. One might be tempted to think that although powers are not mere 'ideas in us', it may turn out that powers are to be understood only in terms of their effects on human perceivers, in which case it might be fair to say there is something subjective about them. Is this what Locke believes? The answer seems to be yes, for the secondary qualities: they are 'nothing in the Objects themselves, but Powers to produce various Sensations in us'. And it might look as though the answer is sometimes yes, for the tertiary qualities as well. The powers of the sun are defined in terms of their effects on the wax, *and* their effects on the perceiver: the sun has the power to alter the parts of the wax so as to 'make them fit to produce in me the distinct *Ideas* of White and Fluid'. This might lead us to think that the tertiary qualities, like the secondary qualities, are alike powers in things *to produce ideas in us*, indirectly, in the case of the former, and directly, in the case of the latter. Locke admittedly encourages such a reading in his tentative classification at the end of chapter 8. He is inclined to label them as 'Secondary Qualities, mediately perceivable', and 'Secondary Qualities, immediately perceivable', respectively. If we pursued this reading, we would interpret the distinction between powers and primary qualities in a modified veil of appearance way: powers (secondary or tertiary) would, unlike primary qualities, be understood only in terms of their connection (immediate or mediate) to human sensory experience.

[22] Ibid.

This, I think, would be a mistake, and we should not infer from such passages that powers are conceptually tied to the (mediated) sensory effects they produce in perceivers. Locke conceives of powers in much more general terms. Powers are relational properties, but they are not subjective properties. They have—let us be vague for a moment—something to do with the ways in which a thing relates to other things, whether human or otherwise. The distinction between powers and primary qualities has nothing to do with the veil of appearance. Powers often do not, and sometimes cannot, produce effects on perceivers. To be sure, 'Powers, *as far as we have any Notice . . . of them*, terminate only in sensible simple Ideas . . . [and] we should have no Notion of any Power [a Load-stone] had at all to operate on Iron, did not its sensible Motion discover it'.[23] But that is a fact about our knowledge of powers, not a fact about the powers themselves. There are many powers whose effects remain inevitably unnoticed, 'a thousand Changes, that Bodies we daily handle, have a Power to cause in one another, which we never suspect'.[24] The tertiary qualities have no subjective aspect. They are as independent of perceivers as are the primary. Whether or not human beings are ever around, the sun will continue to melt the wax, and have the power to do so; the loadstone will continue to attract its ferrous neighbours, and have the power to do so. Not only are the powers as perceiver-independent as the primary qualities: they are also, potentially, of just as much interest to science, as Locke's examples of magnetic power, impenetrability, solubility, and so forth are enough to illustrate. If this is right, then Locke has a distinction which has some claim to the title of the primary/secondary quality distinction, that nevertheless has nothing to do with the veil of appearance distinction with which we began. It is a distinction between powers and primary qualities—and thus, at base, a metaphysical distinction.

Powers are viewed by Locke, and others, as relational properties. Locke describes powers in just these terms in his chapter on our ideas of substances. The properties we commonly ascribe to gold, the properties that constitute what he calls its 'nominal essence', are 'Yellowness, great Weight, Ductility, Fusibility, and Solubility, in *Aqua Regia*'. But these, he says, are 'nothing else, but so many relations to other Substances'.[25] Secondary and tertiary qualities alike are, he says, 'nothing . . . but so many relations'. Secondary and tertiary qualities are powers, and the notion of a power, as Locke says elsewhere, 'includes in it some kind of relation'.[26] What entitles us to ascribe to gold such properties as 'yellow' and 'soluble' is the fact that gold bears certain relations to other substances. Gold's being yellow is constituted by the fact that gold bears a certain relation to human perceivers: it

---

[23] II. xxiii. § 9, p. 300–1, my italics.   [24] II. xxiii. § 9, p. 301.
[25] II. xxiii. § 37, p. 317, my italics.   [26] II. xxi . § 3, p. 234.

produces, in the right circumstances, ideas of yellow in us. Gold's being soluble is constituted by the fact that gold bears a certain relation to aqua regia:
gold will, again in the right circumstances, dissolve in aqua regia. Yellow,
soluble, and so forth are, if not literally 'relations' as Locke says, at any rate
relational properties. In his chapter devoted to the topic of 'Relation' Locke
tells us that when we ascribe relational properties to a thing, we 'imply also
something else separate, and exterior to the existence of that thing'.[27] On
this understanding, the basic idea of a secondary quality, broadly construed,
is the idea of a power, a dispositional relational property.

In what sense are powers relational? Certainly the concept of a secondary
or tertiary quality power is a relational concept: something has such a power
if and only if it relates—or would relate—to other things in certain ways.
But, as we have seen, this relationality at the level of concepts is not synonymous with relationality at the level of properties. When Locke speaks of
powers being 'nothing . . . but so many relations', is he wanting to say that
the concept of a power is relational, or that a power is a relational property?
It depends how we understand the idea that, in ascribing a power to a thing,
we 'imply also something else separate, and exterior to the existence of that
thing'. Do we imply a conceptual connection with certain counterfactual
relations to other things? If so, the *concept* of a power is relational—but a
power may or may not be a relational property, depending on our understanding of intrinsicness, as we saw in Chapter 5. Do we imply relations to
other actually coexistent things? If so, a power will be a relational property
on one conception of intrinsicness. Or do we imply a different sort of 'something else separate, and exterior'—a 'something else' that is not a separately
coexisting *object*, but rather *laws* of nature governing the behaviour of the
thing, laws not fixed by the intrinsic properties of a thing? If so, a power will
be a relational property, on a slightly different conception of intrinsicness.

Perhaps Locke is not interested in a distinction between relationality at
the level of concepts, and relationality, or extrinsicness, at the level of properties. Perhaps he equates them. (Perhaps, too, he is not alert to different
conceptions of relationality at the level of properties.) For the moment we
can leave aside these caveats, since I shall be wanting to suggest that Locke
himself seems to think both that the concept of a power is relational, *and*
that a power is a relational property. Whether this is because he equates the
relationality at the level of concepts with relationality at the level of properties, or whether it is for a different reason, is a question we can return to
in a moment.

The most general conception of a secondary quality, I have suggested, is

---

[27] II. xxv. § 10, p. 323.

that of a power. Of course Locke typically uses the 'secondary quality' label more narrowly, for the powers to produce, for example, sensations of colour in us—and that usage ought to be respected. But the difference between the tertiary qualities and the secondary qualities, narrowly construed, is insignificant at the level of metaphysics. The sun has powers to produce one kind of effect on some items (it melts them), and another kind of effect on other items (it produces ideas of yellow in them). Gold has powers to produce one kind of effect on some items (aqua regia) and another on other items (people). From the perspective of metaphysics, there is little reason to distinguish these. 'Yellow' and 'soluble' are both relational properties. So where do we locate the difference between the two, the difference that motivates a further distinction between secondary and tertiary qualities?[28] It emerges when we take an interest in epistemology. It lies in the fact that 'yellow' and 'soluble' imply relations that have importantly different terms, and the difference is of special interest to human beings. 'Yellow' implies a certain relation to a human perceiver. 'Soluble' implies (in this case) a certain relation to aqua regia. Secondary qualities imply a relation that must take as its second term a human being or beings. Tertiary qualities imply a relation that need not.

Primary qualities, by contrast, are intrinsic properties. This becomes clear when we look in a little more detail at the passage quoted above.

[M]ost of the simple *Ideas*, that make up our complex *Ideas* of Substances, when truly considered, are only Powers, however we are apt to take them for positive Qualities; *v.g.* the greatest part of the *Ideas*, that make our complex *Idea* of *Gold*, are Yellowness, great Weight, Ductility, Fusibility, and Solubility, in *Aqua Regia*, etc. . . . all which *Ideas*, are nothing else, but so many relations to other Substances; and are not really in the Gold, considered barely in it self, though they depend on those real and primary Qualities of its internal constitution, whereby it has a fitness, differently to operate, and be operated on by several other Substances.[29]

What emerges here is a contrast between the powers, qualities that are 'nothing else, but . . . relations to other Substances' and qualities that are in a thing, 'considered barely in it self', 'that particular constitution, which every Thing has within it self, without any relation to any thing without it': a contrast between relational properties and intrinsic properties.[30]

---

[28] One difference that should not distract us is that 'yellow' is monadic in form, where 'soluble in aqua regia' is not. As noted in the discussion of Leibniz (Chapter 4, note 39), and as Locke himself acknowledges by describing *yellow* as a 'relation', the monadic form of a predicate is no proof that the property is not relational.

[29] II. xxiii. § 37, p. 317.

[30] III. vi. § 6, p. 442. There is a prima facie problem. Given that the distinction is cast as a contrast between gold's 'real essence' (its essential properties?) and its 'nominal essence'

We can see how the veil of appearance theme and the intrinsic/relational theme in Locke's views about primary and secondary qualities might connect. Locke's interest in the primary qualities does not simply lie in the fact that they exist independently of human perceivers. After all, the tertiary qualities are as independent of perceivers as are the primary (a fact often neglected in the literature on primary and secondary qualities). However, the primary qualities, unlike the powers as Locke conceives of them, are intrinsic properties. This means that they are indeed the kind of properties a thing can have whether or not there are people around. But, more importantly, they are the kind of properties a thing can have *whether or not there is anything else around*. Their independence from perceivers in particular is just a consequence of their independence from other things generally. Locke's interest in the primary qualities is not, first and foremost, that they are perceiver-independent, but that they constitute metaphysical bedrock.

Locke says that powers are '*nothing else, but* so many relations to other Substances' (emphasis added). The 'nothing . . . but' suggests that powers are supposed to be second rate, metaphysically speaking. Sometimes Locke uses such phrases to signal the subjective character of a property: sweetness and whiteness, pain and sickness, are 'nothing, but the effects' of manna on our bodily organs.[31] But that cannot be the reason here, since there is

---

(its accidental properties?), it may be thought that my characterization needs some more defence, since the intrinsic/relational distinction is not the same as the essential/accidental distinction. I don't want to analyse here the precise connection Locke saw between these two distinctions. For my purposes it is sufficient that Locke's characterization of a thing's 'real essence' is unambiguously a characterization of its intrinsic properties. A thing's 'real essence', according to Locke, consists of those properties it has in itself, independently of other things: that is surely the notion of its intrinsic properties. And, in addition, Locke gives us a thought experiment to help us get a grasp on the notion. We have a deplorable tendency, he says, to imagine that the properties we commonly ascribe to things are the intrinsic properties of the things: 'we are wont to consider the Substances we meet with, each of them, as an entire thing by it self, having all its Qualities in it self, and independent of other Things'(IV. vi. § 11, p. 585). We need a remedy for this tendency, and Locke tries to supply one. If we want to know what a thing's real essence is, we should imagine what the thing would be like in the absence of other things: 'Put a piece of Gold . . . by itself'. Locke asks us to imagine the properties a thing would have by itself: the properties it would have if it were lonely, in the Kim/Lewis sense. This is the thought experiment used to decide what the intrinsic properties of a thing are (on one conception of intrinsicness) and if Locke uses it to try to decide what the 'real essence' of a thing is, then his conception of a real essence can reasonably be interpreted as, at least in part, a conception of its intrinsic properties.

[31] II. viii. § 18, p. 138. In this passage we have sweetness and whiteness identified with effects on us, rather than powers in the objects. Such passages, taken in conjunction with Locke's description of secondary qualities as powers, have motivated the interpretation that colours and tastes are not secondary qualities, as argued by Alexander, 'The Names of Secondary Qualities'.

nothing subjective about the notion of a power as such. If powers are second rate, it must be for some other reason. It is possible that Locke thinks that a property's being relational somehow makes it less than fully real. This is a view Bennett attributes to Locke,[32] citing in its support a remark Locke makes in his chapter devoted to the topic of relation, where he says that relation is 'not contained in the real existence of things, but something extraneous and superinduced'.[33] Guyer attributed a Leibnizian opinion to Kant: Bennett does likewise with Locke. Bennett speculates that Locke may here be expressing a Leibnizian view, according to which relations are not to be included on our list of things that have 'real existence', and that they are therefore not real. If Bennett is right, then that would certainly explain why Locke says of the powers that they are 'nothing . . . but so many Relations'. It would explain Locke's implication that there is something second rate about them. Bennett does not himself apply his interpretation of Locke's remark to the secondary and tertiary qualities, but the implications are easy to see. If the secondary and tertiary qualities are, as Locke says, nothing but so many relations, and relations are not to be counted among things that have 'real existence', then the secondary and tertiary qualities themselves would not be counted among the things that have 'real existence' either. There we would have an argument for the unreality of secondary and tertiary qualities which has nothing whatsoever to do with their being mere sensory states, mere ideas in us. We would have an argument for the unreality of secondary and tertiary qualities which had nothing to do with facts about epistemology, or with facts about human beings and our perceptual idiosyncrasies. Such an argument for the unreality of secondary and tertiary qualities would have its source in metaphysics alone. It would be exactly analogous to the metaphysical argument mistakenly attributed by Guyer to Kant (discussed in Chapter 6). It seems to me that Bennett's speculation accordingly deserves more attention than he himself has given it.

Here I shall simply state a conclusion for which I argue elsewhere.[34] Locke does not hold a Leibnizian view according to which relations and relational properties are unreal, but rather, like Kant, he believes that they are irreducible to intrinsic properties. Applying this to the case of the powers, Locke believes that powers do not supervene on the primary qualities of a

---

[32] Bennett, *Locke, Berkeley, Hume*, 254.

[33] II. xxv. § 8, p. 322.

[34] In 'Locke's Mechanism: Relations and God's Good Pleasure', in progress. An early version has appeared under this title in Knud Haakonssen and Udo Thiel, eds., *Reason, Will and Nature: Voluntarism in Metaphysics and Morals from Ockham to Kant*, Australasian Society for the History of Philosophy Yearbook 1 (1993), 66–88; and as Appendix 1 to 'Kantian Humility', Ph.D. Dissertation, Princeton University, 1995.

thing, but rather have their source in a superadding creative act of God.[35] To ascribe to Locke the doctrine of superadded forces is to ascribe to him the view that God could have made the world exactly as it is with respect to the primary qualities of things, and yet have endowed those things with powers different from the powers they actually have—or perhaps to have endowed them with no powers at all. Translating the same modal point into contemporary terminology, there are possible worlds where things have the same intrinsic properties they actually have, yet possess different powers— or no powers at all. If an intrinsic property is—in accordance with the amended definition raised in Chapter 5—a property compatible with loneliness and *lawlessness*, then powers turn out to be relational properties. That is why I suggested earlier that Locke believes both that the concept of a power is relational, and that a power is a relational, i.e. extrinsic, property. There is, then, an alternative explanation to Bennett's for Locke's use of phrases like 'nothing . . . but'. The explanation is that relational properties are not reducible to intrinsic properties—and if intrinsic properties are the most fundamental properties, then relational properties are not the most fundamental.

We have extracted from Locke a distinction that has good claim to the title of the primary/secondary quality distinction, but which none the less has nothing to do with a contrast between sensory states and things independent of them. It is a distinction between intrinsic and relational properties, a distinction carved at the level of metaphysics rather than epistemology. With this new distinction in mind, we can now return to the passage from the *Prolegomena* with which we started.

4. *A Contradiction Dissolved*

The problem, recall, was this. Kant's comparison between his own and Locke's philosophy appears to yield the conclusion that the qualities of phenomenal objects are exclusively secondary. Kant's scientific realism appears to yield the conclusion that the qualities of phenomenal objects are

---

[35] As Margaret Wilson has persuasively argued, in 'Superadded Properties: The Limits of Mechanism in Locke', *American Philosophical Quarterly* 16 (1979), 143–50. See also Michael Ayers, 'Mechanism, Superaddition, and the Proof of God's Existence in Locke's Essay', *Philosophical Review* 90 (1981), 210–51, and Wilson's reply, 'Superadded Properties: A Reply to Michael Ayers', *Philosophical Review* 91 (1982), 247–52; Michael Ayers, *Locke*, vol. ii, *Ontology* (London: Routledge, 1991), ch. 12; Wilson's review of Ayers's *Locke*, in *Philosophical Review* 102 (1993), 577–84.

exclusively primary. Kant thus appears to be saying that the qualities of phenomenal objects are exclusively primary and exclusively secondary.

We now have two interpretations of Locke's distinction on the table before us, and careful use will resolve the apparent contradiction. The first distinction to be found in Locke is (1) the distinction between the manifest and the scientific: secondary qualities are the manifest qualities, while primary qualities are those attributed to bodies by science. The second distinction to be found in Locke bears a close resemblance to the Distinction I have attributed to Kant, namely (2) the distinction between the relational and the intrinsic: secondary qualities are relational properties (in particular, powers), and primary qualities are intrinsic properties. I take the first distinction to be a veil of appearance distinction, while the second is, at least on the face of it, simply metaphysical. Now to address the contradiction.

According to Kant's scientific realism, the properties of phenomenal objects are exclusively *primary*. This makes perfect sense if we keep the first primary/secondary quality distinction in mind. He means they have exclusively properties attributable to them by *science*. Phenomenal objects have spatial properties, and most importantly, dynamical properties. They have all sorts of properties that we cannot see, and that science can discover. But the manifest image does not apply to the phenomenal world: objects do not have colours and tastes. Hence there is a sense in which all the properties of phenomenal objects are primary.

According to Kant's *Prolegomena* comparison of his philosophy with that of Locke, the properties of phenomenal objects are exclusively *secondary*. This makes perfect sense if we keep the second distinction in mind. He means that they are all *relational*. The properties of objects we had hitherto considered primary—that is to say, properties of objects that we had hitherto regarded as intrinsic properties—are on an equal footing with the secondary: they are relational. Hence there is a sense in which all the properties of phenomenal objects are secondary. Moreover, when Kant says, in the *Prolegomena*, 'Of what things may be in themselves we know nothing', he is expressing Humility: we know nothing of the intrinsic properties of things.

We have, it seems, a resolution of the contradiction. The qualities of phenomenal objects are exclusively secondary, in the Lockean sense that they are all relational properties. And they are exclusively primary, in the different Lockean sense that they are all properties ascribable to bodies by science. Putting the two together: the properties of phenomenal objects are those relational properties ascribed to bodies by science. Viewed from the standpoint of Locke's own distinctions, this comes close to saying that the properties of phenomenal objects are the *tertiary qualities*, in so far as they are relational, but not merely sensory. The implications of this will be the focus of Chapter 8.

We have, it seems, found a way to make the Berkeleian move intelligible without succumbing to the Berkeleian position. The comparison with Locke that I just described is, in the end, nothing like Berkeley at all. If Kant intends something like this by the analogy, then his indignant rhetoric is justified. 'Can this be called idealism? It is the very opposite of it.' Forces are real, and known, but they are not things 'as they are in themselves'. They are real properties, but they are not intrinsic properties. Hence we know something real: our representations of the physical world correspond to the dynamical appearances of substances, and the dynamical appearances are thus known. Moreover, as (relational) properties of substances, forces signify the existence of something that is even more real than themselves. As relational properties they require the existence of relata, substances that have some intrinsic nature.

Concepts of relation presuppose things which are absolutely [i.e. independently] given, and without these are impossible. (A284/B340)

Substances in general must have some intrinsic nature, which is therefore free from all external relations. (A274/B330)

Matter, constituted by forces, requires something that has 'some intrinsic nature' as its substratum. We can know that such a something exists, but we cannot know what it is in itself.

I have sketched, in broad strokes, what I take to be the best way to understand the passage from the *Prolegomena*, and I have shown how the interpretation I offer avoids the Berkeleianism that looked at first inevitable. The alternative understanding of Locke's primary/secondary quality distinction satisfies the three desiderata I raised at that outset: it has a good claim to the title of Locke's primary/secondary quality distinction; it resolves the contradiction posed by the conjunction of Kant's scientific realism with his argument of the *Prolegomena*; and it shows how the Kant who endorses the Distinction between phenomena and things in themselves is quite right to compare himself to Locke. That this application of Kant's Distinction helps to resolve the contradiction we have just considered constitutes an independent piece of support for attributing it to him. Far from undermining the present interpretation, as it seemed at first, the *Prolegomena* argument supports it.

The above sketch was rather swift; and lest the reader imagine that I have lost sight of my text, I propose, in what follows, to fill in some of the finer detail.

5. *A Closer Look*

Here is the first part of the *Prolegomena* passage, this time drawing attention to a hitherto unnoted difficulty, namely Kant's remarkable usage of anaphoric devices, which, for ease of reference, I have numbered:

Things are given to us as objects of our senses situated outside us, but of what they (1) may be in themselves we know nothing; we only know their (2) appearances, i.e. (3) the representations that they (4) effect in us when they (5) affect our senses. Consequently I do indeed admit that there are bodies outside us, i.e. (6) things which, although wholly unknown to us as to what they (7) may be in themselves, we know through the representations which their (8) influence on our sensibility provides for us, and to which (9) we give the name of bodies. This word therefore merely means (10) the appearance of that for us unknown but none the less real object. Can this be called idealism? It is the very opposite of it.

If we follow the chain of Kant's anaphoric devices ('they', 'their', 'which', 'i.e.'), numbered in the text above, we find the following noteworthy assumptions of identity.

(1) Objects of our senses = things that are unknown to us as to what they are in themselves

(2) objects of our senses = appearances of things that are unknown to us as to what they are in themselves

(3), (4), (5) appearances = representations in us produced by things that are unknown to us as to what they are in themselves

(6), (7) bodies outside us = things that are unknown to us as to what they are in themselves

(7), (8) things that are unknown to us as to what they are in themselves = things that are known to us through representations they produce in us

(6), (8) bodies outside us = things that are known to us through the representations they produce in us

(6), (9) bodies outside us = things to which we give the name 'bodies'

(7), (9) things that are unknown to us as to what they are in themselves = things to which we give the name 'bodies'

(8), (9) things that are known to us through the representations they produce in us = things to which we give the name 'bodies'

(10) 'bodies' = the appearance of a real object = the appearance of an object unknown to us as to what it is in itself.

Bodies are identified with things that are unknown to us as to what they are in themselves. Bodies are identified with appearances. Bodies are also identified with representations. This, at first sight, seems to exhibit the very worst of the property/sensation conflation of which Bennett complained, and which we considered in Chapter 2. The series of equivalences here is especially remarkable when one considers that this is an argument whose purported aim is to persuade the reader that Kant is not an idealist. Something here has to give. In the light of the inadequacy of the phenomenalist interpretation of Kant, I suggest a revision of the equivalences suggested in (3), (4), (5) that make appearances identical with representations. Later in the same passage Kant says that bodies are known *through* representations, and that is how we could charitably understand these early references to representations as well. Otherwise we are left with the following incoherent equivalence: bodies, i.e. representations, are identical with bodies, i.e. things that are unknown to us as to what they are in themselves, and by transitivity of identity, representations are identical with things that are unknown to us as to what they are in themselves (3, 4, 5, and 10). Something, I say, has to give, and on this revision, we would be able to make good sense of the passage—in a way that interprets it as presenting the same picture as that of the Amphiboly discussion of *substantia phaenomenon*:

its intrinsic properties are nothing but relations, and it itself is entirely made up of mere relations. We are acquainted with substance in space only through forces which are active in this and that space, either drawing other objects (attraction) or preventing their penetration (repulsion and impenetrability). We are not acquainted with any other properties constituting the concept of the substance which appears in space and which we call matter. As object of pure understanding, on the other hand, every substance must have intrinsic properties and powers which concern its inner reality. (A 265/B321)

With this in mind, let us consider the *Prolegomena* passage again. Things are given to us as objects of our senses. We know nothing of what those things may be in themselves. We know the appearances of those things *through* the representations they produce in us by affecting our senses. (Compare: 'We are acquainted with substance in space only through forces.') Those things are bodies outside us. What those things may be in themselves is wholly unknown to us. (Compare: 'We are not acquainted with any other properties of substance' even though 'every substance must have intrinsic properties and powers which pertain to its inner reality.') We know those things through the representations which their influence on our sensibility provides for us. We give those things the name of bodies. 'Bodies' means the appearance of that real object, which is unknown to us as to what it is in itself. We do know things, but we do not know the intrinsic properties of those things. In short, we have here Kant's Distinction, and an expression of Humility.

The next paragraph contains the explicit comparison with Locke.

That it can be said of many of the predicates of outer things, without detriment to their real existence, that they belong not to these things in themselves but only to their appearances and have no existence of their own . . ., is something that was generally accepted and admitted long before LOCKE'S time, but more so afterwards. To these predicates belong heat, colour, taste, etc. But that I for weighty reasons also count as mere appearances, in addition to these, the remaining qualities of bodies which are called *primariae*, extension, place, and space in general with all that depends on it (impenetrability or materiality, shape, etc.) is something against which not the slightest ground of inadmissibility can be adduced. A man who will not allow colours to be attached to the object in itself as qualities . . . cannot be called an idealist for that; equally little can my doctrine be called idealistic merely because I find that more of, indeed all, the qualities that make up the intuition of a body belong merely to its appearance; for the existence of the thing that appears is not thereby cancelled, as with real idealism, but it is only shown that we cannot know it at all through the senses as it is in itself.[36]

Locke said that certain qualities that we commonly attribute to things do not really belong to the things as they are 'in themselves'—i.e. they are not intrinsic properties of the things. Kant goes further and says that this is true of all properties we are in a position to attribute to things. (Compare: 'the intrinsic properties [of phenomenal substance] are nothing but relations, and it itself is entirely made up of mere relations'.) For example, impenetrability is a property which, as solidity, is usually taken to be an intrinsic property of things: but, as Locke himself would acknowledge,[37] impenetrability is in fact a power, a capacity of repelling other things, a force. (Compare: '[Matter] itself is entirely made up of mere relations . . . forces which are active in this and that space, either drawing other objects (attraction) or preventing their penetration (repulsion and impenetrability).') Matter is constituted by forces, mere relational properties, mere secondary qualities—in one of Locke's senses of 'secondary quality'.

It would be good if the task were as easy as this, but the observant reader will have noted the ominous ellipses, to which we must now in all honesty draw attention. The first set of ellipses is where Kant says that secondary qualities 'have no existence of their own *outside our representations*'; the second set is where Kant compares himself to a man who 'will not allow colours to be attached to the object in itself as qualities *but only to the sense of sight as modifications*'. These are just the kinds of phrases that motivated the disastrous phenomenalist interpretation in the first place, and here again I say

---

[36] *Prolegomena*, Ak. iv. 289, Lucas 45.

[37] Impenetrability, in terms of Locke's distinctions, is a tertiary quality, unlike hardness (secondary) and solidity (primary). The concept of solidity 'carries something more of positive in it' than the concept of impenetrability (II. iv. § 1, p. 123), by which he means that the concept of solidity is the concept of an intrinsic property. For a similar usage of 'positive' see II. xxv. § 6, p. 321. This will be discussed in more detail in Chapter 8.

that something has to give. We have many good reasons for not taking at face value Kant's phenomenalist-sounding talk, and I postpone until the final chapter the task of explaining it.

Before we leave Kant's comparison of his own philosophy with that of Locke, it is worth bringing out one further point of similarity between them. Kant often paints a picture of the endless but ultimately futile human endeavour to discover the intrinsic properties of the world: for example, in the following.

Matter is *substantia phaenomenon*. I search for that which belongs to it intrinsically in all parts of the space which it occupies, and in all the actions it performs, and these of course can only be appearances to outer sense. So I have nothing that is absolutely intrinsic . . . (A277/B333)

I want to suggest that this picture is also reminiscent of Locke: not of the Locke who allegedly creates a veil of appearance, a potentially unbridgeable gulf between percepts and things, but rather of the Locke who sees a gulf between the primary qualities and the powers—a Locke whose concern is with our ignorance, possibly irremediable ignorance, of the real essences of things.

Things, however absolute and entire they seem in themselves, are but Retainers to other parts of Nature . . . Their observable Qualities, Actions, and Powers, are owing to something without them; and there is not so complete and perfect a part, that we know, of Nature, which does not owe the Being it has, and the Excellencies of it, to its Neighbours . . . the real Essences [of Substances] are unknown to us.[38]

Matter *as we know it* consists of 'nothing else, but so many relations' as Locke here seems to say, speaking of the nominal essences of things. Locke's thought is analogous to Kant's epistemic Humility—and it may have the same kind of source. Locke's analogue of Kant's Distinction is a distinction between primary qualities and powers. As an empiricist, he shares Kant's commitment to something like Receptivity. And if he believes that the powers of things must be superadded to the primary qualities by God, he believes that they fail to supervene on the primary qualities: with the result that there is a gap between primary qualities and powers, and between real and nominal essences. Locke thus has an analogue to Kant's thesis of Irreducibility. Our conclusion should be that Kant's comparison of his philosophy with Locke is well justified in the end—but not at all in the way we first supposed.

[38] IV. vi. §§ 11, 12, p. 587. There would be a major difference if Locke believed, as Ayers argues, that the real essence is the source of the other properties, that from which all others flow. Kant thinks that the powers of things do not flow from any inner nature of a substance, understood as a thing in itself. Following Margaret Wilson ('Superadded Properties'), I argue that Ayers is mistaken, in 'Locke's Mechanism'.

8

Kant's 'Primary' Qualities

1. *Introduction*

When Kant says that properties of phenomenal things are all secondary *and* all primary, I interpreted him to mean that they are, like Locke's secondary qualities, relational qualities, and like Locke's primary qualities, the properties ascribed to bodies by science. In so far as they are relational and not merely sensory, they are, I said, something like Locke's tertiary qualities.

If this is correct, then we have in this aspect of Kant's philosophy an interesting and important innovation. There are many different motivations for endorsing a distinction between primary and secondary qualities, but significant among them are the arguments that (a) we need primary qualities for science, and (b) we need primary qualities if we are to have a conception of the physical world as an objective world, distinct from the subjective series of sensations. (These two requirements may be related, but they are presumably not the same.) For Kant, however, the phenomenal world has the properties attributed to it by science, and it is an objective world. If Kant is right, then it is possible to fulfil these two requirements without primary qualities as traditionally conceived—that is to say, without intrinsic properties.

In this chapter I further explain Kant's 'primary'/secondary quality distinction, focusing on the 'primary' side of it.[1] A useful way into the discussion is Bennett's well-known defence of the primary/secondary quality distinction, which is the topic of Section 2. The failure of this argument to prove quite what Bennett thinks it proves has a lesson that bodes well for Kant's approach to the qualities. Section 3 draws a distinction among primary qualities between spatial features and space-filling features. After a brief caveat about space (Section 4) I look at Kant's 'primary' qualities, keep-

---

[1] I am grateful to Frank Jackson and Simon Blackburn for helpful comments on an earlier draft of this chapter. Blackburn finds as troubling as I do the problem described in Section 6 (or his version of it, discussed below). Some discussions of Kant's views about primary and secondary qualities are to be found in Adickes, *Kants Lehre*; Kemp Smith, *Commentary*, App. C; Brittan, *Kant's Theory of Science*; van Cleve, 'Putnam, Kant and Secondary Qualities'. The first two are mainly concerned with its connection with the supposed thesis of 'double affection'. Brittan is especially helpful on the contrast between dynamical and geometrical properties.

ing this distinction in mind. This Section (5) draws on the Anticipations of Perception and the Axioms of Intuition in the *Critique*, and on the dynamical theory to be found in the *Metaphysical Foundations*. In the latter work Kant explicitly draws a contrast between traditional primary qualities and his own by drawing a contrast between solidity and impenetrability. Locke too would have accepted such a contrast: the former is, for him, a primary quality, and the latter is not, but should rather be counted among the 'qualities of a third kind'—the tertiary qualities. Kant, however, rejects the traditional primary quality of solidity. Moreover, he gives an argument for rejecting it, an argument which we briefly considered in Chapter 6, and will attend to in more detail here. It is of special interest, first because it seems to draw heavily on the Irreducibility argument of the *New Exposition*; and second because it has, I think, considerable philosophical merit, with implications, not only for our understanding of Kant, but also for our own contemporary debates about the qualities. As I see it, the argument poses an uncomfortable problem for any philosopher who wants to believe that solidity is a traditional primary quality. Kant's distinction between solidity and impenetrability, and his argument against solidity, is the topic of Section 6.

In the last two sections of the chapter I consider the two roles that have traditionally been assigned to primary qualities, and I ask whether those roles can successfully be played by tertiary qualities. Primary qualities have traditionally been cast as the properties needed for science. That role is considered in Section 7. They have traditionally been cast as the properties needed for objective experience. That role is considered in Section 8. In both cases I argue that tertiary qualities can fill these roles very well. The conclusion is that Kant's 'primary' qualities are quite probably an improvement on the primary qualities.

2. *Bennett's Instructive Mistake*

Bennett imagines a person afflicted with 'size-blindness', and compares such a person to the more familiar victim of colour-blindness. Just as the colour-blind person sees two things as having the same colour when in fact they do not, the size-blind person sees two things as having the same size when in fact they do not. Bennett points out that one has to suppose that the size-blind person does not simply fail to perceive that a particular jug is larger than a particular cup. He fails to perceive the results of various possible size-detecting tests: fails to perceive that the cup is inside the jug, or that water poured from the jug overflows the cup, or that the excess water is thrown at his own face. A failure to detect one primary quality ramifies endlessly into all of the person's other discriminatory capacities. Not so for the colour-blind person, whose other capacities survive intact. This difference, says Bennett, has to do with the fact that a thing's primary qualities interact in countless familiar ways with the other things we encounter, but a thing's secondary qualities do not. 'A thing's being square, or having any other specific primary quality,' says Bennett, 'consists in its relating to many other kinds of things in specific ways.'[2]

Bennett wants to use this argument to defend what he calls the 'Analytic Thesis'. A statement attributing a secondary quality to a thing x is equivalent to a counterfactual conditional of this form: If x stood in relation R to a normal human, the human would have a sensory idea of such-and-such a kind. He wants to defend the view that a secondary quality is a dispositional relational property, and the relation it implies is a particular kind of relation to a human being. The Analytic Thesis applies, he says, to secondary qualities, but not to primary. The Analytic Thesis says that secondary qualities are dispositional, relational, and involve something mental. Putting these features together, a secondary quality is a *power* to produce in *something else* an *idea*. A primary quality is not. Bennett's claim here is strong: it is not simply that the primary qualities do not possess quite all three features, it is that they do not possess *any* of them: 'One notes with pleasure that of the three features credited to the secondary quality greenness, none is credited to the primary quality squareness.'[3] I think Bennett is right in supposing the standard conception of a primary quality to be of a quality that is non-dispositional, non-relational, and involving nothing mental. Primary qualities are thought to be categorical, intrinsic, and independent of the mental. But Bennett is wrong in supposing his argument offers support for such a conception.

The mistake should be plain to see. There is no doubt that Bennett has succeeded in mapping a distinction of some kind. But it is not the distinction between primary and secondary qualities. Consider again what he says. A thing's having any specific primary quality 'consists in its relating to many other kinds of things in specific ways'. Bennett says that the fact that a thing has a particular primary quality 'consists in' the fact that the thing *would relate* to many other kinds of things in specific ways. He says, in other words, that statements about a thing's primary qualities are made true by counterfactual statements about how the thing would relate to other things in certain circumstances. Primary qualities, he thus implies, are *dispositional* and *relational*. They have at least two of the three features of secondary qualities. But they are not secondary qualities: they are tertiary qualities. Bennett

---

[2] Bennett, *Locke, Berkeley, Hume*, 100.

[3] Ibid. 104. As I said in Chapter 4, Bennett considers the powers to be members of the class of ordinary relational properties, though this is not, I think, particularly relevant here.

has turned the primary qualities into powers. He has succeeded in mapping a distinction, not between primary qualities and secondary qualities, but between tertiary qualities and secondary qualities. He has mapped a distinction between dispositional properties that imply systematic relations to a wide variety of things, especially things other than human beings; and dispositional properties that imply an idiosyncratic relation to a human sensory state.

Bennett's mistake here is instructive, for it shows how tertiary qualities might perform exactly the tasks we required of the primary. We thought we needed the primary qualities if we were to distinguish the subjective secondary qualities from the others. We thought we needed the primary qualities if we were to distinguish the properties for which the Analytic Thesis is true, from those for which it is not. We thought we needed the primary qualities for the possibility of (as Strawson says) tracing a subjective path through an objective world. And (though this is not Bennett's main concern) we thought we needed the primary qualities to give a special role to the properties ascribed to the world by science. It seems as though the tertiary qualities may turn out to perform these tasks very well.

3. *Spatial Features and Space-Filling Features*

Although Bennett took the geometrical properties of shape and size as his examples of primary qualities, in describing the typical interaction patterns of differently sized containers of water, square things, and the like, he tacitly made use of a quite different primary quality, which is approximately Locke's quality of *solidity*. Any attempt to identify geometrical primary qualities with their typical interaction patterns will have to make some such assumption. Unless square things were to resist other bodies in various ways, there is nothing we could say about their interaction patterns. Unless the sides of a water jug resist the water it contains, unless the thrown water has an impact on the face of the 'size blind' person, we would have none of the interaction patterns that Bennett supposes to be constitutive of these geometrical primary qualities. These interactions presuppose matter not simply as Cartesian extension, but as something that fills space and resists other bodies. Although I said that Bennett presupposes something like solidity, what he in fact presupposes is a *power* to resist other bodies. That is to say, it is not strictly solidity that is presupposed, but, in Lockean terms, *impenetrability*.

Locke's inclusion of solidity on his list of primary qualities sets him apart from the Cartesians, who believed that a list of primary qualities need include no properties other than purely geometrical properties. In addition to being shaped and extended in space, bodies must, thinks Locke, have some property which, so to speak, provides the stuffing for space. Solidity is that property, a primary quality that 'belongs to body, whereby we conceive it to *fill space*'.[4] Locke distinguishes solidity from hardness, which he takes to be a secondary quality, a power to produce felt sensations of hardness. He also distinguishes solidity from impenetrability, a tertiary quality, a power to resist the approach of other bodies. Hardness and impenetrability are both powers, hardness being a power to produce a particular kind of sensory state in human beings, impenetrability a power to resist things in general. Hardness and impenetrability are dispositional and relational. Solidity, by contrast, is supposed to be categorical and intrinsic. Solidity is supposed to be the ground of the dispositional properties of hardness and impenetrability.

Kant would agree with Locke against the Cartesians that geometrical properties are not sufficient, that one needs in addition a property that will enable matter to fill space. This is evident from many of his arguments in the *Critique*, though it receives its fullest discussion in the *Metaphysical Foundations*. Kant disagrees, though, with Locke's opinion that some property other than a power is needed to satisfy the space-filling requirement. When Kant says, in the *Prolegomena*, that he makes the hitherto primary qualities secondary, one of the things he means is that *he substitutes powers for Locke's intrinsic properties*: and in particular, he substitutes the power of impenetrability for solidity.

4. *A Caveat about Space*

Before I begin considering Kant's views about space and what fills it, I must offer one very large caveat. Among the alleged primary qualities that Kant makes secondary are properties of two kinds: spatial geometrical properties, and space-filling dynamical properties. Kant lists in the *Prolegomena* passage extension, place, space, impenetrability, materiality, shape. I have so far considered only the properties associated with impenetrability and materiality. But if my argument is correct, then we should link this passage with passages in the Amphiboly which say that spatial properties, like forces, 'consist entirely of relations'. If my argument is correct, then we ought to be considering, not simply force, as I have done, and shall continue to do, but space.

Well, my response is that I cannot do that topic justice here. One reason

---

[4] Locke, *Essay*, II. iv. § 2, p. 123, emphasis added. Impenetrability, solidity, and hardness are discussed in II. iv. §§ 1, 2, pp. 123–4. The phrase 'space-filling feature' comes from J. L. Mackie's discussion, in *Problems from Locke* (Oxford: Oxford University Press, 1976), 24, 25.

for the focus on force rather than space has to do with the largeness of the topic of space. A further reason is that Kant's views about space, and their implications for his philosophy, have already received considerable critical attention, whereas his views about force have been comparatively neglected.[5] But the chief reason for the general focus on force, rather than space, is that I believe Kant's views about force, rather than space, provide the key to understanding why he thinks we have no knowledge of things as they are in themselves. And the chief reason for the particular focus on force in this chapter is that I believe Kant's views about force, rather than space, are what provide a distinctive and defensible doctrine of 'primary' and secondary qualities.

Kant does, I suspect, have a relational theory of space. This is something that has, in various guises, been argued for by other commentators.[6] There is no doubt that (the mature) Kant rejected the absolute theory of space advocated by Newton, and some may consider that enough to imply that he has a relational theory of space. However, many different things are involved in the idea, or ideas, of a relational theory of space: that motion is always relative motion; that space itself is always movable relative to some other space; that space has no intrinsic metric but is measurable only relative to sensible measures, rods and clocks; that properties of space superveniently depend on dynamical properties of bodies in space; that apparently intrinsic spatial properties of particular bodies are relational because they can be analysed in terms of the extrinsic spatial properties of their parts. These, it seems to me, are merely the tip of the iceberg. Many of these views are arguably believed by Kant, but whether they really are believed by him, and how they fit together, are questions too big for me, and are questions to which many others have tried to give answers.

Moreover, and most importantly, if spatial properties are relational, they are not relational in the way that dynamical properties are relational. Dynamical properties are relational, because they are powers. But spatial properties are not relational in this sense at all, and I have enough on my plate without them. There is, however, a connection between spatial and dynamical relations. Kant says, as we saw in Chapter 6, that the dynamical relations between substances are 'viewed intuitively' as spatial, and that the formal spatial relations of intuition make possible our experience of real

---

[5] By e.g. Allison in his discussion of substance, *Kant's Transcendental Idealism*; Buroker, in *Space and Incongruence*; van Cleve, 'Putnam, Kant and Secondary Qualities', who despite a minor qualificatory note (108 n. 36) sees Kant's primary qualities as basically Cartesian.

[6] See e.g. Brittan, *Kant's Theory of Science*, ch. 4; Jules Vuillemin, *Physique et métaphysique kantiennes* (Paris: Presses Universitaires de France, 1955); Buroker, *Space and Incongruence*. For a recent and sophisticated discussion of Kant's views about space see Friedman, *Kant and the Exact Sciences* (Cambridge, Mass.: Harvard University Press, 1992).

dynamical relations. The question about this connection—this isomorphism—between space and force will emerge once again in Chapter 10.

5. *Kant's 'Primary' Qualities: Geometrical and Dynamical*

In the *Critique* the contrast between spatial and space-filling properties emerges in the idea of the *real in space*. Space provides a system of formal relations, but space would be nothing to us if it were not for 'the real', that is to say matter, that occupies and fills space. The requirement of the real in space is argued for, at least implicitly, in many places, for example in the First and Third Analogies. Spatial relations provide the formal possibility of reidentifying persisting things by providing the possibility of locations different to our own, but for real reidentification of particulars there must also be substance, occupying space and persisting in space over time. Spatial relations provide the formal possibility of different objects coexisting together, but objects will only really coexist if they are involved in a real community, interacting with each other by means of forces. Kant says, at the end of the Third Analogy, that this means that empty space is not a possible object of experience, a conclusion which he also draws in the Anticipations of Perception.

The contrast between dynamical properties and geometrical properties is made most explicit, in the *Critique* at least, in the contrast between the Anticipations of Perception and the Axioms of Intuition. Kant says in the Axioms of Intuition, that 'all intuitions are extensive magnitudes' (A162/B202). In this section Kant argues that objects must have the Cartesian primary qualities: the 'mathematics of extension' must be applicable to them. 'Pure mathematics, in its complete precision, [is] applicable to objects of experience' (A165/B206).

According to the Anticipations of Perception, things have not only extensive magnitude but intensive magnitude.

In all appearances, the real that is an object of sensation has intensive magnitude, that is, a degree. (B207)

In all appearances sensation, and the *real* which corresponds to it in the object (*realitas phaenomenon*), has an intensive magnitude, that is, a degree. (A166)

Space is not empty, but full, and full to varying degrees. This is a difficult section of the *Critique*, but it is important, and the following features of 'the real', as described here, are worth bringing out.

First, 'the real' in space is not sensation, but what *corresponds* to sensation (A166).[7] It is a feature of the physical world. Second, the real is called *realitas phaenomenon*, a label Kant uses for phenomenal substance (A166). Third, the real is something 'the very concept of which includes being' (A175/B217). Fourth, the real is described in causal terms: it has 'intensive magnitude, that is, a degree of influence on the sense'(A166/B208). Fifth, the real is described in terms of its causal powers not only on ourselves, but also on *other things* in the field of appearance: 'this reality' can be 'viewed as cause, either of sensation or of some other reality in the [field of] appearance, such as change' (A168/B210). Sixth, it is what fills space (A174/B216). Seventh, and finally, Kant thinks of it as *force*, and in particular the force of impenetrability. He cautiously says of the 'real in space' that 'I may not name it here impenetrability or weight, since these are empirical concepts', but in saying that he, of course, names it (A173/B215). We have here, in the Anticipations of Perception, the Kantian doctrine that *matter is force*.

In the Anticipations of Perception Kant argues that in addition to the geometrical primary qualities of the Axioms of Intuition, there is a need for dynamical primary qualities. Matter must have causal powers, in virtue of which it fills space, produces sensations in us, and has parts that can interact with each other. Indeed there is nothing more to matter than this causal power, this *enduring action*, as Guyer suggested, and as we considered in Chapter 3. This discussion in the Anticipations is clearly linked to the remarks in the Second Analogy about the criterion of substance in experience.

The concept of causality leads to the concept of action, this leads to the concept of force, and thereby to the concept of substance . . . I cannot leave unconsidered the criterion of substance in experience, in so far as substance seems to make itself manifest not through the permanence of appearance, but better and more obviously through action. Where there is action, and therefore activity and force, there is also substance . . . Now force proves action, which is, in experience, the adequate criterion of substantiality. (A204/B249–A205/B250)

Kant, as we saw in Chapter 3, explicitly identifies the concept of empirical substance (*substantia phaenomenon*, or *realitas phaenomenon*) with the concept of causal power or force. Implicit in the discussion of the Anticipations of Perception is the nexus of forces assumed in Kant's early *Physical Monadology*. It is a consequence of his matter theory that space is filled, and filled to varying degrees, by forces, where such forces are viewed as realities extending through space in ever-decreasing strengths from their source point: 'A radiation which fills a space—for example, heat—and likewise every other reality in appearance, can diminish in its degree indefinitely,

---

[7] This is also emphasized by Wilson, in 'The "Phenomenalisms" of Berkeley and Kant'.

without leaving the smallest part of this space empty' (A174/B216). Space is filled with a nexus of forces, which enable parts of matter to interact with each other, and produce changes (sensations) in certain thinking substances.[8]

What then are Kant's 'primary' qualities? We have two classes of primary qualities, mathematical and dynamical—or (in honour of their ancestry) Cartesian and Leibnizian.[9] First, there are spatial properties of 'extensive magnitude', shape, size and the geometrical properties; and second, there are the two forces of impenetrability and attraction. All other properties of physical bodies are derived from these.

Kant wants a class of properties that are not simply geometrical. His reason is not the corpuscularian reason for rejecting the Cartesian identification of matter and space, i.e. that the physical world requires a distinction between atoms and the void, absolutely solid particles in otherwise empty space. The Cartesian and Newtonian matter theories are equally misguided, according to Kant. Kant's conception of matter follows that of Leibniz in supposing that the notion of a body in space is essentially the notion of a thing that has certain powers, a thing that engages in causal interactions with other things. This dynamical conception of matter is at odds with the Cartesian view, according to which matter is inert. What may not be so obvious is that the dynamical conception of matter is also at odds with the Newtonian and Lockean views, and that is our present concern. Each of these latter views, while conceding the need for some space-filling feature to be listed among matter's primary qualities, locate that feature in something other than a power. Solidity is not a power. It is the supposed ground of a power. Kant, however, follows Leibniz in saying that it is the power, or force, that is fundamental to the filling of space. Kant's requirement of a force to fill

---

[8] J. F. Rosenberg understands this contrast between space and what fills space as a distinction between form and content. That may be a helpful way of putting it, if one thinks of matter as a kind of stuffing for space, and it is reminiscent of Kant's distinguishing of 'formal' spatial properties from 'real' dynamical ones. Rosenberg also suggests that the contrast between space and what fills it can be thought of as the contrast between the primary and secondary qualities, but that is surely mistaken. Kant's talk of weight and impenetrability make quite clear that the *real* is *physical matter*, and not subjective sensation. It is true that Kant also describes sensation as the matter of experience. The trouble is, we have a pun here on 'matter'. A subjective sense datum can, in a manner of speaking, have form and matter (e.g. an after-image that has both shape and colour). Sensations, in the subjective sense, can thus be matter. But they are not the matter of Kant's physical theory, and physical matter, or force, is the *realitas phaenomenon* that is not identical with, but corresponds to, subjective sensation. See J. F. Rosenberg, *One World and Our Knowledge of it* (Dordrecht: Reidel, 1980), 26, 27.

[9] Kant's second fundamental force (attraction) is really Newtonian rather than Leibnizian. A helpful source on these issues is Brittan, *Kant's Theory of Science*.

space, argued for in the *Physical Monadology*, emerges very clearly again in the *Metaphysical Foundations*.

Matter is the movable in so far as it fills a space. To fill a space means to resist everything movable that strives by its motion to press into a certain space . . . Matter fills a space, not by its mere existence, but by a special moving force.[10]

A material thing is not a space-occupier, but a space-filler. Kant explicitly considers and rejects the conception of something that occupies space, in favour of the conception of something that fills space, since a mere geometrical figure could in principle 'occupy space' without exerting any causal powers. Essential to the notion of filling space is the notion of power or action:

One uses the words 'to occupy a space' . . . in order to indicate thereby the extension of a thing in space. But there is not determined in this concept what action (*Wirkung*), or whether any action at all, arises from this presence as it resists other presences that try to press into it . . . one can say of every geometrical figure that it occupies a space (it is extended).[11]

What is needed for the filling of space is a force of impenetrability (*Zurückstoßungskraft, Undurchdringlichkeit*), which he also calls a force of repulsion (*repulsive Kraft*), and a force of extension (*Ausdehnungskraft*).

Although repulsive force gets the title 'force of extension', Kant ascribes the filling of space to the actions of not one force but two.

Since all given matter must fill its space with a determinate degree of repulsive force, in order to constitute a determinate material thing, only an original attraction in conflict with the original repulsion can make possible a determinate degree of the filling of space, which is matter.[12]

Matter is space filled to a determinate degree: if there were a force of attraction alone, or a force of repulsion alone, matter would either be collapsed to a mathematical point, or dispersed to infinity, so what is really needed for the determinate filling of space is both forces in 'conflict'. Attraction is, in Kant's theory, Newtonian gravitation. As in the *New Exposition*, gravity is thought to be what holds the world together. But Kant still gives a special

---

[10] *Metaphysical Foundations*, Ak. iv. 496–7, Ellington 40, 41. For some commentaries on Kant's dynamism as a physical theory, and for discussion of its contribution to the history of science and to field theory, see the references noted in Chapter 2, i.e. Jammer, *Concepts of Force*; Hesse, *Forces and Fields*; Berkson, *Fields of Force*; and especially Williams, *Michael Faraday*. Boscovich, *A Theory of Natural Philosophy* (1763), makes an interesting comparison.

[11] *Metaphysical Foundations*, Ak. iv. 497, Ellington 41.

[12] Ibid., Ak. iv. 518, Ellington 69.

priority to the force of impenetrability, which is matter's most fundamental property.

Impenetrability, as the fundamental property (*Grundeigenschaft*) of matter whereby it first reveals itself as something real in the space of our external senses, is nothing but matter's power of extension (*Ausdehnungsvermögen*) . . . Impenetrability [is] the primary sign of matter.[13]

Kant's space-filling property is not solidity, but impenetrability. What, exactly, is the difference?

6. *Solidity vs. Impenetrability, and a Problem for a Contemporary Orthodoxy*

At a number of points throughout the *Metaphysical Foundations* Kant explicitly draws a distinction between impenetrability, understood as a power, and solidity, understood as an absolute intrinsic property.

The universal principle of the dynamics of material nature is this: all that is real in the objects of our external senses and is not merely a determination of space (place, extension, and figure) must be regarded as moving force. By this principle, therefore, the so-called solid, or absolute impenetrability, is banished from natural science as an empty concept, and in its stead repulsive force is posited.[14]

Kant's theory of space occupied by forces in varying degrees replaces the need for the Newtonian hypothesis of empty space plus absolutely solid atoms. Solidity, understood as absolute impenetrability, is an 'empty concept', an 'occult quality'.[15] Accusations about occult qualities can fly thick and fast in debates about the fundamental properties of matter. Members of the dynamical tradition, founded by Leibniz, and continued by Kant and Boscovich, may seem to be equally vulnerable to such accusations, when they try to explain that 'matters cannot penetrate one another' because they have 'powers of impenetrability'. Leibnizian physics was ridiculed by its opponents precisely because it was viewed as attempting to resuscitate the scholastic virtues. Kant denies that he makes impenetrability an occult quality, though he offers a cautious acknowledgement of the problem. His own account is, he thinks, an improvement on the Newtonian hypothesis.

For although this [repulsive] force is similar [to absolute solidity] in that its possibility cannot be further explained, and hence must be admitted as fundamental,

[13] Ibid., Ak. iv. 508–9, Ellington 56, 57.
[14] Ibid., Ak. iv. 523, Ellington 77.
[15] It is described as an occult quality at ibid., Ak. iv. 502, Ellington 48.

it nevertheless yields the concept of an active cause and of the laws of the cause in accordance with which the effect, namely, the resistance in the filled space, can be estimated according to the degrees of this effect.[16]

When we come to the fundamental properties, we cannot explain them further. In contrast to the dormitive power of opium, for example, which can be further explained in terms of other more fundamental powers of matter, for the most fundamental properties there is nothing more to be said. The dynamists and mechanists are equally faced with this problem, if it is a problem. The dynamist response is to leave it at that: at the most fundamental level we have, simply, powers, which cannot be further analysed. The response of the opposing mechanists is to hold on, regardless, to solidity as absolute and intrinsic and something other than the power—even if no description could ever capture any alleged difference between them.

There is an assumption in the passage just quoted which seems to draw on a *New Exposition* form of argument: an intrinsic property cannot 'yield the concept of an active cause'. The problem for the Newtonian hypothesis is that absolute solidity—unlike impenetrability—does not yield the concept of an active cause. To borrow the conclusion of the *New Exposition*, the idea here seems to be that it is never through its own intrinsic properties— even the intrinsic property of absolute solidity—that something has the power to determine others different from itself.

Kant makes a similar complaint again, this time directed not against Newton's mechanism, but against Lambert, in a passage briefly considered in Chapter 6. He contrasts his own view to that of someone who holds on to solidity as an intrinsic property:

Matter fills a space, not by its mere existence, but by a special moving force . . . Lambert and others called the space-filling property of matter its solidity (a rather ambiguous expression). They held that solidity must be assumed in everything that exists (substance), at least in the external sensible world. According to their way of thinking the presence of something real in space must by its very concept imply this resistance. They thought that a solid thing must, in accordance with the principle of contradiction, exclude the coexistence of anything else in the space in which it is present. But the principle of contradiction does not drive matter back! . . . Only when I attribute to a space-occupant a *force* to repel every external movable thing that approaches it, do I understand how a contradiction is involved when a space which a thing occupies is penetrated by another thing of the same kind.[17]

Here we clearly have, I think, a version of the Irreducibility argument of the *New Exposition*, but in a very different context. Kant said in 1755 that from

---

[16] Ibid., Ak. iv. 502, Ellington 48.
[17] Ibid., Ak. iv. 497–8, my translation, Ellington 42.

the mere existence of a thing, with its intrinsic properties, no conclusions follow about how that thing will relate to other things. Playing out this form of argument in the context of a theory of matter yields a conclusion about the connection between primary and tertiary qualities. It does not follow from the mere existence of a thing, with its primary qualities, that the thing will have certain tertiary quality powers of relating to other things. And in this particular application, it does not follow from the mere existence of a 'solid' body, where solidity is supposed to be an absolute or intrinsic property, that the body will be impenetrable. Impenetrability does not follow logically from solidity. That is the point of Kant's joke: *der Satz des Widerspruchs treibt keine Materie zurück.* The principle of contradiction doesn't drive matter back![18]

Kant has put his finger on an important problem, even for contemporary philosophical debates about the qualities. (It may be that contemporary physics, having apparently gone Kant's way long ago, has left them far behind.)[19] Supposing that we want to hold on to solidity as a fundamental property of matter, we are faced with the question of its connection, if any, to the power of impenetrability. There are two options: either the connection between them is necessary, or it is contingent.

If the connection is necessary, then solidity *is* impenetrability. This alternative collapses the intrinsic property and the power together. It makes solidity identical with impenetrability. Necessarily, something is solid if and only if it is impenetrable. To take this alternative is, in effect, to give up on solidity as an intrinsic property. To take this alternative is to join the dynamists in all but name.

If instead one maintains that solidity is an intrinsic property distinct from the power of impenetrability, then the connection will be contingent. And this is surely the moral of Kant's argument against Lambert. It does not fol-

---

[18] Whether this argument contradicts Locke will depend on what we take Locke's understanding of the connection between primary qualities and powers to be. He said at least sometimes that impenetrability was a 'consequence' of solidity: suggesting that he thinks, like Lambert, that impenetrability 'follows' from solidity in accordance with the principle of contradiction alone. But if Locke believes that powers must be superadded to matter by God, as discussed in Chapter 7, then there is a sense in which Locke, unlike Lambert, thinks that impenetrability is not after all a 'consequence' of solidity.

[19] A. D. Smith, in a helpful article about the qualities, says that Kant (among others) 'developed the Leibnizian idea that [the space-filling feature] should be understood as *force* . . . Such a line of thought will be seen as momentous in its implications when it is borne in mind both how far an outlook such as this is from the quest for a fully intelligible intrinsic characterization of the material world that dominated the seventeenth century, and also that we are here dealing with a development of ideas that led through Maxwell and Einstein to the theoretical physics of our own day.' 'Of Primary and Secondary Qualities,' *Philosophical Review* 99 (1990), 246–7.

low from the mere existence of a thing, with its intrinsic properties, that the thing will have any power of repelling other things. The powers of things do not supervene on their intrinsic properties: and the power of impenetrability does not supervene on solidity. To borrow an example from Locke, someone acquainted with the intrinsic properties of gold and aqua regia would not be able to deduce that gold has a power of dissolving in aqua regia; for whether gold has that or any other power depends not only on its intrinsic properties, but on the contingent laws of nature. That was the point of Kant's argument from the *New Exposition* (on the second interpretation). From premises about a thing's mere existence, with its intrinsic properties, no conclusions about its powers follow. Applied to this case: from premises about the existence of a solid thing, nothing can be concluded about how that thing will relate to other things. From the thought of the existence of a solid thing, one cannot 'understand how a contradiction is involved when a space which a thing occupies is penetrated by another thing of the same kind'. There is, says Kant, no contradiction involved in asserting that a solid thing is penetrated. It is logically possible for a thing to be solid but not impenetrable. It is logically possible for there to be a world in which human beings—just like us in intrinsic respects—can walk through solid walls. There is no contradiction in supposing such a thing. This seems an unpalatable conclusion, and it may be that Kant is among the first to have drawn it. He takes it to be a kind of *reductio* of the concept of solidity.

In Chapter 5 it was noted that Kant, unlike many contemporary metaphysicians, takes the absence of a necessary connection between intrinsic properties and causal powers to imply that powers do not depend on intrinsic properties *at all*—except in the very general sense that the substance which has the powers must have some intrinsic properties or other if it is to be a substance, a thing capable of existence on its own. He takes it to be a sign that the intrinsic properties are not the causally active features of the world. However, in our own post-Humean days, similar intuitions about the absence of necessary connection between intrinsic properties and causal powers are taken to be a sign that (contrary to Kant) it *is* the intrinsic properties, and not the powers, that are the causally active features of the world. Hume's denial of necessity in nature has become our contemporary orthodoxy.[20] Kant is no successor to Hume in this respect, but his opponent. It is the power, and not any hypothesized intrinsic ground, that has a necessary connection with its effect, namely 'resistance in the filled space'. And *hence* it is the power, in Kant's view, that is the causal agent.

---

[20] A reminder of some statements of what I take to be the contemporary orthodoxy about powers: Jackson, Pargetter, and Prior, 'Three Theses about Dispositions'; Armstrong, *What is a Law of Nature?*; van Cleve, 'Putnam, Kant and Secondary Qualities'; Prior, *Dispositions*.

Our contemporary orthodoxy about powers is as vulnerable as Lambert was to Kant's argument. Our orthodoxy must allow that it is logically possible, as Kant says, for things to be solid but not impenetrable. It must allow that there are possible worlds where we can walk through solid walls.

There is yet a further problem if, despite the contingency of the connection, it is the ground, and not the power, that is regarded as the causally active property.[21] It does not seem to occur to Kant that anyone would adopt this option which has become our own orthodoxy, but it is worth trying to imagine what he would say. If solidity is taken to be the causal ground of impenetrability, and the ground is distinct from the power, and contingently connected with it, then our orthodoxy is faced with a conclusion surprisingly similar to Kantian Humility. Solidity becomes *inscrutable*.[22] We know what impenetrability is, but we do not know what solidity is—except that it is the supposed 'ground' of impenetrability, causally responsible for the behaviour of bodies resisting each other. Solidity is not the same as impenetrability. Solidity becomes the name for a something-we-know-not-what—ominously similar to a Kantian thing in itself. Our contemporary orthodoxy must concede that it, too, is faced with a conclusion similar to Kant's—that there are intrinsic features of the world with which we can never become acquainted. One might think that this version of the conclusion is even worse than Kant's own: for, unlike Kant, the contemporary orthodoxy is purporting to give an *explanation* of a physical phenomenon. What sort of explanation? How does the positing of solidity help to explain anything? What more *could* there be to know? Solidity now has all the defects of a dormitive virtue, obscurity, unobservability, something-we-know-not-whattery—and none of the advantages of a dormitive virtue, since *even if* we were to know what solidity was, we would be unable to infer how it would make something behave. That was the point of Kant's argument against Lambert. There are worlds where solid things do not resist other things, even worlds where solid things—in virtue of their solidity—attract other things, since solidity could as easily have been the causal ground for the power of attraction as for the power of repulsion. In short, we do not know what solidity is; and even if God were to tell us, that would help us not a

[21] Simon Blackburn has an excellent discussion of this problem in 'Filling in Space', reprinted in *Essays in Quasi-Realism* (New York: Oxford University Press, 1993), 255–8, and my understanding of the problem is much indebted to him. However, he ought to distinguish powers from counterfactuals in describing the problem; contrary to what he says, the differences do matter, if powers can be causal agents.

[22] I borrow this term from John Foster, and use it in roughly the sense he gives it in his chapter on 'The Inscrutability of Matter', in *The Case for Idealism* (London: Routledge & Kegan Paul, 1982), 51–72.

whit. One can surely find some sympathy for Kant's view that intrinsic properties have no role to play in explaining the order of nature.

Kant, unlike the proponents of our orthodoxy, demands that the fundamental property of impenetrability should have a necessary connection with its effect; and he places the causes of things in the knowable, phenomenal, world: powers, forces, are causes. And I conclude this section by suggesting that Kant's rejection of solidity, and his replacement of solidity with the power of impenetrability, has its advantages for a doctrine of 'primary' qualities.

7. *Science: Primary vs. Tertiary Qualities*

One of the traditional requirements on a primary/secondary quality distinction is that it distinguish the properties attributed to matter by *science* from the unscientific sensory qualities. The accusations and counter-accusations between dynamists and mechanists about occult qualities are not unrelated to the science issue. The break with scholastic occult qualities, and a search for the fundamental properties needed for science, were thought to go hand in hand.[23]

When one attributes a dormitive power to opium, one attributes a very specific property: a power of putting someone to sleep. One attributes it on the basis of one kind of dispositional manifestation, and this piecemeal way of identifying properties is at odds with what was needed by the developing mechanistic science: first because it fails to explain why opium puts someone to sleep, and second because it fails to allow opium's sleep-inducing qualities to be systematically integrated with other properties it might have, or with its other possible interactive effects. What is needed instead of these specific properties are qualities that are, as Boyle says, 'catholick', and as Locke says 'utterly inseparable from body': qualities that are universal and essential, possessed by every material object. Each body will have a quality that is a determinate instantiation of all the determinable primary qualities. Not all bodies will have the determinate property of triangularity, but all will have the determinable property of extension. Primary qualities, as universal and essential qualities of matter, can serve as the foundation for

---

[23] See e.g. Smith: 'The making of the [primary/secondary] distinction was an integral part of the most significant feature of seventeenth century thought: the break with Aristotelianism . . . Distinguishing [the qualities] was part of the search for the requisite concepts to employ in a genuinely explanatory science' ('Of Primary and Secondary Qualities', 225). I follow Smith closely on the contrast between the scholastic view and mechanism; he describes the 'piecemeal' nature of scholastic powers on p. 225.

mechanism. They are, moreover, the qualities in terms of which the scholastic virtues can be explained. The primary qualities, in serving their purpose for science, are supposed to be properties that are universal, 'catholick'; and they are supposed to be properties that characterize the intrinsic nature of physical objects.[24]

The conflict between dynamism and mechanism, viewed in relation to disputes about primary versus tertiary qualities, can be seen to hinge on a disagreement about the requirements that primary qualities be both intrinsic and catholic. Mechanism, in turning its back on occult qualities, was turning its back on specific powers. What is wrong with occult qualities, according to the mechanist, is that they are specific, not catholic; and powers, not intrinsic properties. The dynamist can in turn reply that the demand for something better than specific powers can be met by properties that are not intrinsic. *Certain powers are catholic*, and herein lies the essence of matter.

That is exactly what Kant does, when he argues for his two fundamental forces. Attraction and repulsion are universal, essential properties of matter, and they thus fulfil the requirement of catholicity on primary qualities. But they are none the less powers. Perhaps Kant can say that the mechanists already accept one fundamental, otherwise inexplicable power, namely gravity, and thus their programme is already crumbling. Moreover as we have seen, Kant can say with respect to the mechanist's space-filling property that if the mechanist holds on to solidity as a 'something-I-know-not-what' distinct from a power of impenetrability, that is nevertheless responsible for observed resistance, then the mechanist is himself engaging in the disreputable practices of his scholastic enemies. The dynamists leave impenetrability as a *power*: that is enough to provoke angry cries of 'occult qualities!' from the mechanists. But if the mechanists in turn make solidity a *hidden something*, an unknown ground for the power of impenetrability, then that is enough to provoke the same accusation from the other side.

There is a second problem for the mechanists. Kant's argument against Lambert showed that if solidity is something other than impenetrability, then it is in principle possible for a thing to be solid but not impenetrable. But this has implications for the relevance of solidity for its supposed role in science. The primary qualities are supposed to be intrinsic and catholic, or essential to matter. Solidity is, *ex hypothesi*, intrinsic and catholic. All matter, according to the mechanists, must be solid. But, if Kant's argument against Lambert is correct, this is by no means to say that all matter must be impenetrable. It is possible for matter to be solid, but not impenetrable. If solidity is intrinsic and catholic, then impenetrability is not catholic. If

---

[24] See again Smith, sects. IV and V.

matter is solid in all possible worlds, and if the connection between solidity and impenetrability is contingent, then matter is not impenetrable in all possible worlds. To be sure, as a matter of good luck, all bodies in the world in which we happen to live may be both solid and impenetrable. But if solidity is essential to matter, then, given Kant's argument, impenetrability is not.

The requirement on primary qualities was a requirement for properties that are both essential to bodies and necessary for the science of mechanics. Imagine how mechanics would be in a world where, as is possible on the mechanist account, things are solid but not impenetrable. In such a world there could be no mechanics. What is needed for mechanics is impenetrability: not a primary, but a tertiary quality.

This is to suggest not simply that tertiary qualities can indeed perform the tasks required by mechanics, assuming that they are catholic enough. It is to suggest that, as Kant believes, they can perform the tasks better than the traditional primary qualities. Like the traditional primary qualities, they are distinct from secondary qualities. Like the primary qualities, they can be catholic. And unlike the primary qualities, they can be properties that are necessary for science. I have simplified discussion by focusing on the contrast between solidity and impenetrability, but what I say connects with a much more general point about the causal powers of matter. It has been noted, and worried about, by contemporary philosophical descendants of the mechanist tradition:

if we look at the properties of physical objects that physicists are prepared to allow them such as mass, electric charge, or momentum, these show a distressing tendency to dissolve into relations that one object has to another. What, then, are the things that have these relations to each other? Must they not have a non-relational nature if they are to sustain relations? But what is this nature?[25]

David Armstrong's thought here is, it seems to me, half-way to Kant's. As far as physics is concerned, Kant's advice is that we should accept the lesson of the dynamist tradition: the properties of bodies that physics delivers are indeed, as Armstrong says, understood only in relational terms, as increasingly detailed knowledge of the causal powers of things.[26] If we want to say that there is nevertheless some part of the physical world that grounds

[25] David Armstrong, *A Materialist Theory of Mind* (London: Routledge & Kegan Paul, 1968), 74–5.

[26] See Smith, 252. See also Blackburn, 'Filling in Space'; Foster, 'The Inscrutability of Matter', in *The Case for Idealism*. For a development of a powers ontology, see R. Harré and E. H. Madden, *Causal Powers* (Oxford: Blackwell, 1975). Foster has an interesting appendix to his chapter on the inscrutability of matter that offers a fairly widely accepted (e.g. by Smith) argument aiming to refute the powers thesis. In so far as I understand the argument I disagree, since it appears to treat powers as equivalent to bare dispositions.

these causal powers, then we are left with an occult something. Simon Blackburn describes the same problem.

> [A]ny conceivable improvement in science will give us only a better pattern of dispositions and powers. That's the way physics works . . . [the ground of these powers] will remain, therefore, entirely beyond our ken, a something-we-know-not-what identified only by the powers and dispositions it supports.[27]

It is ironic to find in this contemporary orthodoxy of science an implicit commitment to Kantian Humility—or a commitment, at any rate, to the conclusion that there are intrinsic properties of which we can have no knowledge. The conclusion can be made to look very uncomfortable. According to this contemporary view there are intrinsic properties that physics can never grasp. If physical properties are those properties that physics can discover, then the conclusion is that there are *non-physical* intrinsic properties of which we can have no knowledge. The difference between this epistemic humility and Kant's is that, on this view, the properties are supposed to be causes, and are supposed to explain something. That, as I said, makes our own contemporary view if anything even more mysterious than Kant's, since it posits something that seems on a par with a scholastic virtue—something that is causal, hidden, unknowable, non-physical, a something that purports to explain, but does not.

In this chapter I have so far painted Kant as a champion of dynamism, who sees no need for primary qualities as traditionally conceived in his theory of matter. However Kant shares the mechanists' desire to find firm footing in some properties that are not relational. In expressing this desire, Armstrong said that things must 'have a non-relational nature if they are to sustain relations': but this requirement is ambiguous between a requirement that things have some intrinsic properties or other; and a requirement that things have intrinsic properties which are the causal grounds for relational powers. Kant rejects the second requirement, as we have seen. But he accepts the first. That is why he says that the understanding, when it entitles an object in a relation mere phenomenon, at the same time must form a representation of an object in itself (B307). That is why he says that concepts of relation presuppose things which are independent (A284/B340). That is why he says that substances must have some intrinsic nature (A274/B330), even if that intrinsic nature is unknown (A277/B333). So Kant too is left with an occult something, though he refuses to say it explains anything in the physical world. There are things that have a non-relational nature, but they are not to be found in the field of experience. The things that have a non-relational nature are not part of the physical world, nor do they have

---

[27] Blackburn, 'Filling in Space', 256.

any explanatory role to play in understanding what matter is. As far as physics is concerned we need no such thing.

This latter conclusion, that as far as physics is concerned we need no such thing, seems to have been Michael Faraday's when, influenced by Kantian philosophy, he began to develop field theory as a science. Suppose, he says, we distinguish a particle *a*, from the powers or forces *m*, with which it is endowed. The properties which can in principle be encountered in scientific practice are

the properties or forces of the *m*, not those of the *a*, which, without the forces, is conceived of as having no powers. But then surely the *m* is the *matter* . . . To my mind, therefore, the *a* or nucleus vanishes, and the substance consists of the powers, or *m*; and indeed what notion can we form of the nucleus independent of its powers? all our perception and knowledge of the atom, and even our fancy, is limited to ideas of its powers: what thought remains on which to hang the imagination of an *a* independent of the acknowledged forces? . . . why then assume the existence of that of which we are ignorant, which we cannot conceive, and for which there is no philosophical necessity?[28]

Faraday's argument has something in common with Kant's argument, in the *Metaphysical Foundations*, against mechanism. Faraday thinks that in physics there is no need for any such substantial core, no need for properties other than powers, and if one is a physicist, that is all that matters. Faraday feels no need for Kant's thing in itself.

In this section I have tried to explain how a Kantian replacement of primary qualities with tertiary qualities might perform the scientific task traditionally required of primary qualities. If Kant attributes to matter powers that are essential and universal, without having thereby attributed to matter the traditional primary qualities, then it seems that Kant's proposal is not only adequate, but an improvement on its competitors.[29] It has often been held that we need primary qualities for science: and we have just seen how well Kant's tertiary qualities might perform this first task. It has sometimes been held that we need primary qualities for objectivity. Let us turn to consider how well they might perform this second task.

---

[28] Michael Faraday, 'A speculation touching Electric Conduction and the Nature of Matter', in *Experimental Researches in Electricity*, vol. ii (London: Richard & John Edward Taylor, 1844), 290–1. This remark by Faraday is discussed by Berkson, *Fields of Force*, and P. M. Heimann and J. E. McGuire, 'Newtonian Forces and Lockean Powers: Concepts of Matter in Eighteenth Century Thought', *Historical Studies in the Physical Sciences* 3 (1971), 233–306.

[29] As a matter of (mere) fact, dynamism seems, historically, to have had greater potential for bringing systematicity into science than mechanism did. Kant's belief in the unity of forces, and the derivability of all properties from the two fundamental forces, motivated much research, first in chemistry inspired by the *Naturphilosophen*, and then, most significantly, in the work of Humphry Davy and Michael Faraday, who discovered the unity of electrical and magnetic 'force', and developed field theory as a result. (See Williams, *Michael Faraday*.)

8. *Objectivity: Primary vs. Tertiary Qualities*

The Kantian task of identifying what is needed for us to have experience of an objective world should lead one to a distinction between primary and secondary qualities. That conclusion has been argued for by Gareth Evans, building on the work of Strawson.[30] Kant argues, according to Strawson, that in order to be able to trace a subjective path through an objective world we must be able to employ certain objectivity concepts. To think of the world as objective, and as independent of the subjective stream of experience, we must be able to locate things in a spatial, or quasi-spatial, framework. Only if we think of particulars as located in space, and in a location different to our own, can we have a basis for reidentifying them as the very same things previously encountered. Thinking of things as located in space enables us to think of things as persistent and identical over time. Thinking of things as *outer* enables us to think of them as *other*.

In response to Strawson, Evans argued that much more is needed than Strawson allowed, if we are to have a conception of 'things without the mind'. In his paper of that title, Evans takes up Strawson's Kantian project, saying that what is needed for objectivity is not simply space or quasi-space, but space-occupying *matter*, and along with matter, a full blooded distinction between primary and secondary qualities. We have seen that there is a sense in which Kant does indeed have a primary/secondary quality distinction within the world of experience, and if Evans is right, Kant's discussion of it ought to play a more central role than it is usually taken to do. However, that is not my main concern. For Kant's supposed primary/secondary quality distinction is, we have seen, more like a *tertiary*/secondary quality distinction, and this raises the question of whether this distinction could in principle fulfil the tasks required of it by such commentators as Strawson and Evans. That is what I propose to explore now.

Evans distinguishes primary from secondary qualities in a manner that is reminiscent of Bennett's discussion, though Evans traces it to Thomas Reid. Secondary qualities, or properties, are dispositional properties of a particular kind. 'For an object to have [a secondary property] is for it to be such that, if certain sensitive beings were suitably situated, they would be affected with certain experiences.'[31] They are sensory and dispositional. Primary qualities, he says, are neither sensory nor dispositional, but are involved in the notion of matter as space-occupying stuff: position, shape, size, motion,

---

[30] Strawson, *Individuals* and *The Bounds of Sense*; Evans, 'Things Without the Mind', 76–116, see especially Pt. III.

[31] 'Things Without the Mind', 95.

and in addition to these, the space 'fillers', mass, weight, hardness. The primary qualities are associated with a primitive mechanics, and they are partly theoretical. To understand them one must have a grasp of the way 'bodies compete for the occupancy of positions in space, and of the resistance one body may afford to the motion of another'. To grasp the primary qualities of a thing is to understand, at least in part, various 'propositions about its characteristic behaviour and interaction with other bodies'. It seems to me that Evans has so far done precisely as Bennett did: he has said that it is constitutive of the concept of a primary quality that it satisfy a particular functional role, specified by a set of propositions describing a complex set of actual and potential interactions with other things. Although the primary qualities are not sensory, Evans has turned them into powers. He has made them dispositional and relational: he has made them tertiary qualities.

Evans nevertheless proceeds to use 'dispositional' as a synonym for 'secondary'. Evans takes up Strawson's starting-point, which is that objectivity requires reidentifiable particulars. He argues that if we are to have the concept of a persisting and reidentifiable particular, we need to be able to assert certain counterfactual statements, such as, 'If I were at location L, I would hear sound S.' There needs to be something that makes that counterfactual true, and that something cannot merely be a universal regularity of the form: 'Anyone at L always hears S.' These conditionals require a ground in the world, a relatively abiding property of a thing which is causally responsible for the manifestation of the disposition, and which makes the counterfactual true. Objectivity requires the possibility of reidentifying independent particulars, and it thus requires more than universal generalizations about the course of experience: it requires the application of the concept of 'persisting space-occupying substances in whose primary qualities the dispositions to produce experiences may be regarded as grounded'.[32]

There are really two parts to Evans's requirement of properties associated with a primitive mechanics: one is that they are not sensory; and the other is that they are intrinsic and categorical, rather than relational and dispositional. He imagines that these must coincide. But there is no reason for thinking so. Properties do not become less dispositional simply by becoming more theoretical, as Strawson rightly says in his reply to Evans.[33] While the properties associated with a primitive mechanics will be non-sensory, there is no reason for thinking they will be non-relational and categorical, and hence no reason to think they will be primary qualities in the sense required by Evans. Tertiary qualities can serve well enough as properties

---

[32] Ibid. 104–5.
[33] P. F. Strawson, 'Reply to Evans', in Zak van Straaten, ed., *Philosophical Subjects: Essays Presented to P. F. Strawson* (Oxford: Oxford University Press, 1980), 280.

associated with a 'primitive mechanics', so well indeed that Evans seems accidentally to have brought them in already.

This point is brought out by Strawson.

> It seems that our search for the properties of the categorical base must finally lead us to the undeniably theoretical properties which physics assigns to the ultimate constituents of matter—perhaps force, mass, impenetrability, electric charge. But these properties themselves seem to be thoroughly dispositional in character.

This echoes the points made by Armstrong and Blackburn, and (barring the anachronistic example of electric charge) is in principle so far something with which Kant would entirely agree. Kant thinks that intrinsic properties do not have a role to play in science: that was the point of his argument against Lambert and Newton. Strawson continues: 'If the argument is from dispositional properties conceived as objective to the need for a categorical base, then the categorical base is still to seek.'[34] Strawson himself seems to agree with Evans that sensory properties, conceived of as objective, require a non-relational basis: but he does not, it seems, look to science for that basis. He suggests that one can refuse to think of sensory properties as merely dispositional without thereby requiring 'a categorical base of different character from themselves'.[35] And he admits that his own solution does not save us altogether 'from intellectual discomfort'.

An alternative, and literally Kantian, solution is to accept that objectivity requires properties that are not sensory, but that objectivity does not require these to be non-relational. Objectivity requires, if Evans is correct, a distinction between sensory properties and properties associated with something like a mechanics—but these latter properties can be powers. They can be as relational and dispositional as you like, provided that the relations and dispositions concern things other than ourselves and our sensory states. What is needed is a conception of ourselves as tracing a path through a world that contains things that interact not just with us but with each other—whether or not we are there. Kant says of force that it interacts with ourselves *and with other things*: 'this reality' can be 'viewed as cause either of sensation *or of some other reality* in the field of appearance, such as change' (A168/B210, emphasis added). Strawson acknowledges this crucial difference between the dispositional properties of science, and the sensory dispositional properties, though he does not pursue it. He says, of the properties of theoretical physics, that 'these properties themselves seem to be thoroughly dispositional in character, though the dispositions in question relate to the *operations of objects upon each other* rather than, directly, to their operations upon the human sensibility'.[36] This difference, though, is just

---

[34] Ibid.   [35] Ibid.   [36] Ibid., emphasis added.

what is needed if a distinction is to be made between the sensory and the non-sensory. Things must be thought to have powers that they exert on things *other than ourselves*: that is to say, they must be thought to have tertiary qualities. We think of the sun as melting the wax, and having the power to do so; we think of the loadstone attracting the iron filings, and having the power to do so; and we think of the world as being this way whether or not we are there to see it. When we think this way, we are making a distinction between the subjective and the objective—even if we are thinking of 'mere powers'.

Evans's demand that there be a ground for dispositions is, then, quite different to the demand that there be an alternative to the merely sensory. Although both demands have their source in deep metaphysical intuition, or at any rate, 'deep conceptual prejudice',[37] they are quite distinct. And failure to meet those demands will have different results. To abandon an alternative to the sensory would be to take the path of phenomenalism, or something like it. To abandon intrinsic, categorical grounds for dispositions would be, perhaps, to take the path of Faraday, and field theory. Kant, I have been suggesting, has far more in common with the latter than the former.

Primary qualities have traditionally been thought to be needed as the properties that can fulfil the twin tasks associated with science and objectivity, because they have been thought to be intrinsic, catholic, and distinct from the sensory. What we have seen in this chapter is that the *intrinsicness* of primary qualities seems to be quite irrelevant to their success in fulfilling these tasks. What is needed to fulfil the task of scientific properties are properties that are catholic, shared by all material things.[38] What is needed to fulfil the task of objective properties are properties distinct from the sensory. It is a mistake to think that primary qualities are needed for these two tasks, since tertiary qualities can also be catholic, and distinct from the sensory. And that is why Kant's tertiary qualities—Kant's powers or forces—can very well fulfil the twin tasks traditionally assigned to the primary qualities. I conclude that Kant's 'primary'/secondary quality distinction has much in its favour.

---

[37] Evans's words, in 'Things Without the Mind', 102.

[38] Well, at least on certain visions of science, shared by the old mechanists and dynamists alike. A. D. Smith suggests that the catholicity requirement has now been abandoned (in 'Of Primary and Secondary Qualities').

9

The Unobservable and the Supersensible

1. *Experience and the Unobservable*

Commenting on Kant's scientific realism, Margaret Wilson remarks that 'Kant is a very peculiar sort of phenomenalist indeed', a phenomenalist for whom 'the world of science, and not the world of sensation' is 'empirically real'.[1] This remark connects with an issue raised towards the end of Chapter 2, namely, that Kant's understanding of Receptivity has the potential to yield an empiricism which has more in common with causal theories of knowledge than with phenomenalism. For Kant, the fundamental fact about sensibility is that it is *passive*: and therefore the fundamental fact about an 'object of possible experience' is not that it is an object of which we can become *aware*, but that it is an object that can *affect* us.

There is a profound difference between these two ways of thinking about experience. Faced with the question: what could possibly be an object of human experience? the most natural tendency is an introspective one: of what could I, and beings like me, become aware? The answers will be various, but they will all tend to come from this imaginative first-person standpoint, the standpoint of Descartes inspecting the furniture of his mind, the standpoint of Locke reflecting on his ideas, the standpoint of Berkeley forcing us to acknowledge the reality of what is given to sensory awareness, the standpoint of a sense-datum theorist who thinks he encounters only flashes and buzzes. When we read Kant, we have an antecedent, though rough and ready, conception of what experience is, and that conception is inextricably tied up with the idea of things of which one can become aware. Kant has an antecedent conception of what experience is too, but it is not the same. Instead of the introspective question: of what could I become aware? there is the neutral third-person question: by what could a receptive creature be affected? That is a very abstract question, and it can have an abstract and trivial-looking answer: namely, everything with which it causally interacts.

It seems to me that much philosophical commentary on Kant brings our common and garden conceptions of experience to its interpretations of

---

[1] Wilson, 'The "Phenomenalisms" of Berkeley and Kant,' 170, 169.

Kant. Bennett and Strawson are examples, but there are others. A sophisticated and interesting argument is offered by Charles Parsons, for example, against the Kantian grounding of geometrical knowledge in the forms of intuition. Geometrical knowledge, and knowledge of objects with geometrical properties, requires a grasp of space as infinitely divisible. If that fact is to be explained by space's being a form of intuition, then infinity must be revealed in the way that objects present themselves to us in perception: 'everything about the object which we can know must be able to show itself in experience and must therefore be limited by the general conditions of possible experience.'[2] Infinitely small and infinitely distant things in space are not given in any actual experience, and in any ordinary sense of 'possible' could not be given in any possible experience either. Parsons extends the notion of 'possible experience' in various directions on Kant's behalf, but he concludes that none of them, in the end, will save Kant from the problem. This particular problem is not my topic here, but it is quite evident that Parsons, like anyone else who addresses this kind of question, reasonably takes Kantian experience to require that an object of experience 'show itself' to the light of experience, where experience is taken to require conscious awareness. This is indeed a reasonable conception of experience, but it is not, I think, Kant's. The question that needs to be answered, for Kant, is a question about what can in principle affect a receptive creature. If infinitely small or infinitely distant things could affect a receptive creature, then they are objects of possible experience—no matter if we could never become aware of them.

Very many objects of which we can never become aware none the less count for Kant as objects of possible experience. Consider the following list of candidate objects of possible experience:[3]

  (a) colours, tastes
  (b) ordinary middle-sized objects: houses, ships
  (c) gravitational force, Newtonian *lamellae*, or light particles
  (d) absolutely solid Newtonian atoms
  (e) things as they are in themselves.

Which of these are really objects of possible experience? Empiricists, presented with such a list, may make different choices, depending on their theoretical commitments. A strict sense-datum theorist might accept only

---

[2] Charles Parsons, 'Infinity and Kant's Conception of "The Possibility of Experience"', *Philosophical Review* **73** (1964), 182–97.

[3] (a) A28, A29/B45; (b) the Second Analogy; (c) *Metaphysical Foundations*, Ak. iv. 508–11, Ellington 56–60; 'On a Discovery', Ak. viii. 205, Allison 122; (d) *Metaphysical Foundations*, Ak. iv. 523, 532 ff., Ellington 77, 90 ff.; (e) *Critique*, *passim*.

(a), and treat (b) to (d) as potential logical constructions out of sense data. Colours and tastes are real, everything else (at least from (b) to (d)) can be logical constructions out of sense data. Berkeley might accept as real (a) and (b), the sensory qualities and the ordinary objects—cherries and the like—which are constituted by them. And he might be sceptical about all the rest, regarding force, gravity, attraction, and so forth as at best 'useful for reasonings and reckonings'.[4] No ordinary empiricist would accept the theoretical entities of (c) as straightforwardly 'empirically real', and at the same time reject the sensory qualities in (a). But Kant does. No ordinary empiricist would class the theoretical entities listed in (c) as objects of possible experience, and then draw the line at the theoretical entities of (d) on partly epistemological grounds. But Kant does. Newtonian light particles can in principle be objects of possible experience, but not Newtonian atoms. Kant does indeed have a very unusual conception of experience, if it persuades him to rule out colours, rule in invisible forces, rule out Newtonian atoms, and rule out things in themselves.

The banishing of solid Newtonian atoms has its source in the epistemological consequences of the Irreducibility argument as applied, in the *Metaphysical Foundations*, to the case of solidity. Kant believes, on the basis of the Irreducibility argument, that causal powers do not supervene on the intrinsic properties of things, and he believes that intrinsic properties therefore cannot be causally efficacious: that is why he says, in the *New Exposition*, 'A substance never has the power through its own intrinsic properties to determine others different from itself, as has been proven.'[5] And that is why, in the *Metaphysical Foundations*, Kant ridicules Lambert's idea that solidity as an intrinsic property could be causally efficacious—

that a solid thing must, in accordance with the principle of contradiction, exclude the coexistence of anything else in the space in which it is present. But the principle of contradiction does not drive matter back! . . . Only when I attribute to a space-occupant a *force* to repel every external movable thing that approaches it, do I understand how a contradiction is involved when a space which a thing occupies is penetrated by another thing of the same kind.[6]

If such properties cannot be causally efficacious, then a receptive creature cannot be affected by them. This, I suggest, is part of the reason behind Kant's rejection of Newtonian atoms, which he says cannot 'be discovered by any experiment'.[7] It is not the small size of the postulated atoms that concerns Kant, but the absoluteness of their solidity. Absolutely solid atoms

---

[4] Berkeley, *De Motu*, § 17, p. 255.   [5] *New Exposition*, Ak. i. 415.
[6] *Metaphysical Foundations*, Ak. iv. 497–8, my translation, Ellington 42.
[7] Ibid., Ak. iv. 533, Ellington 92.

cannot be discovered by any experiment since no absolute or intrinsic properties of a thing can be discovered by any experiment. Fields of force are to replace solid atoms.

All that is real in the objects of our external senses and is not merely a determination of space . . . must be regarded as moving force. By this principle, therefore, the so-called solid, or absolute impenetrability, is banished from natural science as an empty concept.[8]

Kant has nothing against theoretical entities that are difficult, even impossible, to perceive because of their size or other accidental features. Invisible forces, and very tiny bodies themselves constituted by forces, are all empirically real, and they are real because they can affect us. Kant's realism about these unobservable theoretical entities follows from the thesis of Receptivity. We can in principle have experience of whatever affects us, regardless of how remote the possibility of our ever being directly *aware* of it.

That was evident in the passage considered in Chapter 7 about magnetic matter:

the knowledge of things as real does not, indeed, require immediate perception (and therefore, sensation of which we are conscious) of the object whose existence is to be known. (A225/B272)

From the perception of the attracted iron filings we know of the existence of a magnetic matter pervading all bodies, although immediate perception of this stuff is impossible because of the constitution of our organs. For if our senses were finer, we would come upon a direct empirical intuition of it in an experience, in accordance with the laws of sensibility and the context of our perceptions. The grossness of our senses does not in any way decide the form of possible experience in general. Our knowledge of the existence of things reaches, then, as far as perception and its advance according to empirical laws can extend. (A226/B273)

Kant is quite frank here that possible experience has nothing at all to do with what we are actually capable of sensing. We have no sixth 'magnetic sense'— but this has no relevance whatsoever to the question of whether magnetic matter is an object of possible experience.

Kant is here drawing a contrast between two classes of 'non-sensible' entities, the contingently unobservable, and things in themselves. This distinction is raised in the Amphiboly, as the following passage shows. The first

---

[8] Ibid., Ak. iv. 523, Ellington 77. Compare Brittan, *Kant's Theory of Science*, 152. I do not suggest that the intrinsicness of solidity is Kant's only reason for rejecting atomism: other reasons include Newton's positing of a vacuum, which is incompatible with Kant's views in the Third Analogy and the Anticipations of Perception.

part is familiar enough, but what is important to emphasize now is the contrast between the comparatively hidden properties of the phenomenal realm, revealed little by little as we 'penetrate to nature's inner recesses', and the absolutely hidden properties of things as they are in themselves:

Matter is *substantia phaenomenon*. I search for that which belongs to it intrinsically in all parts of the space which it occupies, and in all the actions it performs, and these of course can only be appearances to outer sense. So I have nothing that is absolutely intrinsic, but only what is comparatively intrinsic, and that is itself again constituted by external relations . . . If the complaints that 'we have no insight whatsoever into the intrinsic nature of things' are supposed to mean that we cannot grasp by pure understanding what the things which appear to us may be in themselves, they are completely unreasonable and stupid. They want us to be able to be acquainted with things without senses . . . and thus to have a faculty of knowledge altogether different from the human. They want us not to be human beings, but beings of whom we are unable to say whether they are even possible, much less how they are constituted. Through observation and analysis of appearances we penetrate to nature's inner recesses, and who knows how far this knowledge in time may extend. But even if the whole of nature were revealed to us, with all this knowledge we would still never be able to answer those transcendental questions which go beyond nature. (A277/B233)

It is a striking symptom of the level of abstraction of Kant's conception of sensibility that he appears to think that different sensory organs required for acquaintance with magnetic matter (A226/B273) would *not* require 'a faculty of knowledge altogether different from the human' (A277/B233). Creatures who encountered their world through sensitivity to magnetic fields and electric currents (eels, platypuses), or ultraviolet light (bees), or sonar (bats, whales)—none of these would require a faculty altogether different from the human. Creatures who had knowledge of things as they are in themselves, on the other hand, would require a faculty altogether different from the human. Bees and bats, whales and platypuses, must all be affected by their world if they are to have knowledge, or any kind of belief, about it: and in this respect at any rate their faculties of sensibility are no different from our own.

The contrast between contingent and necessary unobservability emerges in a revealing part of Kant's dispute with Eberhard, published in 1790, where Kant draws a similar contrast between the contingent unobservability of theoretical entities and the necessary unobservability of things as they are in themselves. This discussion has, in part, been the subject of our attention in Chapter 4, but this time our focus will be on the contrast it draws between the two different ways something can be beyond the bounds of experience.

2. *The Kant–Eberhard Controversy: Unobservable vs. Supersensible*

Eberhard had attacked Kant's philosophy, claiming that any supposed merits of the *Critique of Pure Reason* had already been anticipated by Leibniz. Kant's response provides us with a very explicit comparison of his own philosophy with that of Leibniz, which makes it an interesting text if we think—as I have argued—that Kant's view about things in themselves is motivated in part by an acceptance of some aspects of Leibnizian philosophy, and in part by a rejection of others: an acceptance of a broadly Leibnizian conception of substance, combined with a rejection of Leibnizian reductionism.

Eberhard reiterated the Leibnizian orthodoxy that the sensible world is a composite whose parts are simple substances or monads, and he complained that, despite Kant's rhetoric, the critical philosophy offered nothing new. Eberhard defends the Leibnizian view that

there is . . . no other difference between a thing as phenomenon and the representation of the noumenon which underlies it than between a crowd of men which I see at a great distance and the same men when I am so close that I can count the individuals. It is only . . . that *we could never come so close to it*.[9]

According to Eberhard (or Kant's version of him), the monads are intelligible entities that, as far as our senses are concerned, are like the very distant men: they cannot be grasped as individuals, through the senses, though they can be grasped in a confused and indistinct manner. Nevertheless, they are the grounds of the appearances. Monads are thus *non-sensible grounds* of appearances. But, according to Eberhard, this is exactly what Kant has argued in his *Critique*, in saying that things in themselves are non-sensible grounds of appearances. Eberhard concludes that Kant's 'New Critique of Pure Reason has been made Superfluous by an Earlier One', as his title announces.

Kant rejects Eberhard's construal of the Kantian philosophy. Kant's complaint to Eberhard is the complaint he made in the *Critique*, namely that this Leibnizian view 'takes the appearances for the things themselves', as he said in the Amphiboly. It reduces the phenomenon to the noumenon: it makes the appearance like a flock, that is nothing over and above its constituent members. This, as Kant says, 'makes no difference in the thing, but only in the degree of our power of perception'. And in response Kant says that while the claim that monads are non-sensible grounds of appearances

---

[9] This is Kant's version of Eberhard's view, and emphasis is added. 'On a Discovery', Ak. viii. 208, Allison 124-5.

bears a superficial resemblance to his own claim that things in themselves are grounds of appearances, it hides two equivocations.

The first is in the notion of 'ground' (*Grund*). There is a sense in which parts can be thought of as 'grounds' of the wholes they constitute, and there is a quite different sense in which a Kantian thing in itself is a 'ground', or 'substrate', of the appearances.[10] The first sense of 'ground' is reductive, and has to do with the parts and wholes. We can add that it also has to do with the way that one class of things can form the 'ground' for a supervenient class of things: in the way that, in Kant's example, the crowd supervenes upon the individuals that constitute it, so that there can be no change in the crowd without a change in the men. This first sense of 'ground' reduces the appearance to the ground of the appearance: it 'makes no difference in the thing', it takes the appearances for things in themselves. The phenomenon is nothing over and above the ground of the phenomenon. The second sense of 'ground' has to do with substances and properties. Kant says that things in themselves are 'ultimate grounds which are not appearances', they are 'the supersensible which grounds each appearance as *substrate*' (emphasis added). Eberhard has the former usage of 'ground', Kant has the latter, and Kant denies that things in themselves are grounds of phenomena in the Leibnizian sense. This is an important statement, because it explicitly rejects the view that things in themselves are grounds of phenomena in the way that one class of things can be 'ground' for a supervenient class of things. It explicitly endorses the view that things in themselves are, instead, the 'substrate' of phenomena: they are substances, bearers of properties that make up the physical world, but not themselves parts of the phenomenal world. It does not say that things in themselves are the same as phenomena, but regarded differently. A 'difference *in the thing*'—not merely in our attitudes to the thing—must be allowed. And it does affirm, once again, the reason for the unknowability of this substrate: 'intuition, through which the thing can alone be given to us, does not provide us with the properties that belong to it as it is in itself'.[11]

The second equivocation is in the notion of the 'non-sensible' (*nicht-empfindbar*), which in Eberhard's usage, according to Kant, slides between *supersensible* and *unobservable*. It equivocates between the idea of something 'completely beyond the sphere of sensibility', and the idea of something 'of whose representation one is not conscious'.[12] The proper meaning of 'non-

---

[10] *On a Discovery*, Ak. viii. 208, 209 n., Allison 124, 125.

[11] Ibid., Ak. viii. 209, 210, Allison 125.

[12] The contrast is between something that is *völlig außerhalb der Sphäre der Sinnlichkeit* and something *dessen Vorstellung man sich nicht bewußt ist*, the latter being illustrated by the example of what Allison translates as *lamellae*: ibid., Ak. viii. 204–5, Allison 121–2.

sensible' is 'completely outside the realm of sensibility'. But monads, according to Eberhard, are really present in the appearances just as individual men are really present in a crowd seen from afar. In what sense are they then 'non-sensible'? In Eberhard's usage, says Kant,

a *non-sensible* part . . . means a part of an empirical intuition, i.e. a part of which one is not *conscious* . . . [I]f something is an object of the senses (*Sinne*) and sensation (*Empfindung*), all of its simple parts must be so, even though they may lack clarity of representation. Thus, the obscurity of the partial representations of a whole, as a result of which only the understanding can determine their presence in this whole and in its intuition, does not raise them above the sphere of sensibility and convert them into objects of reason. Newton's *lamellae*, of which the colored particles of bodies consist, have not yet been seen through a microscope. Nevertheless, the understanding not only recognizes (or supposes) their existence, but also that they really are represented in our empirical intuition, albeit without being consciously apprehended. Yet this is no basis for regarding them as non-sensible, and hence as objects of reason, and they have never been understood in this way by his followers. There is, however, no difference between such small parts and completely simple parts, save in degree of diminution. If the whole is an object of the senses, all of its parts must necessarily be so likewise.[13]

Newton's *lamellae* are, on this hypothesis, the sub-microscopic particles that are the physical basis for colour. According to Kant, Eberhard's interpretation of Leibniz makes the monads just like Newton's *lamellae* only smaller—indeed, infinitely small. Thus while monads, on this account, are unobservable, in the contingent sense in which Newton's *lamellae*—and presumably magnetic matter also—are unobservable, they are none the less sensible, since they are parts of the sensible world. In Eberhard's usage, a thing becomes a non-sensible object, hence an intelligible object, hence a thing itself, merely in virtue of its being too small or distant to perceive. This, says Kant, is absurd.

According to the *Critique*, everything in an appearance is itself still appearance, however far the understanding may continue to divide it into its parts and demonstrate the existence of parts which the senses are no longer capable of clearly perceiving. According to Mr Eberhard, however, they then immediately cease being appearances and become the things themselves.[14]

Eberhard's conflation of the unobservable with the supersensible is responsible for his misunderstanding. His claim that Kant was simply plagiarizing from Leibniz, by saying that things in themselves are the *non-sensible grounds*

---

[13] Ibid., Ak. viii. 205, Allison 122. Kant complains that Eberhard tends to use the even more ambiguous word *unbildbar* which Allison translates as 'unimageable'.

[14] Ibid., Ak. viii. 210, Allison 126.

of appearances, is thus shown to be mistaken: things in themselves are grounds, yes, but not parts of the appearance; things in themselves are non-sensible, yes, but not contingently unobservable.

While this round of the debate sees Kant as the winner, what is particularly interesting about it is the implication for Kant's beliefs about observability. Kant believes that tiny objects such as *lamellae*, which have 'not yet been seen through any microscope' (as true in our day as it was in Kant's), and of which no one has ever been directly 'conscious' or aware, are none the less 'really represented in our empirical intuition, albeit without being consciously apprehended'.[15] Note that Kant does not, this time, say that they *could* be represented in our intuition, 'if our senses were finer' (cf. A226/B273): Newton's *lamellae* already *are* represented in our intuition, and if our senses were finer we would then become *conscious* of them.

Kant speaks of something similar, I think, in the *Critique*, when he says, of the gradual increase in our knowledge of the phenomenal world, that we are able to

advance from appearances . . . to appearances; for even if these latter yield no actual perception (as is the case when for our consciousness they are too weak in degree to become experience), as appearances they none the less still belong to a possible experience. (A522/B550)

The idea here is comparable to that in his discussion of magnetic matter (A226/B273). The absence of actual perception—even the absence of empirically possible perception—has no bearing whatsoever on the issue of whether the object belongs to possible experience. Here Kant says that the only reason that these things are not *already* objects of actual perception is that their influence on our senses is 'too weak in degree to become experience'. The implication here, as in Kant's discussion of Newton's *lamellae*, is that these unobserved things *already affect us*, and hence *are already represented* in intuition, but their influence is too weak in degree for us to become aware of them.

This is a striking feature of Kant's understanding of the notion of experience, and it seems to be closely linked to his realism about these theoretical entities. But there is surely something puzzling about it. Kant's thesis of Receptivity entitles him to the conclusion that things that could affect our sensory organs are in principle objects of possible experience; but that surely is not sufficient for their being *already* 'represented in empirical intuition', albeit unconsciously.

---

[15] Ibid., Ak. viii. 205, Allison 122.

3. *Observability and Community*

There is a possible explanation for this striking feature of Kant's notion of experience, and I offer it as a speculative hypothesis. First, recall a distinctive thesis from Kant's early works. Each substance is in mutual interaction with *every other substance* with which it makes up a world. Each substance exerts forces on every other substance in its world. Unless this were so the substances would not co-exist in the same world. This thesis survives in the *Critique* as the thesis of community, in the Third Analogy, and as we saw in Chapter 6, parts of the argument there resemble very closely the argument of the *New Exposition*:

All substances, in so far as they can be perceived to coexist in space, are in thoroughgoing reciprocity (B256). All substances, so far as they coexist, stand in throughgoing community, that is, mutual interaction (A211).

Each substance must therefore contain in itself the causality of certain properties in the others, and at the same time contain in itself the effects of the causality of others, that is, they must stand in dynamical community if their co-existence in a possible experience is to be known. Now, with respect to objects of experience, something is *necessary* if experience of the objects themselves would be impossible without it. Therefore it necessary that substances in the [field of] appearance, in so far as they are co-existent, should stand in a thorough-going community of mutual interaction . . . Only thus by means of their reciprocal influence can the parts of matter establish their simultaneous existence, and thereby . . . their coexistence, even to the most remote objects. (A212/B259–A213/B260)

The substances here are not the monads of the *New Exposition*, but phenomenal substances, constituted by forces of attraction and repulsion. There seem to be some unnoticed epistemological implications here for Kant's conception of what is given to intuition, and this in turn has unnoticed implications for the issue of observability. Human sensory organs, and in general, human bodies, are after all parts of matter in the field of appearance.

We may easily recognize from our experiences that only the continuous influences in all parts of space can lead our senses from one object to another. The light, which plays between our eye and the celestial bodies, produces a . . . community between us and them, and thereby shows us that they coexist . . . (A213/B260)[16]

---

[16] A remark about the ellipses, which I have substituted for the word 'mediate'. Some may wonder whether the talk of 'mediate' community undermines the idea that there is *direct* causal influence between every coexistent thing. But I think that Kant has something quite different in mind: a contrast between the (temporal) relation of 'simultaneous existence', which is an immediate community, with the (metaphysical) relation of 'coexistence' which is mediate, i.e. epistemically speaking one is aware first of simultaneous existence, and then

Each part of matter, according to the requirement of community, reciprocally interacts with every other part of matter, regardless of its small size
and remote distance. Let us be literal-minded about this. My fingernail reg-
isters the effects of events in distant nebulae, and in turn produces effects
in them. If it were not so, they would not coexist. The fluttering sparrow
outside my window has its small influence on the fiery heart of the sun, and
the influence is reciprocal. That is why sparrow and sun inhabit the same
world. My retinas register the effects of the tiniest sub-microscopic *lamellae*, and in turn produce effects on them. That is required by the fact of their
coexistence. Things are members of the same world only in virtue of interacting dynamically with each other. That was the conclusion of the *New
Exposition*, and it is a conclusion that survives in the mature Kant. Human
bodies and their sensory organs therefore receive effects from *everything* in
the physical universe. That is why Newton's *lamellae* are *already represented*
in our intuition, even though we are not conscious of them. Magnetic matter, the inhabitants of the moon, gravitational force, all these, if they coexist with us, are already represented in our intuition in virtue of the effects
they produce in us: although it may be the case that 'for our consciousness
they are too weak in degree to become experience' (A522/B550). If our
senses were finer, then—quite literally—'the whole of nature would be
revealed to us' (A277/B233).

   If this is correct, then Kant has an even more peculiar conception of sensory experience than Wilson noted. It has almost nothing in common with
Berkeley, as Wilson rightly said. But it does have something in common with
Leibniz. According to Leibniz, each solitary monad, despite its solitude,
represents the entire universe within itself: its perceptions mirror, from its
own point of view, all the events occurring within all the other substances,
even though the perceptions (*petites perceptions*) are not events of which we
are, in the usual sense, *conscious*. That is not, of course, what Kant thinks:
we know nothing at all of events intrinsic to substances, either in ourselves
or other substances.

   However it must not be forgotten that the Leibnizian mirror thesis applies
to *bodies* just as much as it applies to monads. Leibniz says that

all matter is bound together, and every motion in this plenum has some effect on
distant bodies in proportion to their distance . . . As a result every body responds
to everything which happens in the universe, so that he who sees all could read in
each everything that happens everywhere . . . each monad . . . represents more distinctly [its] body . . . And as this body expresses the whole universe by the connec-

because of that, coexistence. (Note that these two ideas were always distinct, for Kant, even
in the *New Exposition*, where the order of priority is reversed.) This is admittedly a bit strange,
but consideration of the full passage will show that this seems to be what Kant means.

tion between all matter in the plenum, the soul also represents the whole universe in representing the body.[17]

This physical version of the Leibnizian mirror thesis seems to be implied by Kant's own Third Analogy—the crucial difference being, of course, that Kant's version of this thesis is unequivocally *causal*. If all parts of matter register the effects of all other parts of matter, then any given part of matter will, in a sense, be a mirror of the entire physical cosmos. In so far as our bodies are parts of matter, we too will receive influences from every other thing with which we coexist, although the forces exerted upon us and represented in our intuition may be 'too weak to come to consciousness'. Kant's belief that Newton's *lamellae* are really represented in intuition, albeit unconsciously—his belief that the tiniest and most distant parts of the physical world are likewise sensed, but too weakly to come to consciousness— has something in common with the *petites perceptions* of Leibniz. This descendant of the mirror thesis, and with it the disdain for the lived conscious experience of human beings, comes from Kant's Leibnizian heritage. The Irreducibility argument that leads Kant to abandon knowledge of things in themselves gives him no reason, after all, to abandon this part of his own philosophical tradition.

　　This provides an additional reason for Kant's being so apparently offhand about knowledge of the unobserved entities of science. Everything that *can affect us* is in principle an object of possible experience. Receptivity takes us that far. Moreover, everything with which we coexist *does in fact* affect us. Community takes us this much further. Everything with which we coexist is therefore an object of possible experience, and 'if our senses were finer', or 'infinitely sharpened', would be an object of awareness. That, I suggest, is Kant's view—and it helps to explain, I think, why scientific realism comes so naturally to him.

4. *Monadology, Well vs. Badly Understood*

No matter how refined our senses, we could never have knowledge of things as they are in themselves. This statement of the thesis of Humility appears in Kant's argument against Eberhard, in a passage where Kant, as in the Amphiboly, identifies the Leibnizian monad with the thing in itself in his own philosophy.

Even if our senses were infinitely sharpened, it would still remain completely impossible even to come nearer to the simple [monad], much less to finally arrive at it,

---

[17] Leibniz, 'Monadology', Loemker 649.

because it is not to be found in such objects [bodies]. Therefore, no choice remains but to admit that bodies are not things in themselves at all, and that their sensible representation, which we call corporeal things, is nothing but the appearance of something, which as thing in itself can alone contain the simple, but which for us remains entirely unknowable.[18]

Appearance does not contain anything simple (i.e. not consisting of parts), the Leibnizian monad is *ex hypothesi* simple, and hence it is not an appearance but a thing in itself. Kant is interpreting Leibniz in a way that breaks with the interpretation offered by Eberhard, for whom monads were imperceptible parts of appearances. What is remarkable now, though, is that Kant goes on to say that with a charitable interpretation of Leibniz in place, one can after all view the *Critique of Pure Reason* as a *vindication* of Leibniz.

What Kant says about Leibniz in the final paragraph of his reply to Eberhard is something that could well be on the banner of any philosopher interested in the task of rational reconstruction.

The *Critique of Pure Reason* can . . . be seen as the genuine apology for Leibniz, even against his partisans whose eulogies scarcely do him any honour . . . Many historians of philosophy, with all their intended praise, let the philosophers speak mere nonsense. They do not guess the purpose of the philosophers . . . They cannot see beyond what the philosophers actually said, to what they really meant to say.[19]

We have here a rare comment by Kant on the methodology of the history of philosophy. Kant suggests here that interpretive charity will yield interpretive authenticity. If we avoid, where possible, attributing 'mere nonsense' to the philosophers we study, even at the price of ignoring 'what the philosophers actually said', we will thereby discover 'what they really meant to say'. As I said in the Introduction, this gives us apparent Kantian licence, should we ever desire it, for the rational reconstructions of all the Strawsons, Bennetts, and Allisons of this world. A paradoxical licence admittedly: a licence in 'what the philosopher actually said' for *ignoring* 'what the philosopher actually said' is a licence that renders itself superfluous—a ladder that kicks itself away.

What then did Leibniz 'really mean to say', according to Kant? When Leibniz spoke of monads, he did not mean to say that they were parts of bodies: 'He did not mean the physical world, but its substrate, the intelligible world, which is unknown to us.'[20] Here we have Kant's charitable reconstruction of Leibniz, clearly at odds now with the interpretation he gave in the Amphiboly, according to which Leibniz 'took' the appearances

---

[18] *On a Discovery*, Ak. viii. 209, Allison 125, 126.
[19] Ibid., Ak. viii. 250–1, my translation, Allison 160.
[20] Ibid., Ak. viii. 248, Allison 158.

for things in themselves—in other words, 'took' the physical world for the monadic world. Kant says that the best interpretation of Leibniz will not after all attribute to him the view that monads are grounds of the physical world in the way that individual men are the grounds of a crowd. Instead, it will attribute to Leibniz the view that the monadic realm is the *substrate* of the physical world—a substrate which is unknown to us as to what it is in itself. It will attribute to Leibniz the view that the monads are substances, some of whose properties constitute the physical world—while the substances as they are in themselves, intrinsically, remain unknown to us. Kant's rational reconstruction of Leibniz paints a Leibniz who resembles Kant. Monads are substances, whose intrinsic properties are unknown to us, but whose non-intrinsic properties appear to us in the guise of the physical world. This Kantian reconstruction of Leibniz appears elsewhere in the debate with Eberhard too:

[T]he simple [in appearances] is absolutely impossible. Hence if Leibniz at times expressed himself in such a manner that his doctrine of simple being can be interpreted as implying that matter is a composite thereof, it is none the less fairer to him, as long as it is reconcilable with his express teachings, to understand him to mean by the simple not a part of matter but the non-sensible, and to us fully unknown ground of the appearance which we name matter (which may be a simple being even if the matter which constitutes the appearance is composite). If we cannot interpret Leibniz in this manner, we must reject his claims.[21]

Leibniz really 'meant to say' what Kant himself said in the *Critique*: not the 'nonsense' attributed to him by Eberhard, according to which the monads are grounds of the appearances in the way that men are grounds of crowds, but the Kantian thesis that monads are things in themselves, the 'non-sensible, and to us fully unknown ground of the appearance which we name matter'. In this ironic twist, Kant accepts the Eberhardian charge: Kant *is* like Leibniz, but like a Leibniz moulded in Kantian image.

The Kant–Eberhard discussion can help us to respond to a different challenge to the interpretation for which I have argued. Michael Friedman, in charting the progress of Kant's philosophy from his early monadology to the mature position of the *Critique*, finds in Kant's attitude to substance his 'truly decisive break with the Leibnizian–Wolffian tradition':

Substance is now '*substantia phaenomenon* in space': that is *matter* . . . [S]ubstance is no longer in any way simple. This becomes especially clear in the *Metaphysical Foundations of Natural Science* of 1786, where Kant argues that material substance is infinitely divisible and explicitly points out the incompatibility of this with his own earlier *Physical Monadology* in particular and with Leibnizean metaphysics in

---

[21] Ibid., Ak. viii. 203, Allison 120.

general . . . Kant . . . in explicitly rejecting the simplicity of substance . . . has broken with the monadology completely.[22]

Against this I have argued that Kant has *not* broken with the monadology completely. He endorses a Distinction according to which things in themselves are substances, in something close to the Leibnizian sense, while phenomenal substance, *substantia phaenomenon*, is a 'merely comparative' subject. Kant inherited his Distinction, in broad outline, from Leibniz, and his later epistemology is inscribed upon it. Leibniz and Kant alike distinguish true substances—beings that conform to the 'pure concept' of substance—from phenomenal substance, namely matter. That has been among the central arguments of this book. How then to reply to Friedman's particular objection?

In the passage cited by Friedman from the *Metaphysical Foundations*, Kant appears to recapitulate his argument of the *Physical Monadology*, only to reject it.

[I]f a monadist might want to assume that matter consists of physical points each of which (for this reason) has no movable parts but yet fills a space by mere repulsive force, he would be able to grant that this space, but not the substance acting in it, is at the same time divided, and hence that the sphere of substance's activity is divided, but not that the active movable subject itself is at the same time divided by the division of the space. Accordingly, he would compound matter from physically indivisible parts and yet allow it to occupy space in a dynamical way. By [my] argument, however, this subterfuge is completely taken away from the monadist.

Kant's objections to this argument are essentially his objections to Eberhard. The mistake here is to use the monadology in 'the explication of natural appearances', as Kant says a little later, by making the monads parts, even if indivisible parts, of the physical world, the realm of appearance. The mistake is in a 'badly understood' monadology.

The ground of this aberration lies in a badly understood monadology, which does not at all belong to the explication of natural appearances . . . The composite in the appearance does not consist of the simple . . . It was not Leibniz' intention, as far as I comprehend, to explain space by the order of simple entities side by side.[23]

Here again we find the charitable reconstruction of Leibniz's 'intention', at odds with the view that Leibniz simply took the natural appearances for the the monads.

Friedman says that Kant's own early *Physical Monadology* is the target of attack in the above passage from the *Metaphysical Foundations*. However it is not entirely clear whether Kant, even in 1756, placed the monads in the

---

[22] Friedman in ch. 1 of *Kant and the Exact Sciences*, 38.
[23] *Metaphysical Foundations*, Ak. iv. 507–8, Ellington 55–6.

appearances in the way that he later rejects. There is discernible ambivalence on this question. On the one hand, monads in 1756 are admittedly defined as 'parts' of matter—but on the other hand Kant is extremely cautious about whether monads are *in the physical world*, that is to say, the dynamical and spatial world.

Proposition VII. Whatever is intrinsic to substance, i.e. *the substantial itself, is not properly defined by space*. The substance itself is the subject of extrinsic properties [forces], and those extrinsic properties are something properly to be sought in space. But, you say, substance is present in a small portion of space, and present everywhere within it; therefore if one divides space, does not one divide substance? *I answer: space is the field of the external presence* [force] of the element (monad) . . . But besides external presence, i.e. relational properties of the substance, there are other intrinsic properties, without which the relational properties [forces] would not exist, because there would be no subject in which they inhered. But *the intrinsic properties are not in space, precisely because they are intrinsic.*[24]

Certainly the monads *as they are in themselves* are not in the physical world. Kant says in 1756 that monads are present in the world in the way that God is present in the world: and this presence is a virtual, not an actual, presence. The analogy is not easy to follow. But to take this suggestion seriously is to cast doubt upon the idea that the physical monads are in the physical, phenomenal world: God, after all, is not in the world, although his causally efficacious power may be present within it. The fact that their intrinsic properties are not in space shows that even at this stage monads are not in the appearances in the sense that individual men are in a crowd. The monads are 'the substantial itself', they are in a certain way *identified* with their intrinsic properties: the 'substantial itself' is taken to be 'whatever is intrinsic to substance', the 'intrinsic properties' without which 'there would be no subject'. So while there is some ambivalence about monads in 1756, in the idea that they are parts of the physical world, and yet 'in themselves' absent from the physical world, this ambivalence is resolved by abandoning the idea that they are parts of the physical world. Friedman is right only to this extent: Kant does indeed turn his back on a monadology whose aim is the 'explication of natural appearances' in terms of simple substances and their intrinsic properties.

Notice that Kant describes such a view in the *Metaphysical Foundations* as a 'badly understood monadology'. He thinks here, just as he thinks in his debate with Eberhard, that there is a monadology that can be better understood. The true monadology, he says,

[24] (Emphasis added) Prop. VII., *Physical Monadology*, Ak. i. 481, Beck 123. Friedman agrees that there is a sense in which the physical monads are not, for Kant, in space.

does not at all belong to the explication of natural appearances but is a platonic concept of the world carried out by Leibniz. This concept is correct in itself insofar as the world is regarded not as an object of the senses but as a thing in itself, i.e. as merely an object of the understanding which nevertheless lies at the basis of the appearances of the senses . . . [T]he order of simple entities . . . [belongs] to a merely intelligible (for us unknown) world.[25]

Here Kant says that the Leibnizian monadology is *correct*—interpreted as referring to things in themselves, and not to appearances. Leibnizian substances are what must be thought to 'lie at the basis of the appearances', and they are unknown to us. This is just what Kant said in his defence of Leibniz against Eberhard. Leibniz, in referring to monads, 'did not mean the physical world, but its substrate, the intelligible world, which is unknown to us',[26] and once this charitable interpretation of Leibniz is allowed, the *Critique of Pure Reason* can be seen as the 'true apology for Leibniz'. Contrary to Friedman, Kant has by no means 'broken with the monadology completely'.[27] The monads remain as the things in themselves, the substratum of appearances, the substances whose relational properties we can know but whose intrinsic properties remain unknown.

This revision of the monadology has implications for Kant's physics, and thus for the discussion of the preceding chapter. Kant's dynamical theory of matter, argued for in the *Metaphysical Foundations*, bears many resemblances to the theory of force of the *Physical Monadology*: both posit forces of attraction and repulsion whose 'conflict' or interaction constitutes the physical world. But conspicuously absent from the later theory is any talk at all of the 'physical' monad, the unextended point or particle that one might at least be tempted to say is a part of the physical world. No intrinsic properties belong to the physical world, or to any part of it. That was a premise of Kant's argument against the 'absolute solidity' of the mechanists, and it is here directed against the different target of a badly understood monadology. Forces are not attributed to unextended substantial points, but are—as far as the physical world is concerned—viewed as autonomous. Their points of origin can be viewed as mathematical abstractions: the force of impenetrability is, he says, 'an immediate repulsion, whereby a point (in its merely mathematical presentation) fills a space

[25] *Metaphysical Foundations*, Ak. iv. 507, Ellington 55.

[26] *On a Discovery*, Ak. viii. 248, Allison 158.

[27] It may be that Kant has broken with the monadology as far as his interest to Friedman's project of exploring Kant's science is concerned. As far as I can tell, Friedman makes no reference at all to Kant's distinction between phenomena and things in themselves in discussing the writings of Kant's mature philosophy, notwithstanding Kant's insistence that things in themselves are required as the 'substrate' of matter. Despite his interest in Kant's theory of science, Friedman pays little attention to Kant's dynamical theory of matter, and none that I know of to Kant's idea that matter 'consists entirely of relations'.

dynamically'.[28] The cautious qualification of the phrase 'in its merely mathematical presentation' is there, I take it, precisely to rule out the substantial indivisible points of a 'badly understood monadology'. Whatever one's conclusions about Kant's theory of matter, one thing is unambiguously clear: the monad has been banished from it. Points of matter are centres of force; and that is how Kant's theory of matter comes to be a field theory.[29]

5. *Final Comments*

My chief interest in this chapter has been to explore Kant's views about observability, in order to gain a better understanding of the connections between Kant's scientific realism, and his epistemic Humility: a better understanding of the contrast between two very different ways that theoretical entities, and things as they are in themselves, are beyond the bounds of experience. In the process of this exploration, additional support has been found for attributing the Distinction to Kant, and for attributing to Kant a considerable sympathy for certain Leibnizian assumptions about substance—a sympathy that is strong enough to lead him to describe his own philosophy as the true vindication of Leibniz.

The significant change in Kant's physical theory, the abandoning of the substantial physical monad, is something that demands an explanation, no matter what interpretation of Kant one favours. The explanation that I have suggested is very simple. It is well supported in Kant's writings, especially in the Amphiboly, the *Metaphysical Foundations*, and the debate with Eberhard. Monads are now Kantian things in themselves, things that are not located in the appearances, but that are none the less the substratum of appearances: that is to say, they are substances, which are the bearers of properties that constitute the physical world. To be the ultimate bearers of properties, they must be substances: which means that, in addition to the merely relational properties that constitute the physical world, they must have intrinsic properties. But their intrinsic properties are unknown to us. The best explanation for the change in Kant's physical theory is that Kant always assumed the Distinction implicit in his early monadology, assumed a distinction between substances and their forces, and then came to endorse Humility, which relegated the substances—that is to say, the substances as they are in themselves, intrinsically—to the realm of the unknowable. This

---

[28] *Metaphysical Foundations*, Ak. iv. 520, Ellington 72.

[29] Useful references here are Berkson, *Fields of Force*; Joseph Agassi, *Faraday as a Natural Philosopher* (Chicago, Ill.: University of Chicago Press, 1971); Jammer, *Concepts of Force*; Williams, *Michael Faraday*, and *The Origins of Field Theory* (New York: Random House, 1966); Hacking, *Representing and Intervening*, 100.

left Kant with a physics with fields of force, and no substance—at least as far as his physical theory is concerned.

Kant has a strange conception of the objects of experience, which excludes colours (as sensations), Newtonian atoms, things in themselves, but includes invisible forces and sub-microscopic Newtonian *lamellae*. I have tried, in this chapter, to show why Kant's notion of what can be given to experience is very much guided by his belief in Receptivity. Anything that can in principle affect us is a possible object of experience. Since the theoretical entities of science are constituted by forces, they are possible objects of experience, no matter how small or remote. This, I think, is enough to explain Kant's attitude. However, I suggested a second hypothesis. Kant's understanding of community leads him to believe that every coexistent object reciprocally produces effects in every other, so that each part of matter produces effects in all others. This, I suggested, has epistemological implications. A human organism is affected by everything in the physical universe. This, conjoined with the thesis of Receptivity, ensures that everything in the physical universe is *already* represented in empirical intuition, 'albeit without being consciously apprehended'. This descendant of the Leibnizian mirror thesis is an additional reason for Kant to ignore, as he so evidently ignores, the contingencies of what can actually be given to our senses.

The same Receptivity which permits a very generous scientific realism at the same time prohibits knowledge of things as they are in themselves. The properties of things as they are in themselves are not given to experience at all. The intrinsic properties of substances are not simply unobservable, but 'supersensible'. They are supersensible because they cannot be given, as they are in themselves, to creatures whose sensibility is passive. It is not 'through itself' that a substance has the power to 'determine others different from itself', as Kant says in the *New Exposition*. Substances do have causal powers, and we can come to have knowledge of them in so far as we are receptive to their causal powers. But our receptivity yields no knowledge of the substance as it is in itself, since it is not through itself, not through its own intrinsic properties, that it has those causal powers. Kant's commitment to Receptivity, his commitment to scientific realism, and his commitment to Humility, thus go hand in hand.

Realism or Idealism?

1. *Summing Up*

One task of this enquiry has been to show that there is a way of understanding Kant's distinction between phenomena and things in themselves which is nothing like a veil of appearance, with Berkeleian ideas on this side of the veil, and things in themselves on the other. The distinction I have drawn from Kant's writings is, basically, a distinction between two classes of properties of things. Kant thinks that phenomena are real properties, albeit relational properties, of substances. I have tried to show that there are advantages to this way of understanding Kant. A famous problem disappears, as I suggested in Chapter 1. Things in themselves exist, and affect us, and we have no knowledge of things as they are in themselves. That is to say, there exist things that have intrinsic properties, and they affect us by means of their forces, and we have no knowledge of their intrinsic properties. My main interest, in the early chapters, has been in finding an explanation for the fundamental unargued premise of which Strawson complained. Kant believes that our ignorance of the intrinsic properties of things follows from the receptivity of our knowledge, because he takes the irreducibility of causal powers for granted. Since it is not through a thing's intrinsic properties that it has the power to affect us, acquaintance with its causal powers will not give us acquaintance with its intrinsic properties. This way of understanding Kant, then, finds an argument for the unargued premise. It is also possible to make good sense of Kant's unpromising claim that his philosophy makes all the qualities secondary. Although this seems to make Kant look very like Berkeley, when one sees Kant means something like Locke's tertiary qualities, we have a philosopher who has more in common with Faraday than with the bishop. Moreover, the 'primary'/secondary quality distinction that then emerges has many advantages over its competitors—even its current competitors. That was among the arguments of Chapters 7 and 8. Finally, we have an explanation for why Kant believes things can be objects of possible experience when they can never be seen, or heard, or tasted, or touched: we have an explanation for Kant's striking realism about the unseen realm that science can unveil.

What I have said is so far compatible with thinking that Kant is not an idealist at all. To be sure, Kant has a Distinction between phenomena and things in themselves: but that is not idealism. Philosophers who would like to distinguish fundamental entities from less fundamental ones may wish to make a distinction of a similar general kind. Kant says that we have no knowledge of things as they are in themselves: but that is not idealism either. Philosophers who would like to allow that some features of the real world are knowable, some are unknowable, may wish to express their epistemic humility in a similar general manner. Kant says that he makes all the qualities secondary: but that does not make him like Berkeley. Philosophers who would like to say that the qualities of the physical world are, contrary to Locke, all powers, may find themselves expressing their views in a similar way too. It is not idealism to make a distinction between phenomena and things in themselves, or to say that the qualities of bodies are all secondary, or to deny that we have knowledge of things as they are in themselves. Many philosophers and interpreters of Kant have wished to take the insights of Kant's arguments in the Aesthetic and Analytic without paying the idealist price. From what I have said so far, it may seem that it is possible to do so, and in a way that does full justice to Kant. But that impression would be misleading.

Kant gives us some licence to look beyond 'what the philosophers actually said, to what they really meant to say'. It can be sorely tempting to use that licence, but restraint is called for. It is better to see what Kant meant to say by seeing what he actually said. To stop at this point would be to succumb to temptation: it would be to use, and perhaps to abuse, the licence he rashly gives. For there are many things that Kant actually said that do not sit well at all with what I have argued that he meant to say. And Kant's optimistic suggestion that interpretive charity will always yield interpretive accuracy is, to say the least, far-fetched.

2. *Idealism: First Impressions*

Kant says that 'external things, namely matter, are . . . nothing but mere appearances, that is, representations in us, of whose reality we are directly conscious' (A371–2), that 'objects . . . in themselves remain unknown to us' (A379), that 'if I remove the thinking subject, the whole corporeal world must vanish' (A383). This kind of talk is difficult to explain away. The easiest solution would perhaps be to say, with Bennett, that Kant—like everyone throughout philosophy's history—is very apt to conflate properties with ideas, and that when he speaks of *representations in us*, he ought to be speaking of *properties of something else*. There is certainly some reason for thinking Kant is confused in the way Bennett describes, and as we considered in Chapter 2. Worse in this respect than the passages considered by Bennett is the *Prolegomena* passage discussed in Chapter 7, where Kant seems to use the one chain of anaphoric devices to refer to ideas in us, appearances, and properties of things in themselves.

That would perhaps be the easiest solution. But to adopt it would be to do Kant an injustice of a different kind. While the realist interpretation of Kant that I have made possible may remove the sting from much that is traditionally associated with the doctrine of idealism, limitations must be acknowledged if we refuse to make use of the licence of rational reconstruction. None of the main arguments of the preceding chapters need be retracted: Kant's distinction between phenomena and things in themselves is still the Distinction; Kant's claim that we are ignorant of things as they are in themselves is still epistemic Humility. But Kant's apparent idealism—his assertion, for example, that the entire corporeal world will at once vanish on the removal of the thinking subject—ought to be confronted and, if possible, explained.

Idealism comes in different shapes and sizes, and Kant's idealism—to the extent that he is an idealist—emerges in two rather different dimensions. One has to do with the nature of things in themselves, I believe; and the other has to do with the nature of space. Before closing, I want to consider each of these—all too briefly I am afraid—and to assess their implications for the interpretation offered in the foregoing chapters.

3. *Idealism: Things in Themselves*

Kant's views about things in themselves may imply that ultimate reality is not physical in its nature. This might make Kant count as an idealist in the eyes of many. Suppose we say that the physical world is the world that is in principle discoverable by physics. Kant thinks that the physical world is the phenomenal world, and that things as they are in themselves are not physical. To be sure, things in themselves are physical in a certain sense: the things that have an intrinsic nature have extrinsic, physical properties. But things *as* they are in themselves are not physical: for their intrinsic properties are not physical. Physics can discover nothing about things as they are in themselves. If things in themselves are substances, each of which has a nature and existence that is independent of others, then things in themselves, and not phenomena, are the most fundamental existents. The physical world is a dependent world; things in themselves are independent. Kant thus thinks that the most fundamental existents are—in this sense—not physical.

To say that the physical world is real, and that there is something nonphysical besides, is to deny physicalism. It is to deny that reality is exhausted by physical reality. But that is not sufficient for idealism. To say that physics fails to snare every aspect of reality is hardly to be an idealist. To go further, and say that the non-physical things are more basic and fundamental than the physical things, brings one perhaps a little closer to idealism. To go further still, and not only deny that the fundamental things are physical but assert that they are *mental* in nature, would be to come much closer to idealism. It might be to embrace a certain sort of idealism, and also to violate the constraints of epistemic Humility. Here we must record that Kant comes close to doing both of these.

Let us consider one such passage. Despite its problems, it has the merit of pointing to the Leibnizian background to Kant's views about things in themselves, and of suggesting what Kant had in mind when he said in the *Metaphysical Foundations* that the Leibnizian monadology was true as an account of things in themselves. In the Second Paralogism of the *Critique* Kant attempts to refute rational psychology's claim that what is distinctive about the soul is that it is simple. Kant's reply to this claim is that simplicity may well not be distinctive of souls, since things in themselves, *as the substratum of matter*, may, for all we know, equally be simple. That Kantian idea we have encountered already in the debate with Eberhard, and on its own, it may not be a violation of Humility (though I say this with some caution).[1] However, Kant now goes further, and speculates that things in themselves are Leibnizian *souls*. He speculates that their intrinsic properties—about which so little has been and can be said—are the sorts of properties possessed by souls or thinking beings.

Extension, impenetrability, cohesion, and motion—in short, everything which outer senses can give us—are not thought, feeling, desire, or resolution, nor contain them, since these are never objects of external intuition. It could nevertheless be that the something which lies at the ground of external appearances, which affects our sense so that our sense receives representations of space, matter, shape, and so on—it could be that this something, when regarded as noumenon (or better, as transcendental object), is at the same time the subject of thoughts. (A358)

Kant raises, somewhat hesitantly, the possibility that the substance which 'lies at the ground' of external appearance, may be a thinking thing. He continues:

This may be so, even though the way our external sense is affected by it gives us no intuition of representations, will, and so on, but only of space and its properties.

---

[1] I imagine, on Kant's behalf, an argument that proceeds like this. To be simple means not to be divisible. To be divisible is to be in space. Reason requires that there exists something that has an intrinsic nature. On the premise that nothing in space can have an intrinsic nature, the thing that has an intrinsic nature is non-spatial and hence simple.

For this something is not extended, nor impenetrable nor composite, since all these predicates concern only sensibility and its intuition, in so far as we are affected by certain objects that are otherwise unknown to us. These expressions, however, do not enable us to know what kind of an object it is, but only to know that if it is considered as it is in itself, apart from a relation to external senses, these predicates of external appearances cannot be attributed to it. But the predicates of inner sense, representations and thought, are not inconsistent with it. So even if we grant the human soul to have a simple nature, such simplicity is not enough to distinguish it from matter—in view of the substratum of matter . . .

Matter is mere external appearance, whose substratum cannot be known through any predicate we can assign to it. So I can well assume that matter in itself is simple . . . and that the substance which possesses extension with regard to our outer sense, possesses thoughts in itself, which can be consciously represented through its own inner sense.

The substratum of matter may well be a conscious being that possesses thoughts. Having taken very seriously the Leibnizian conception of substances as thinking souls, Kant then distances himself:

Without allowing these hypotheses, however, one can note the following general point: if I understand by 'soul' a thinking being in itself, it is useless to ask whether or not it is similar to matter (matter not being a thing in itself but only a kind of representation in us). For it is obvious that a thing as it is in itself has a nature that is different from the properties that only make up its situation. But if we compare the thinking 'I' not with matter but with the intelligible which lies at the ground of the external appearance we call matter, we cannot say that the soul is intrinsically any different from it, since we know nothing at all of it. (A360)

This is the passage encountered in Chapter 2 which irritated Bennett, with its identification of matter with 'a kind of representation', and also with the 'properties that make up the situation' of a thing—where that thing is thought to have an intrinsic nature quite different from those properties. Let us consider the implications of Kant's suggestion that *the substratum of matter is a thinking being*.

Kant suggests that the intrinsic properties of substances are thoughts— that things as they are in themselves are thinkers. This does come very close to an idealism—but an idealism that is not a phenomenalism. It opens the way for an entirely different understanding of Kant's startling declaration that 'if I remove the thinking subject, the whole corporeal world must vanish' (A383). If the substratum of matter is a thinking monad, then Kant's declaration would be perfectly accurate. And it would be accurate for a reason very different to the reason it would be accurate when applied to a phenomenalistic idealism. The reason would *not* be the following familiar reason: 'To be is to be perceived; if I remove the thinking, perceiving subject, I remove both perceiver and perceived. Therefore if I remove the think-

ing, perceiving subject the whole corporeal world must vanish.' Instead, the
reason would be something like this: 'To be a substance is to be a being that
has thoughts; if I remove the thinking being, I remove the substance and *all*
of its properties; if the substance has physical properties as well as thoughts,
then if I remove the substance I remove its physical properties too. Therefore if I remove the thinking subject, the whole corporeal world must vanish.' If the substratum of matter is a thinking being, then the vanishing of
the substratum would be the vanishing of matter and the whole corporeal
world—even if the properties consituting matter are *not mental at all*. We
have something of an irony here: Kant's unwise speculations about the
intrinsic mental properties of the substratum permit a more realistic understanding of this apparently extreme declaration of idealism. Physical properties may be real, not mental, not things for which to be is to be perceived;
and yet it may be true that if the thinking subjects were removed, the physical world would also be removed.

Kant is usually more cautious than he is in this Second Paralogism, so
this dimension to Kant's idealism can, perhaps, be regarded as an unwise
and atypical aberration. Humility should be sufficient to guard against idealism of this kind. For Humility counsels silence on the question of the
intrinsic properties of matter's 'substratum'.

4. *Idealism: Space*

There is no doubt that Kant believes that space is ideal. If we are to take
seriously what the philosopher 'actually said', as opposed to what he might
have 'meant to say', this cannot be denied. Kant says repeatedly throughout
the *Critique* that space is a merely subjective form of intuition. The goal of
the Aesthetic is to establish the ideality of space.[2] This dimension to Kant's
idealism can hardly be dismissed as an unwise and atypical aberration.

Now it might be thought that this admission demolishes the interpretive
hypothesis offered here. Surely, it might be said, if space is ideal, then bodies in space are ideal, and we need no alternative understanding of what it
is to be a phenomenon. Surely if space is ideal, we need no alternative understanding of Kant's conclusion that we have no knowledge of things in themselves. The phenomenalist Kant triumphs. Space, as Kant says, is 'in us'
(A370); spatial bodies are likewise 'in us'; and we have no knowledge of anything else.

This response may be tempting, but it would be, I think, a mistake. There

---

[2] Kant says the same about time, but, like other commentators, I shall find it convenient
here to focus just on space.

are some crucial questions to answer before one settles for so easy a response. First: is Kant's idealism about space the explanation for his conclusion that we have no knowledge of things in themselves? If the answer to this question is no, we must look elsewhere for an explanation, and the explanation I have offered may well be the right one. Second: is idealism about space detachable from Kant's philosophy? If the answer to this question is yes, then a realist understanding of phenomena of the kind suggested here may well be compatible with what the philosopher *ought* to have said about space. Third: is idealism about space compatible, in Kant's view, with realism about bodies in space? If the answer to this question is yes, then a realist understanding of phenomena may well be compatible with what the philosopher *actually* said about space. Let us consider these one at a time.

Kant believes that we have no knowledge of things as they are in themselves. Why? He thinks that our ignorance of things as they are in themselves follows from the fact that human knowledge is receptive. That has been a fundamental assumption of the foregoing enquiry, and it is an assumption shared by many, including commentators as different as Strawson and Heimsoeth. Kant says that the demand for knowledge of things as they are in themselves is a demand that we should be able to be acquainted with things 'without senses' (A277/B333). He says that properties belonging to things as they are in themselves 'can never be given to us through the senses' (A36/B52). Our ignorance of things in themselves is supposed to follow from Receptivity, and not from any particular Kantian doctrine about space. To say this is not to deny that Kant's views about space deserve detailed attention in their own right—attention of a kind that they have certainly received from others, and cannot receive here. This assumption, and its methodological consequence, is what has made it possible to pursue this enquiry without addressing the large and complex topic of space. Kant would deny that we have knowledge of things in themselves no matter what he thought about space: the conclusion about Humility is independent of any conclusion about space. So Kant's idealism about space cannot be the explanation for his conclusion that we have no knowledge of things in themselves. We must, it seems, look elsewhere for an explanation: and I have suggested where it is to be found.

Is idealism about space detachable from the rest of Kant's philosophy? Some commentators have argued that the answer to this question is a clear yes. Among these, Guyer is perhaps especially interesting. Kant infers from the a priori character of our knowledge of space to the subjectivity and ideality of space, but according to Guyer his argument rests on a modal error. Kant's argument rests on a conflation of the following propositions: (a) Necessarily, if we are to perceive an object, then it is spatial; and (b) If we perceive an object, then it is necessarily spatial. The first, according to

Guyer, is sufficient for the claim about our a priori knowledge of space. The second, he says, implies the subjectivity of space. But to move from the first proposition to the second is to commit a modal scope fallacy. So the idealist conclusion about space is indeed detachable from Kant's arguments about our a priori knowledge of space.[3] One might have questions about the details of Guyer's argument. Suppose, plausibly enough, that spatial objects are necessarily spatial. Then the second proposition would follow from the first, without error. If we perceive an object, it is necessarily spatial, if spatial objects are necessarily spatial. And the second proposition would be true without implying the subjectivity of space. The point is though that Guyer's strategy, or something like it, might show that Kant's idealism about space is based on a philosophical mistake. It would then be quite possible to disentangle the Kantian idealism which has its source in the supposed subjectivity of space from the other parts of Kant's philosophy, just as Guyer recommends. And on such an understanding, there would be no temptation whatsoever to regard phenomena as ideal. Phenomena would be wholly real. A realist understanding of phenomena would be perfectly compatible with what the philosopher *ought* to have said about space.

However, notice that on such an understanding, the interpretation offered here would remain entirely intact—and this is where I part company with Guyer, and with others who pursue a realist Kant through the pages of the *Critique*. Kant would still make the Distinction between phenomena and things in themselves: he would distinguish the relational properties of substances from the substances in themselves, the substances as bearers of intrinsic properties. He would still insist on Humility: he would insist on our inevitable ignorance of the intrinsic properties of things, for this, as he says, follows from Receptivity. And human knowledge is inevitably receptive, whether or not space is ideal.

We turn now to the third question. Is Kant's idealism about space compatible, in Kant's own view, with realism about bodies in space? If it is, then phenomena may be real, even though space is ideal. The suggestion might be thought outrageous: surely if space is ideal, then space and *everything in space* is ideal. It must be said that Kant himself seems to think this way in many places: for example, in the phenomenalistic argument of the Fourth Paralogism. Matter is 'only a species of representations . . . which are called external . . . because they relate perceptions to the space in which all things are external to one another, while yet the space itself is in us' (A370). Such representations have this 'deceptive property that, representing objects in space, they detach themselves as it were from the soul and appear to hover

---

[3] Guyer, *Kant and the Claims*, 364.

outside it' (A385). But elsewhere we find a very different train of thought, as Guyer has shown.

Kant says in a letter to Beck of 1792:

> Messrs. Eberhard and Garve's opinion that Berkeley's idealism is the same as that of the critical philosophy (which I could better call 'the principle of the ideality of space and time') does not deserve the slightest attention. For I speak of ideality in reference to the *form of representations*; but they interpret this to mean ideality with respect to the *matter*, that is, the ideality of the *object*.[4]

Kant wants to contrast his own philosophy with the phenomenalism of Berkeley by saying that the Kantian philosophy makes merely 'the form' ideal, and not the objects presented in spatial form. Guyer argues convincingly that Kant viewed his idealism as 'formal' rather than 'real'; he considered it an idealism with respect to the form but not the object of intuition.[5]

Kant clearly thinks, at different stages of his philosophical career, that there is in principle no contradiction in holding both that space is ideal, and that what is represented in space is real. In the *Inaugural Dissertation* of 1770 Kant holds that space is subjective and dependent on the human mind, and that the objects sensed in spatial form are real and independent of the human mind. He says, 'Space is not something objective and real . . . but it is subjective and ideal and proceeds from the nature of the mind' (§ 15). He also says that knowledge of phenomena is veridical, since phenomena 'are witnesses, as being things caused, to the presence of an object, and this is opposed to idealism' (§ 11). Idealism about the form of intuition is not taken to imply idealism about the things represented in intuition.[6] Guyer says that this basic allegiance to realism—notwithstanding the commitment to the ideality of space—returns to the fore in the mature Kantian philosophy, and especially in the Refutation of Idealism written for the second edition of the *Critique*. According to Kant, we cannot have knowledge of ourselves without having knowledge of some thing that exists independently of ourselves: and this conclusion, so Guyer argues, should be taken at face value.[7] In short, there seems to be good reason for thinking that in Kant's own opinion, idealism about space is compatible with realism about phenomenal objects;

---

[4] Letter to J. S. Beck (4 Dec. 1792), Ak. xi. 395, Zweig 198. See Guyer, *Kant and the Claims*, 414.

[5] Guyer, *Kant and the Claims*, 414.

[6] As Guyer comments, ibid. 21. Quotations are from *Inaugural Dissertation*, Ak. ii. 403, 397, Kerferd and Walford 70, 61.

[7] I oversimplify: the argument is that we cannot have knowledge of ourselves as determined in time without knowledge of some independent thing. Guyer's excellent analyses of Kant's Refutations of Idealism form Pt. IV of Guyer, *Kant and the Claims*.

and that precisely this combination is suggested in his claim that he is an idealist about spatial 'form', but not about the 'matter' or object that is represented in spatial form. If this is so, then a realist understanding of phenomena is compatible not only with what the philosopher *ought* to have said about space, but with what the philosopher *actually* said about space.

Kant's claim, though, deserves closer attention, if we are to see what this realism amounts to. What is this 'matter' for which space provides the 'form'? We would do well, at this point, to remind ourselves of Kant's contrast between 'formal' and 'real' relations. Kant says that space, with all that it contains, 'consists solely of relations, formal or, it may be, also real' (A284/B340). Among these 'relations' are some that are abiding, persistent, and 'through these we are given a determinate object' (A285/B341). This abiding appearance in space is 'impenetrable extension' (A284/B339), it is 'the real in appearance (*realitas phaenomenon*)', it is '*substantia phaenomenon* in space', which is 'entirely made up of mere relations', entirely made up, that is to say, of the forces of attraction and repulsion (A265/B321). Kant says that we are acquainted with substance through forces. He says that forces are properties of substances; but he does not say this about space. Space is ideal in a way that force is not. A 'real predicate', Kant says, is a force, an 'action of a substance' (*R* 5296). Forces are, while spatial properties are not, properties of substances. The ideality of space is compatible with the reality of bodies, constituted by forces. This, I think, may be what Kant means when he says, 'Bodies would be things, even if they were not present [to us]. But space is always only form' (*R* 5320).[8] The contrast between the formal and the real is also made in the Axioms of Intuition, and the Anticipations of Perception: the former concern extensive magnitudes, spatial properties, hence 'appearances in their formal aspect' (A162/B202), and the latter concern intensive magnitudes, dynamical properties, forces, 'the *real* which corresponds to sensation in the object (*realitas phaenomenon*)' (A166).

Kant is thus saying that 'real relations' provide the 'matter' for 'formal relations': that is, *force* provides the 'matter' for *space*. In terms of Kant's two classes of primary qualities, discussed in Chapter 8, the dynamical qualities provide the matter, and the geometrical qualities provide the form. 'Matter' is of course being used in two senses here: one contrasting with form, the other contrasting (perhaps) with mind. But Kant is bringing these two together. The 'matter' for which space provides the 'form' is matter in the sense of *physical substance*, the real. The stuff which fills space is physical stuff. Matter in both of Kant's senses of 'matter' is *the real* in space. Matter is force, and force is the 'real relation' which is represented to us in the formal and subjective relations of space.

[8] Ak. xviii. 146, 151, M 1777–80.

To suggest this is to disagree, now, with Guyer, who seems to take 'the real' that is subjectively represented in space to be the thing in itself. The 'matter' for which space provides the form is not ideal, but neither is it the thing *as* it is in itself—contrary to Guyer. Rather, the matter for which space provides the form is force, a relational property of the thing in itself. It is important that force is a relational property, to which space, itself a system of relations, is in some way *appropriate*. Kant says in the *Prolegomena* that space is 'appropriate' (*gemäß*) to the 'relations' that link our receptive sensibility with objects.[9] Such relations are the forces or causal powers of objects. So space, a system of formal and ideal relations, is in some way appropriate to the real relations of force. But as a system of formal relations it is by no means appropriate to the real but non-relational features of things as they are in themselves. The matter for which space provides the form is not the thing *as* it is in itself, which could never be presented in spatial form. What Kant said in the *Physical Monadology* about the thing *as* it is in itself would apply as much to the later Kant as to the former, notwithstanding his later commitment to the ideality of space. 'Besides external presence, i.e. the relational properties of the substance, there are other intrinsic properties, without which the relational properties [forces] would not exist, because there would be no subject in which they inhered. But the intrinsic properties are not in space, precisely because they are intrinsic' (Prop. VII). That is part of the reason for Kant's saying that through mere relations we cannot be acquainted with a thing as it is in itself, and that spatial intuition therefore cannot capture the intrinsic properties of what it represents (B67).

If, as Guyer suggests, there is continuity between the realism of Kant's mature philosophy and the realism of the *Inaugural Dissertation*, then that is further support for the view that force—not the thing as it is in itself—is the 'real' that is represented in ideal space. For, as Guyer points out, there Kant seems to say that phenomena are real, but that they 'do not represent the intrinsic and absolute quality of objects' (§ 11); he says that they are the dynamical, interactive 'relation' of substances, and he says that this 'relation, when viewed intuitively, is called space' (§ 16).[10] The real dynamical relations among substances are viewed intuitively as spatial. The substances have, in addition, intrinsic and absolute qualities: but these are not captured by the formal spatial relations through which we view the dynamical relations among the substances. The result is that phenomena are not ideal, but real, and independent of perceivers; but they are not independent *tout court*. Bodies, constituted by forces, are *phaenomena substantiata*, real but dependent beings, which we treat as independent substances.

[9] *Prolegomena*, Ak. iv. 290, Lucas 46.
[10] Ak. ii. 397, 407, Kerferd and Walford 61, 75.

The question of the connection between the formal (spatial) relations, and the real (dynamical) is a large one, too large adequately to address here. And there is something peculiar to any modern reader in the idea that force may be real, even if space is ideal. Doesn't the notion of force presuppose the notion of space? What sense can be made of forces that are real, and perceiver-independent—but are spatial only in so far as they are 'viewed intuitively'? Perhaps this is indeed a peculiar idea: but it may not seem so peculiar to Kant. We know that, from his earliest days, Kant saw a very close isomorphism between spatial relations and dynamical, and that he by no means took it for granted that dynamical relations among substances pre-suppose spatial relations. The history of his views about space seems, in many respects, to be a playing out of the different possible directions of dependence, and kinds of dependence, between space and force. At first he thinks that dynamical relations are the more fundamental, and that they are what make spatial relations possible.[11] In his first work, indeed, Kant attempted to infer properties of space (its three dimensionality) from properties of force (gravitation's inverse square law).[12] Later he wonders whether the dependence is the other way: whether spatial relations are what make dynamical relations possible.[13] Later still, he supposes that spatial relations are ideal, but are the real dynamical relations of substances 'viewed intuitively'.[14] In the *Critique*, this thought is linked to a transcendental argument about human experience: spatial relations are ideal, but they make *experience* of real dynamical relations possible.

This last thought seems to be present in some of the texts considered in Chapter 6. Recall that we saw a later incarnation of Kant's Irreducibility argument in the Postulates of Empirical Thought, and the solution offered there draws on Kant's views about space. Causal powers of substances do not supervene on the mere existence of substances—on the assumption that a substance is an absolute subject, that conforms to the pure concept of substance. Given this problem, identified in the *New Exposition*, it is difficult to see how there could ever be any community or interaction amongst substances. However, says Kant,

we can make quite comprehensible the possibility of a community of substances— substances as *appearances*—when we represent them to ourselves in space, in external intuition. For this already contains in itself a priori formal external relations as conditions of the possibility of [experience of] real external relations (action and reaction) and thus community. (B293–4)

---

[11] *Living Forces* (1747), *New Exposition* (1755), *Physical Monadology* (1756).
[12] *Living Forces* (1747).
[13] *Regions in Space* (1768).
[14] *Inaugural Dissertation* (1770).

Space, as a system of a priori formal relations, makes it possible for us to experience the real relations of forces. We saw that the same argument is made again in a later work.

It is already in the [Leibnizian] concept of substances, that, if nothing is added to them, they must be represented as completely isolated . . . If they should stand in community as substances of a world, this community can only be ideal and cannot be a real physical influence. The possibility of this latter interaction cannot be understood from the mere existence of the substances . . . But if, by contrast, one begins with the pure intuition of space, which lies *a priori* at the ground of all [experience of] external relations . . . then all substances are thereby bound in relations that make [experience of] physical influence possible.[15]

Kant, in his mature philosophy, is especially interested in the conditions of our *experience* of relations, and of physical influence, hence my bracketed interpolations in the above quotations. The interpolations perhaps need more argument than I can give them here, but they are quite in keeping with Kant's focus on conditions of our *experience* in the Analogies, particularly in the similar argument of the Third Analogy (discussed in Chapters 6 and 9). The link Kant wants to make between spatial and dynamical relations concerns not the existence of the latter, but our experience of them. If we have experience at all, it must be because we are affected by something: that follows from the fact that our intuition is passive, sensible. This receptive experience reveals the existence of something distinct from ourselves. Given the fact of receptivity, what affects us must be the causal power of something distinct from ourselves: what affects us must be the forces of substances. Forces are not themselves substances, for they are not absolutely independent things. But forces can do duty for substance in a manner which is 'empirically serviceable' (A349). Spatial relations—even subjective, ideal spatial relations—enable us to represent these dynamical relations as matter: not as an absolute subject, but as an 'abiding picture' of an absolute subject. Spatial relations provide us with a kind of grid, or map, or blueprint, that enables us to represent material things as objects that are distinct from us, and distinct from each other.

By means of external sense . . . we represent to ourselves objects as distinct from us, and all without exception in space. (A22/B37)

Many complex and difficult issues are raised by these last suggestions, and I do not hope to resolve them here. The connection Kant sees between dynamical and spatial relations must be regarded as unfinished business. But despite the difficulties, it seems to me that even granting what this

---

[15] *What Real Progress?*, Ak. xx. 283–4.

philosopher actually said, the ideality of space does not, in his own opinion, undermine the reality of what is presented in space: namely bodies, constituted by forces that are mind-independent properties of absolutely independent substances, things in themselves. That, it seems to me, is what Kant said, and meant to say.

BIBLIOGRAPHY

1. *Works by Kant*

Gesammelte Schriften, ed. Königlich Preussischen Akademie der Wissenschaften, 29 vols. Berlin and Leipzig: de Gruyter, 1922.

Gedanken von der wahren Schätzung der lebendige Kräfte (1747) (*Thoughts on the True Estimation of Living Forces*), Ak. vol. i.

Principiorum primorum cognitionis metaphysicae nova dilucidatio (1755), Ak. vol. i. English translation: *A New Exposition of the First Principles of Metaphysical Knowledge*, in L. W. Beck *et al.*, eds., *Kant's Latin Writings: Translations, Commentaries and Notes*. New York: P. Lang, 1986.

Metaphysicae cum geometria iunctae usus in philosophia naturali, cuius specimen I. continet monadologiam physicam (1756), Ak. vol. i. English translation: *Physical Monadology*, in L. W. Beck *et al.*, eds., *Kant's Latin Writings: Translations, Commentaries and Notes*. New York: P. Lang, 1986.

Von dem ersten Grunde des Unterschiedes der Gegenden im Raume (1768), Ak. vol. ii. English translation: *Concerning the Ultimate Foundation of the Differentiation of Regions in Space*, in G. B. Kerferd and D. E. Walford, eds., *Kant: Selected Pre-Critical Writings*. Manchester: Manchester University Press, 1968.

De mundi sensibilis atque intelligibilis forma et principiis (1770), Ak. vol. ii. English translation: *On the Form and Principles of the Sensible and Intelligible World (The Inaugural Dissertation)*, in G. B. Kerferd and D. E. Walford, eds., *Kant: Selected Pre-Critical Writings*. Manchester: Manchester University Press, 1968.

Reflexionen zur Metaphysik, Ak. vols. xvii and xviii. Dates given are those suggested by Erich Adickes (Preface to Ak. vol. xvii), or by Arthur Melnick (*Space, Time and Thought in Kant*, 547–9), signified by 'A' or 'M' respectively.

Metaphysik L₁ (mid-1770s), Ak. vol. xxviii. English translation: *Immanuel Kant: Lectures on Metaphysics*, trans. and ed. Karl Ameriks and Steve Naragon. Cambridge: Cambridge University Press, 1997.

Prolegomena zu einer jeden künftigen Metaphysik (1783), Ak. vol. iv. English translation: *Prolegomena*, trans. and ed. Peter G. Lucas. Manchester: Manchester University Press, 1953.

Kritik der reinen Vernunft (1781/1787), Ak. vols. iv and iii. Also ed. Raymund Schmidt. Hamburg: Felix Meiner Verlag, 1956. The customary practice of citing the pagination of the 1781 (A) edition and/or the 1787 (B) edition is followed. English translation: *Critique of Pure Reason*, trans. Norman Kemp Smith. London: Macmillan, 1929.

Metaphysische Anfangsgründe der Naturwissenschaft (1786), Ak. vol. iv. English translation: *Metaphysical Foundations of Natural Science*, trans. J. Ellington. Indianapolis, Ind.: Library of Liberal Arts, 1970.

Über eine Entdeckung nach der alle neue Kritik der reinen Vernunft durch eine ältere entbehrlich gemacht werden soll (1790), Ak. vol. viii. English translation: *On a Discovery according to which any New Critique of Pure Reason has been made Superfluous by an Earlier One*, in *The Kant–Eberhard Controversy*, trans. with a commentary by Henry Allison. Baltimore, Md.: Johns Hopkins University Press, 1973.

Welches sind die wirklichen Fortschritte, die die Metaphysik seit Leibnizens und Wolf's Zeiten in Deutschland gemacht hat? (Kant's submission for a Prize Essay of 1791, published in 1804) (*What Real Progress has Metaphysics made in Germany since the Time of Leibniz and Wolff?*), Ak. vol. xx.

Kant's Briefwechsel, Ak. vols. x–xiii. English translations of selected letters in *Kant: Philosophical Correspondence, 1759–99*, trans. and ed. Arnulf Zweig. Chicago, Ill.: University of Chicago Press, 1967.

II. *Other Sources*

ADAMS, ROBERT MERRIHEW. 'Phenomenalism and Corporeal Substance in Leibniz', in Peter French, Theodore Uehling, and Howard Wettstein, eds., *Midwest Studies in Philosophy*, viii. 217–57. Minneapolis, Minn.: University of Minnesota Press, 1983.

ADICKES, ERICH. *Kants Lehre von der doppelten Affektion unseres Ich als Schlüssel zu seiner Erkenntnistheorie*. Tübingen: J. C. Mohr, 1929.

AGASSI, JOSEPH. *Faraday as a Natural Philosopher*. Chicago, Ill.: University of Chicago Press, 1971.

ALEXANDER, PETER. 'The Names of Secondary Qualities', *Proceedings of the Aristotelian Society* 77 (1976–7), 203–20.

ALLISON, HENRY. *Kant's Transcendental Idealism*. New Haven, Conn.: Yale University Press, 1983.

ARMSTRONG, DAVID. *A Materialist Theory of Mind*. London: Routledge & Kegan Paul, 1968.

—— *What is a Law of Nature?* Cambridge: Cambridge University Press, 1983.

AYERS, MICHAEL. 'Mechanism, Superaddition, and the Proof of God's Existence in Locke's Essay', *Philosophical Review* 90 (1981), 210–51.

—— *Locke*, vol. ii: *Ontology*. London: Routledge, 1991.

BAUMGARTEN, A. G. *Metaphysica* (1757), reprinted in the Academy edition of Kant's works, Ak. xvii.

BENCIVENGA, ERMANNO. *Kant's Copernican Revolution*. New York: Oxford University Press, 1981.

BENNETT, JONATHAN. *Kant's Analytic*. Cambridge: Cambridge University Press, 1966.

—— *Kant's Dialectic*. Cambridge: Cambridge University Press, 1974.

—— *Locke, Berkeley, Hume: Central Themes*. Oxford: Oxford University Press, 1971.

—— 'Substance, Reality and Primary Qualities,' *American Philosophical Quarterly* 2 (1965), 1–17.

BERKELEY, GEORGE. *De Motu* (1721), trans. A. A. Luce, in *Berkeley's Philosophical Writings*, ed. David Armstrong. London: Collier Macmillan, 1965.

—— *Three Dialogues between Hylas and Philonous* (1713), in *Berkeley's Philosophical Writings*, ed. David Armstrong. London: Collier Macmillan, 1965.

—— *A Treatise Concerning the Principles of Human Knowledge* (1710), in *Berkeley's Philosophical Writings*, ed. David Armstrong. London: Collier Macmillan, 1965.

BERKSON, W. *Fields of Force*. London: Routledge & Kegan Paul, 1974.

BIGELOW, JOHN, ELLIS, BRIAN, and PARGETTER, ROBERT. 'Forces', *Philosophy of Science* **55** (1988), 614–30.

BLACKBURN, SIMON. 'Filling In Space', reprinted in *Essays in Quasi-Realism*, 255–8. New York: Oxford University Press, 1993.

BOSCOVICH, R. J. *A Theory of Natural Philosophy* (1763), trans. J. M. Child. Cambridge, Mass.: MIT Press, 1966.

BRITTAN, GORDON. *Kant's Theory of Science*. Princeton, N.J.: Princeton University Press, 1978.

BUCHDAHL, GERD. *Metaphysics and the Philosophy of Science*. Oxford: Blackwell, 1969.

BUROKER, JILL VANCE. *Space and Incongruence*. Dordrecht: Reidel, 1981.

CAMPBELL, KEITH. *Abstract Particulars*. Oxford: Blackwell, 1990.

COSTABEL, PIERRE. 'Newton's and Leibniz' Dynamics,' in R. Palter, ed., *The Annus Mirabilis of Sir Isaac Newton*. Cambridge, Mass.: MIT Press, 1970.

COVER, J. A. 'Relations and Reducibility in Leibniz', *Pacific Philosophical Quarterly* **70** (1989), 185–211.

DRYER, D. P. *Kant's Solution for Verification in Metaphysics*. London: George Allen & Unwin, 1966.

DUNN, J. M. 'Relevant Predication 2: Intrinsic Properties and Internal Relations,' *Philosophical Studies* **60** (1990), 177–206.

ELLIS, BRIAN and LIERSE, CAROLINE. 'Dispositional Essentialism', *Australasian Journal of Philosophy* **72** (1994), 27–45.

EVANS, GARETH. 'Things Without the Mind', in Zak van Straaten, ed., *Philosophical Subjects: Essays Presented to P. F. Strawson*, 76–116. Oxford: Oxford University Press, 1980.

FARADAY, MICHAEL. 'A speculation touching Electric Conduction and the Nature of Matter,' in *Experimental Researches in Electricity*, vol. ii. London: Richard & John Edward Taylor, 1844.

FLAX, JANE. 'Philosophy and the Patriarchal Unconscious', in S. Harding and M. Hintikka, eds., *Discovering Reality: Feminist Perspectives in Epistemology, Metaphysics, Methodology, and Philosophy of Science*. Dordrecht: Reidel, 1983.

FOSTER, JOHN. *The Case for Idealism*. London: Routledge & Kegan Paul, 1982.

FRIEDMAN, MICHAEL. *Kant and the Exact Sciences*. Cambridge, Mass.: Harvard University Press, 1992.

FURTH, MONTGOMERY. 'Monadology', in Harry Frankfurt, ed., *Leibniz*, 99–36. New York: Doubleday, 1972.

GARVE, CHRISTIAN. Review of Kant's *Critique of Pure Reason* (with editorial changes by J. G. H. Feder), in *Göttinger Anzeigen von gelehrten Sachen*, Jan. 1782.

GEACH, PETER. *Logic Matters*. Oxford: Blackwell, 1972.

—— *Truth, Love and Immortality*. London: Hutchinson, 1979.

GUYER, PAUL. *Kant and the Claims of Knowledge*. Cambridge: Cambridge University Press, 1987.

HACKING, IAN. *Representing and Intervening*. Cambridge: Cambridge University Press, 1983.

HARRÉ, R. and MADDEN, E. H. *Causal Powers*. Oxford: Blackwell, 1975.

HEIMANN, P. M. and McGUIRE, J. E. 'Newtonian Forces and Lockean Powers: Concepts of Matter in Eighteenth Century Thought', *Historical Studies in the Physical Sciences* 3 (1971), 233–306.

HEIMSOETH, HEINZ. 'Metaphysical Motives in the Development of Critical Idealism,' in Moltke Gram ed., *Kant: Disputed Questions*, 158–99. Chicago, Ill.: Quadrangle Books, 1967.

HESSE, MARY. *Forces and Fields*. London: Thomas Nelson, 1961.

HINTIKKA, JAAKKO. 'Leibniz on Plenitude, Relations, and the "Reign of Law"', in Harry Frankfurt, ed., *Leibniz*, 155–90. New York: Doubleday, 1972.

HUMBERSTONE, I. L. 'Intrinsic/Extrinsic', *Synthese* 108 (1996), 205–67 (accepted in 1992).

ISHIGURO, HIDÉ. *Leibniz's Philosophy of Logic and Language*. London: Duckworth, 1972.

—— 'Leibniz's Theory of the Ideality of Relations', in Harry Frankfurt, ed., *Leibniz*, 191–214. New York: Doubleday, 1972.

JACKSON, FRANK, PARGETTER, ROBERT, and PRIOR, ELIZABETH. 'Three Theses about Dispositions', *American Philosophical Quarterly* 19 (1982), 251–7.

JACOBI, F. H. *Werke*. Leipzig: Gerhard Fleischer, 1815.

JAMMER, MAX. *Concepts of Force*. Cambridge, Mass.: Harvard University Press, 1957.

KHAMARA, E. J. 'Indiscernibles and the Absolute Theory of Space and Time', *Studia Leibnitiana* 20 (1988), 140–59.

KEMP SMITH, NORMAN. *Commentary to Kant's Critique of Pure Reason*, 2nd edn. London: Macmillan, 1923.

KIM, JAEGWON. 'Concepts of Supervenience', *Philosophy and Phenomenological Research* 45 (1984), 153–76.

—— 'Psychophysical Supervenience', *Philosophical Studies* 41 (1982), 51–70.

LANGSAM, HAROLD. 'Kant, Hume, and our Ordinary Concept of Causation', *Philosophy and Phenomenological Research* 54 (1994), 625–47.

LANGTON, RAE. 'Kant and Scientific Realism', B.A. Honours thesis, Department of Traditional and Modern Philosophy, University of Sydney, 1985.

—— 'Kantian Humility', unpublished Ph.D. dissertation, Princeton University, 1995.

—— 'Locke's Mechanism: Relations and God's Good Pleasure', in progress, and in draft form in Knud Haakonssen and Udo Thiel, eds., *Reason, Will and Nature: Voluntarism in Metaphysics and Morals from Ockham to Kant*, Australian Society for the History of Philosophy Yearbook 1 (1993), 66–88.

—— and LEWIS, DAVID. 'Defining "Intrinsic"', *Philosophy and Phenomenological Research* 58 (1998).

LAYWINE, ALISON. *Kant's Early Metaphysics and the Origins of the Critical Philo-sophy*, North American Kant Society Studies in Philosophy, vol. iii. Atascadero, Calif.: Ridgeview, 1993.

LEIBNIZ, G. W. *Die Leibniz-Handschriften der königlichen öffentlichen Bibliothek zu Hannover*, ed. E. Bodemann. Hanover, 1895; repr. Hildesheim: G. Olms, 1966.

—— *Mathematische Schriften*, ed. C. I. Gerhardt, 7 vols. Berlin, 1849–55; repr. Hildesheim: G. Olms, 1962.

—— *New Essays on Human Understanding* (1765), trans. and ed. P. Remnant and J. Bennett. Cambridge: Cambridge University Press, 1981.

—— *Opuscules et fragments inédits de Leibniz*, ed. Louis Couturat. Paris: Presses Uni-versitaires de France, 1903; repr. Hildesheim: G. Olms, 1961.

—— *Philosophical Essays*, trans. and ed. R. Ariew and D. Garber. Indianapolis, Ind.: Hackett, 1989.

—— *Philosophical Papers and Letters*, trans. and ed. L. Loemker, 2nd edn. Dor-drecht: Reidel, 1969.

—— *Die philosophischen Schriften*, ed. C. I. Gerhardt, 7 vols. Berlin, 1875–90; repr. Hildesheim: G. Olms, 1960–1.

—— *Textes inédits d'après les manuscrits de la bibliothèque provinciale de Hanovre*, ed. G. Grua, vol. ii. Paris: Presses Universitaires de France, 1948.

LEWIS, DAVID. 'Extrinsic Properties', *Philosophical Studies* **44** (1983), 197–200.

—— *On the Plurality of Worlds*. Oxford: Basil Blackwell, 1986.

LLOYD, GENEVIEVE. *The Man of Reason*. London: Methuen, 1984.

LOCKE, JOHN. *Essay Concerning Human Understanding* (1689), ed. P. Nidditch. Oxford: Oxford University Press, 1975.

LOUX, MICHAEL J. *Substance and Attribute*. Dordrecht: Reidel, 1978.

MACKIE, J. L. *Problems from Locke*. Oxford: Oxford University Press, 1976.

MARTIN, C. B. 'Dispositions and Conditionals', *Philosophical Quarterly* **44** (1994), 1–8.

MARTIN, GOTTFRIED. *Kant's Metaphysics and Theory of Science* (1951), trans. P. Lucas. Manchester: Manchester University Press, 1955.

MATES, BENSON. *The Philosophy of Leibniz: Metaphysics and Language*. New York: Oxford University Press, 1986.

MELNICK, ARTHUR. *Space, Time, and Thought in Kant*. Dordrecht: Kluwer, 1989.

MONDADORI, FABRIZIO. 'Solipsistic Perception in a World of Monads', in Michael Hooker, ed., *Leibniz: Critical and Interpretive Essays*. Manchester: Manchester University Press, 1982, 21–44.

PARKINSON, G. H. R. *Logic and Reality in Leibniz's Metaphysics*. Oxford: Oxford University Press, 1965.

PARSONS, CHARLES. 'Infinity and Kant's Conception of "The Possibility of Experi-ence"', *Philosophical Review* **73** (1964), 182–97.

PATON, H. J. *Kant's Metaphysic of Experience*. London: Allen & Unwin, 1936.

PLATO. *Phaedo*, trans. Hugh Tredennick, in *The Collected Dialogues of Plato*, ed. Edith Hamilton and Huntingdon Cairns. Princeton, N.J.: Princeton University Press, 1961.

POLONOFF, IRVING. *Force, Cosmos, Monads and Other Themes of Kant's Early Thought*. Kant-Studien Ergänzungsheft No. 107, 1973.

PRIOR, ELIZABETH. *Dispositions*. Aberdeen: Aberdeen University Press, 1985.

PUTNAM, HILARY. *Reason, Truth and History*. Cambridge: Cambridge University Press, 1981.

RESCHER, NICHOLAS. *The Philosophy of Leibniz*. Englewood Cliffs, N.J.: Prentice-Hall, 1967.

ROBINET, A. 'Leibniz: Lecture du treatise de Berkeley', *Études de philosophie* (1983), 217–23.

—— *Malebranche et Leibniz: Relations personnelles*. Paris: J. Vrin, 1955.

ROSENBERG, J. F. *One World and Our Knowledge of it*. Dordrecht: Reidel, 1980.

ROYSE, JAMES. 'Leibniz and the Reducibility of Relations to Properties', *Studia Leibnitiana* 12 (1980), 179–204.

RUSSELL, BERTRAND. *A Critical Exposition of the Philosophy of Leibniz* (1900), 2nd edn. London: George Allen & Unwin, 1937.

—— 'The Philosophy of Logical Atomism' (1918), in *Logic and Knowledge*, ed. R. C. Marsh, 175–281. London: George Allen & Unwin, 1956.

—— *The Principles of Mathematics* (1903), 2nd edn. London: George Allen & Unwin, 1937.

SELLARS, WILFRID. *Essays on Philosophy and its History*. Dordrecht: Reidel, 1974.

—— *Science, Perception and Reality*. New York: Humanities Press, 1962.

SMITH, A. D. 'Of Primary and Secondary Qualities', *Philosophical Review* 99 (1990), 221–54.

SHOEMAKER, SYDNEY. 'Causality and Properties', in Peter van Inwagen, ed., *Time and Cause*. Dordrecht: Reidel, 1980.

STRAWSON, P. F. *The Bounds of Sense*. London: Methuen, 1966.

—— *Individuals*. London: Methuen, 1959.

—— 'Reply to Evans,' in Zak van Straaten, ed., *Philosophical Subjects: Essays Presented to P. F. Strawson*, 273–82. Oxford: Oxford University Press, 1980.

SWOYER, CHRIS. 'The Nature of Natural Laws', *Australasian Journal of Philosophy* 60 (1982), 203–23.

TURBAYNE, COLIN. 'Kant's Refutation of Dogmatic Idealism', *Philosophical Quarterly* 5 (1955), 225–44.

VALLENTYNE, PETER. 'Intrinsic Properties Defined', *Philosophical Studies* 88 (1997), 209–19.

VAN CLEVE, JAMES. 'Incongruent Counterparts and Things in Themselves', in G. Funke and T. M. Seebohm, eds., *Proceedings of the Sixth International Kant Congress*, vol. ii. Pt. 2, 33–45. Washington, D.C.: Centre for Advanced Research in Phenomenology and University Press of America, 1989.

—— 'Inner States and Outer Relations: Kant and the Case for Monadism', in Peter H. Hare, ed., *Doing Philosophy Historically*. Buffalo, N.Y: Prometheus Books, 1988.

—— 'Putnam, Kant, and Secondary Qualities', *Philosophical Papers* 24 (1995), 83–109.

VLEESCHAUWER, HERMAN J. DE. *The Development of Kantian Thought*, trans. A. R.

Duncan. London: Thomas Nelson, 1962. Originally published as *L'Évolution de la pensée kantienne*. Paris: Presses Universitaires de France, 1939.

VUILLEMIN, JULES. *Physique et métaphysique kantiennes*. Paris: Presses Universitaires de France, 1955.

WILLIAMS, L. P. *Michael Faraday: A Biography*. London: Chapman & Hall, 1965.

—— *The Origins of Field Theory*. New York: Random House, 1966.

WILSON, CATHERINE. *Leibniz's Metaphysics*. Princeton, N.J.: Princeton University Press, 1989.

WILSON, MARGARET. 'Kant and "the *Dogmatic* Idealism of Berkeley"', *Journal of the History of Philosophy* **9** (1971), 464–70.

—— 'On Kant and the Refutation of Subjectivism', in L. W. Beck, ed., *Kant's Theory of Knowledge*, 208–17. Dordrecht: Reidel, 1974.

—— 'The "Phenomenalisms" of Berkeley and Kant', in Allen Wood, ed., *Self and Nature in Kant's Philosophy*, 157–73. Ithaca, N.Y.: Cornell University Press, 1984.

—— Review of Michael Ayers, *Locke*, *Philosophical Review* **102** (1993), 577–84.

—— 'Superadded Properties: The Limits of Mechanism in Locke', *American Philosophical Quarterly* **16** (1979), 143–50.

—— 'Superadded Properties: A Reply to Michael Ayers', *Philosophical Review* **90** (1982), 247–52.

YOLTON, JOHN. *Locke and the Compass of Human Understanding*. Cambridge: Cambridge University Press, 1975.

INDEX